W9-BAH-886

MY FARAWAY HOME

Christmas Day, 1940, Mindanao. Mary McKay, seven years old, with her parents Harriet and Douglass, and her brother, Bob.

MY FARAWAY HOME

AN AMERICAN FAMILY'S WWII TALE OF ADVENTURE AND SURVIVAL IN THE JUNGLES OF THE PHILIPPINES

MARY McKAY MAYNARD

The Lyons Press
Guilford, CT
An Imprint of The Globe Pequot Press

ACKNOWLEDGMENTS

I dedicate this book to the heroes of World War II—young men then—who fought the war and won it, and to the gentle Filipinos who bore so much and were so kind to us. There is no way to thank any of them for what they did.

I can thank Charles Stabinsky, who asked me every year when I came in for a check-up, "Have you started that book yet?" and all the readers of the manuscript, published writers among them, who told me the book was wonderful. Elizabeth Hilts said, "It *is* wonderful, but tell me more here and less there."

I am grateful for the gentle and intelligent editing by Enrica Gadler and Mark Weinstein at The Lyons Press and for Mark's bright-eyed discovery of the manuscript.

Thanks most of all to my husband, Howard, who politely read two pages every day for three years and then cried when he read the finished *My Faraway Home*.

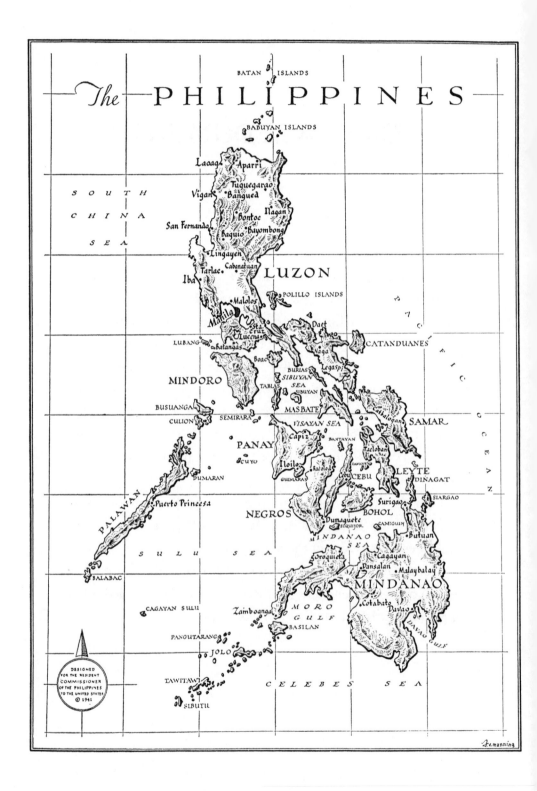

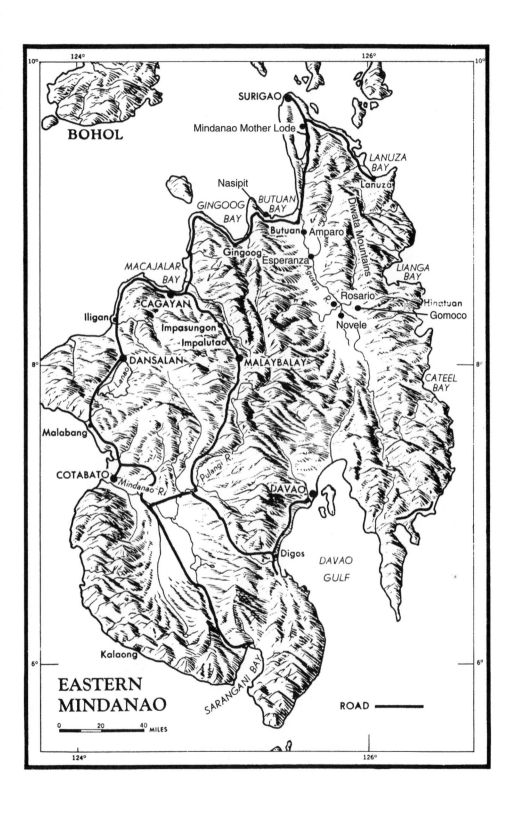

BOHOL

SURIGAO

Mindanao Mother Lode

LANUZA BAY

Lanuza

Nasipit

BUTUAN BAY

GINGOOG BAY

Butuan   Amparo

Diwata Mountains

Gingoog

Esperanza

MACAJALAR BAY

LIANGA BAY

CAGAYAN

Rosario   Hinatuan

Iligan

Gomoco

Impasungon

Agusan R.

Impalutao

Novele

DANSALAN

MALAYBALAY

CATEEL BAY

Lanao

Malabang

Pulangi R.

COTABATO

Mindanao R.

DAVAO

Digos

DAVAO GULF

Kalaong

SARANGANI BAY

EASTERN MINDANAO

ROAD ■■■■■

0   20   40 MILES

CONTENTS

PART
1

WAITING AND RUNNING

I had been forlorn and uneasy for three days. At breakfast on Monday, I had watched two forks laden with scrambled eggs stop in midair, then slowly drop to my parents' plates as we listened to the morning news from Manila.

The Japanese had bombed Pearl Harbor.

That same morning, without any opposition, the Japanese attacked Luzon, the main island of the Philippines. Now, on Thursday, our island of Mindanao was still untouched, but already there were new words to learn: "declaration of war" "blackout" "evacuation."

It hadn't taken long for a seven-year-old to figure out that evacuation meant leaving a familiar life at a jungle gold mine where the days followed one after another in calm procession, where cicadas sang all day long in the heat, and where the *wak-wak* cried out in the jungle night. It meant leaving the familiar sounds of the mill across the canyon humming at its work of refining gold, and the *chuff-chuff* of the donkey engine that pulled mine cars through the tunnel.

I was alone on the screened porch that ran the length of our house, listening to my mother and Mrs. Feigel make lists for the evacuation. I sat right at the end of the rattan sofa so that I could move to a cool place on the cushion when the spot I was sitting on grew too warm and damp.

(I slept that way, too, in my wide bed with the mosquito net tucked in tight. Starting at one edge and keeping my arms away from the netting because the mosquitoes could bite me through it, I moved in careful distances back and forth across the bed. I could keep a cool spot waiting as the heat built up under me. Early in the morning, I caught the bloated mosquitoes that flew heavily at the top of the net and smashed them. I was careful not to smear the mosquito nets with blood because the nets were heavy and hard to wash, and Marta, our *lavandera,* was so little.)

I listened to my mother's rich voice and Mrs. Feigel's sharper one as they made lists and packed bags in the *sala.* I ran in to join them.

"I thought of something we'll need, Mommy. Candles."

"They're already on the list, dear."

"Oh."

I lingered near them, but they went on with their planning. Mrs. Feigel's husband, Fred, worked for my father, who was general manager of Mindanao Mother Lode, and ran the mill that worked all the hours of the day. Jean had no children and found them annoying, and that was why I was left alone to take care of myself.

My mother wasn't always so distant; her preoccupation with the war was the greatest cause of my unease. We had always spent long mornings on the porch doing my lessons, which came from the Calvert System in Baltimore. Sometimes during our sessions, clans of monkeys passed by high in the jungle near our house. We would run out to the garden hoping to see them, but the monkeys traveled so high that we usually had to be content to hear their chatter and to see the branches move as the families passed through the trees. Hornbills called to one another from the highest trees, "Callao, callao," and the cicadas sang louder in the increasing heat until finally they were all that sang during the hottest hours.

I thought to play with Pat, Mrs. Feigel's large German shepherd, who was never far from her side, but he raised his lip at me as he always did, so I wandered down to the building behind our house where the servants lived and worked. Consuelo, our houseboy's wife, who was usually happy to play with me, was busy with a sick child, and Marta, the *lavandera,* was working hard ironing a white linen suit of my father's. For a while, I watched her fill the hollow Chinese iron with red coals from the kitchen fire and pass it over the wet and wrinkled linen. Slowly, the jacket took shape, but I didn't stay.

I went back to my spot on the porch—at least I could hear my mother's voice, even if her attention was not on me. From our house I could see most of the buildings of Mindanao Mother Lode. Right across from us was the mill that ground rocks torn from tunnels inside the mountain and turned them into concentrate. Small canvas bags of concentrate went to a smelter in Oregon, where the pure gold finally appeared. In Mindanao, we never saw the gold ingots; we saw only the early steps in the process. Men with paintbrushes were creeping along the length of the mill's long galvanized iron roof. They were painting it black so it wouldn't attract enemy bombers. Looking into the mill, I could see huge rolls of khaki fabric turning slowly as they accepted and filtered the crushed rock.

To the right of the mill and beyond the tunnel where the gold ore was found stood the mess house where the single men lived and where we often went in the evenings for cocktails and dinner. Even so many years later, the hollow rattle of dice shaken in a leather cup and the click as dice roll on a tabletop bring back to memory the evenings spent on the mess house veranda where the grown-ups drank and gossiped and I listened. It was there I heard Mr. Ortega, the assistant mill manager, say, "Franco, he's just bloffing!" I thought about "bloffing" for a long time, remembering the argument his remark caused.

Long ago, it seemed to me now, we had come home from the beach on a Sunday afternoon to see a row of men leaning over the railing of the mess house porch. They told us that Germany had marched into Poland. Waldo Neveling and Mr. Heidepreim, the two Germans on the staff, looked funny that night. Mr. Neveling's silver tooth didn't show because he wasn't laughing the way he usually did, but Mr. Heidepreim's eyes glistened behind his gold-wire glasses. He seemed excited. Everyone else was scared and silent, and I knew it was bad for Germany to invade Poland. Bad for us, too, even though we were far away in a jungle.

Below the mess house, where the river turned in its valley and made a flat space, the smaller buildings stood. My father's office was in a three-room building built on stilts to allow cool air to circulate through it. He shared the building with Fred Feigel, the mill man, and Larry Smith, the mine man, though often I found them in the assay office, a smaller building where they tested rock taken from the lode vein in the mountain.

Beyond the small buildings, and running below the long porch of the mess house, the road ran out past the workers' barrio

toward the village of Mabuhay. A right turn at Mabuhay led down
the white coral-paved road to Surigao, where our supplies arrived
on the Thursday boat. Twice a year we boarded that interisland
steamer, the *Corregidor*. She stopped at island ports along the way
as she picked up passengers and cargo on her way to Manila. My
mother loved those leisurely trips through the islands. The tropical clouds piled high in the sky in the daytime, and phosphorus
glowed in the sea at night as the ship cut the water.

At the barrio there was a large building that loomed over the
miners' shacks that clustered at the edge of the jungle. The company gave Christmas parties in the big building for the miners
and their families. On payday the men lined up for their en-
velopes of money and then lined up again to buy supplies and
canned goods at the *tienda* window. It was a rare thing among
Filipinos to be able to buy food other than rice and dried fish
from the coasts.

Men came from far away, bringing their families and belongings, hoping to find work at the mine. They were willing to
work deep inside the mountain in tiny spaces to earn cash to
buy Coca-Cola for their children. Men begged for jobs and
pulled all the strings they could. One man boasted, "I am the
husband of Mr. McKay's *lavandera!*" Our Marta, the man's wife,
earned a sack of rice and twelve pesos a month for washing our
clothes under a cold-water faucet and ironing them with a charcoal iron. Her husband wanted work, too.

Dionisio, our houseboy, waxed our floors daily with John-
son's wax from black-and-orange cans. He polished the floors
by skating over them on dried coconut husks cut in half. He
was polishing the floors now, the husks strapped to his feet.
Shuuush, shuuush, he skated over the shining floors.

"Mommy, are Marta and Dionisio coming with us when we are evacuated?"

"No, Mary, we can't take them with us."

"But why not? Who'll wash our clothes and who'll cook for us and polish the floors?"

"I don't think we'll be gone very long, dear. Just for a few days until the Air Force and Navy can get here from Hawaii. Now, run along and play. Mrs. Feigel and I want to get this done before lunch and siesta."

The radio told of the British battleships *The Prince of Wales* and *The Repulse* being sunk, of bombings, and of Guam falling. Guam, I knew, was an island where the Pan American clipper stopped to refuel on its flights from San Francisco to Manila; but, I wondered, how could an island "fall"? Could our huge island fall, too?

———⟫·◆·⟪———

My parents were born in the 1890s to Canadians who were drawn to North Dakota by the Homestead Act. They met at the University of North Dakota and married in 1920.

Even though he was the football star and she was the most popular girl in the university, the match was not a perfect one. Douglass McKay was quiet, serious, and moody. Raised by Scottish Presbyterian parents who had emigrated from Ontario, Douglass learned responsibility and a basic distrust of frivolity. His mother died of cancer when he was young, and a younger sister whom he loved very much died in her teens. I think the Battle of Belleau Wood in World War I left marks on his soul as well.

Harriet Mills was beautiful and gregarious. Though her parents homesteaded in North Dakota in the late 1880s and were struggling dirt farmers, their children inherited from them the idea that they came from a heritage of privilege. Harriet was the youngest of five children, and was doted on and protected by everyone in the family from the hardest aspects of life on a homestead. She could be frivolous and impractical, but she was observant enough to have had witnessed hardship firsthand. Given a choice, she chose the upbeat and hid her dark side in lightheartedness.

My father's first job as an engineer was in Park City, Utah, when it was a true Wild West mining camp. My father worked too much, leaving his wife alone most of the time. In winter, she skied the mountains so fast that the wind whistled as she flew by; in summer, she hiked alone. She begged her young husband to spend more time with her and not to leave her vulnerable to the attentions of his boss.

In a pattern he repeated often in their marriage—resisting her requests in silence and then overreacting and giving her much more than she wanted—he announced one day that he had quit his job because she was so unhappy and that they were now partners in a resort business in Longview, Washington.

They took their six-week-old baby, Bob, and drove west, only to find that they and many other people had been scammed. There was nothing for them there but a barracks to live in with strangers. It rained constantly, and they had no money left to make a change.

Harriet and the baby got sick; she couldn't nurse him. Douglass retreated into dark silence, and Harriet fell apart. She went home to her Fundamentalist mother in North Dakota—another disastrous move—and soon was in a hospital in Minneapolis while one of her sisters took care of Bob.

My father, from then on, distrusted her. He never saw that he had any responsibility for her illness; he learned only that she was fragile and untrustworthy in a crisis. He wanted no more children.

A year later, after she recovered, they went back to Park City. In 1927, when Bob was four, my father became manager of a silver mine in the Sierra Nevada in California. For a while life was easier, though my mother was lonely much of the time. She and Bob spent winters in Reno when he was old enough to go to school.

The Depression put Silverado Mine into receivership, and my father remained as watchman and caretaker. He and Bob hunted and fished to eke out a living while they waited for a paycheck. Those years were happy for my brother; he learned to hunt and to improvise and to keep a Model A running by using his ingenuity.

My birth in 1934 put an additional strain on my parents' finances and—I am sure—their relationship.

Late in 1936, a job opportunity appeared in the Philippines, but by the time my father got to Manila and to the mine that offered the position, the mining boom there was on its way out. He found several short-term jobs over the next two years—one of them mining manganese on a tiny island called Siquijor. Between each of these jobs, my mother and I—and, sometimes, Bob—would live at a Mrs. Kane's Boarding House in Manila. There we met other out-of-work mining families and made friendships that outlasted a war. My mother suffered in each new mining camp, missing the muted colors of the desert and feeling suffocated by the dark green jungles that encircled the mining camps.

Finally, late in 1938, the perfect job came up: general manager of Mindanao Mother Lode, a rich and promising mine on the southernmost and largest island in the archipelago.

At last, life was easy. My mother fell in love with the slow pace of the Islands, the twice-yearly trips to Manila, the gentle Filipinos. Bob was in boarding school, but I was there for her; and my father was in love with his job.

When talk of war became louder in 1940 and 1941, they couldn't tear themselves away from the Philippines—not so soon after finding peace in their lives. War was theoretical. Their private peace was too precious to risk. That is how we came to be caught in a war.

———⟫◆⟪———

I saw my father leave his office and begin to walk home for lunch. He always walked slowly in the noontime heat, but today his shoulders seemed to carry weights. Mother and I watched him cross the wooden bridge, then disappear as the road followed the fold in the hill. He coughed, as he always did, as he climbed the long wooden stairs to our house. During a long spell without a job in Nevada, he had polished quartz and semiprecious stones as a way to pass the time. Too stubborn to respond to my mother's pleading, he had refused to wet the stones. The cough that resulted from inhaling quartz dust was now a part of him, like the line between his eyebrows and his black mustache. My mother called it catarrh, but it was really silicosis.

"You didn't send a boy with a note, so I guess there's no answer to your cable," my mother said.

"No, nothing from anyone. I tried to send another cable this morning, but the post office in Surigao wouldn't take it. They said that nothing has gone in either direction since late on the twelfth. Messages are piled up waiting to go if anything opens up."

In a few days my brother, Bob, would have been home for Christmas vacation. He was a senior at Brent School in Baguio, north of Manila. The main Japanese landing had been to the north and west of Baguio, aimed at Manila. It seemed impossible, but he could already be a prisoner.

Dionisio served our lunch, padding softly on the shining floor in his bare feet, while my father tuned the Philco radio to the noon news from Manila. He leaned over the veneered cabinet, coaxing the green cat's eye to narrow and erase the howls of static. We listened to reports of the Japanese advance on Manila. The Japanese had bombed Davao, the largest city on Mindanao and to our south. I felt fear tighten as my parents looked at each other in silence. The enemy had attacked on all sides of us.

"I know Bob's fine," my mother said. "I just know he is. He's strong and young and resourceful. You did put money in his account, didn't you, when you were in Manila? He'll maybe make his way here. He may even be on the *Corregidor* at this very moment!"

In the first few days, reports were that damage at Pearl Harbor and at Clark Field near Manila had been light, but now that didn't ring true. Where, my mother kept asking, was the Air Force, those clouds of Flying Fortresses? The Japanese were free to attack anywhere in the western Pacific. They were now bombing Singapore.

From my room at siesta time, I heard them talking. They kept their voices low, but I crept away from my bed and under the house, which was built on concrete pilings, where I could hear better.

"God, I wish I'd sent you and the kids home in April when the Army wives went!"

"But I wouldn't go then, and I wouldn't go now, either. We'll be all right, even if it takes a year. We can live off the land."

"Live off the land with white skins? We'd be turned in in a minute!"

"I don't think so. I think the Filipinos will be loyal, and I think we'll be all right. I just want Bob here with us. I can't stand not knowing where he is. I want us all together for this. I know this is just panic. MacArthur said, when you saw him in May, any war would be over in three weeks, and I believe him. He said it again last week when you saw him in Manila. I'd just like to see one of our planes, though. Even one would make me feel better."

General Douglas MacArthur was commander of the U.S. Armed Forces of the Far East at the time, and he was also a stockholder in Mindanao Mother Lode. In May, before the war started, my father had made an appointment with the general in Manila to ask what he should do about evacuating his family from the Islands. Many Americans—including the U.S. Army—were sending their dependents home in 1941, and he had wanted to do the responsible thing. MacArthur had told him not to worry: any war, if it came, would be over within a month. Just the week before the bombing of Pearl Harbor, MacArthur told my father the same thing, though he advised not sending any gold concentrate by ship for a few weeks.

"Plowman wants to buy a *lorcha* and sail for Australia," my father said. I always strained to hear his low voice.

"My God, that's crazy! Does he know anything about boats? He's from Texas! And the Japanese are already bombing Singapore between here and Australia."

"There's a mine in Agusan we could probably go to while we wait for the Navy. It's pretty far up into the hills. I don't like staying out here on this peninsula. The Japs could pen us up here, easy."

"I just want to see one airplane!" my mother said, "Just one." They talked for a while, until the heat lulled them off to sleep.

I stayed under the house, where it was always cooler than anywhere else. Our house was built on concrete pilings so that air could circulate beneath it and so that animals and insects could not enter it easily. The pilings had little moats filled with oil that were supposed to keep the ants from climbing into the house. I knew that the ants walked over the bodies of the first ones, but I never told the grown-ups. The earth was safe, and I was used to the green jungle around us, but I liked the idea of the sailboat.

———⟫◆⟪———

After siesta, Maximo, our chauffeur, drove my mother and me to Surigao to buy supplies. The servants needed rice, and the lists made that morning in the *sala* were long.

I was glad finally to find out what "yousaffy" meant. The adults had been using the word even before the Emergency (as we were calling the war), but it hadn't seemed important enough to learn. Now there was a sign across the doors of our car, taken over this morning, my father had told us at lunch, by the U.S. Armed Forces of the Far East. USAFFE, read the side of our black Studebaker. The Army was allowing us to use our car for the last time before they took it into service.

Along the road to Surigao the farmers were planting rice. Bending under the sun to spear young green shoots of rice into muddy water, they didn't seem to be afraid of snakes in the murky paddies the way I would have been. Though I couldn't hear the chanting through the car windows, I knew they were singing:

> Planting rice is never fun,
> Bent from morn 'til the set of sun
> Cannot sit and cannot stand,
> There's no rest for anyone!

As we approached Surigao, people on the way to rice-rich valleys inland walked toward us carrying bundles, and the buses we passed were heavy with passengers. Pigs tied upside down to poles squealed hopelessly as they were carried. Chickens, also tied to poles, were more patient; they held their heads in proper alignment with the earth, beaks open in thirst. Babies nestled hotly against their mothers' bodies and slept as they could.

Along Bilang-Bilang Street, under the canopy of the trees planted two hundred years before by Spaniards, brightly painted horse-drawn *carretelas* carried panicky people to the harbor. Carved chests, treadle sewing machines, songbirds in cages sat among the riders. The sounds of cracking whips and shouting drivers joined with the sounds of animals and crying children. I think it was then my mother finally realized that we were truly caught in a war. The scene in Surigao, though color-ful and tropical, was not different from the pictures of refugees leaving Paris or Warsaw that we had seen in *Life* magazine.

We went first to buy drinking glasses at the Japanese Bazaar, always our first stop in town, and stood stupidly before the CLOSED sign. The Japanese in the area had been rounded up and interned in the rooms above the store. Nagata and Katahari, who had built cabinets in our house at the mine, looked down at us. My mother's hand rose to greet them, then sank slowly when she realized they were enemies now.

Ong Bon Pin, however, was still trading, though his shelves were showing and the overhead beams weren't holding many baskets and mats to wrap things in. The smell from large glass jars filled with fermented dried fish made me cover my nose as it always had, and I turned away from the *baluts,* unhatched chicks buried in their shells for months, which are a delicacy for Filipinos.

I watched the storekeeper wrap lamp chimneys; heard my mother gasp at the new high price of rice. She bought two sacks of rice, his last packet of needles, some spools of thread. Ong Bon Pin sold mother the glasses that she couldn't buy from the Japanese Bazaar; then, just as the afternoon rains began, we went to the harbor to buy kerosene.

The scene there was even more frantic than the one on Bi-lang-Bilang Street. Prices for places on the few remaining boats rose constantly as newcomers arrived on the pier to escape to Siargao or Bucas Grande, islands we could see on clear days from Surigao. One boat, laden to the gunwales, sailed out of the harbor as we watched and vanished into the slanting rain.

We stopped at the Cosmos Hotel for tea, as we always did, and met some of the twenty-eight Norwegian sailors from the freighter *Ravenaas* who had come ashore in lifeboats the day before. They had been steaming through the Islands, not knowing anything about a war with Japan. When a Japanese bomber attacked them, the ship sank quickly. The survivors were tall, most of them, and blond. They spoke among themselves but were silent with us. It was strange for me to see them as silent as natives in from the hills; I had never before seen white men who could not speak English. I wanted to know what it felt like to be bombed out in the middle of the ocean when you didn't even know there was a war, but there was no way of finding out. We gave them shirts and trousers collected at the mine; they bowed and seemed grateful.

This was the day the *Corregidor* usually arrived on its circuit through the Islands, bringing travelers and supplies. It had not arrived, nor had there been any news of it. We returned to the mine without the fresh fruit and vegetables and the Australian meat we depended upon.

At home we found Dionisio quietly hanging the blackout curtains at the windows. Not much was said at dinner, and before long we were tucked under our mosquito nets listening to the drumming rain on our galvanized-iron roof.

———◆———

There are no rules for being caught in a war. Tension builds, fear grows. Decisions are made and unmade, changed, and acted upon. Mainly there is waiting. The waiting gave an appearance of normality, but the reality was change and erosion.

Dionisio asked my mother one morning, "Ma'am, is there still war?" That was early, before too many decisions had been made. For a few days, the mine kept to its shifts, but in less than a week workers began to be laid off and the mine worked only one shift. The silence of the mill was unsettling; it added to the feeling of everyday life being suspended. I hadn't known how used to the noisy mill I was—the growl of rock being shattered and the pop of larger rocks breaking—until it stopped running.

Some of the single men on the staff left to volunteer with US-AFFE. It was better than waiting around, they said. There was a lot to be done, but it was too late, really, to make any difference. My father took me with him one afternoon, racing in a company car over the white crushed-coral roads, to watch the constabulary begin basic training for Filipino troops. He had fought in World War I, and I imagine he thought he could contribute something to the war effort. The recruits carried sticks instead of guns. Americans rarely bothered to learn the Filipino languages, and orders of "Left! Right! Present Arms!" were meaningless to the raw troops who spoke a variety of dialects but little English.

One afternoon, a car bristling with guns came to take our Germans away. Waldo Neveling left with a wave and a silvery smile, but Mr. Heidepreim stayed with us. My father trusted him and vouched for his loyalty. I don't know where Germans and Italians were taken to be prisoners; in the Far East in those days it would not have occurred to anyone to put white men with Japanese, even if they were now all our enemies.

The worst news was of the sinking of the *Corregidor* in Manila Bay. She hit a mine and sank in ten minutes, the radio said. Once, a few months before, standing at the ship's rail with my mother, I heard a man say, "Only a few layers of paint on this old tub keep us from sinking."

I had no difficulty picturing the paint shattering in the midnight sea and imagining the steamer slipping under the water.

Sometimes, I would catch sight of my mother standing still with her hands over her face.

"What's wrong, Mommy?"

"Nothing, really, dear. I guess I was just thinking about Bob."

"Do you think Bob is all right. Was he on the boat, Mommy?"

"We don't know. But you mustn't worry. Remember what a good swimmer he is, and how he taught you to swim underwater? Remember how fast he can run? I know he's all right, so you must know that, too."

I worried anyway and wanted to hear his name on the radio. Bob was ten years older than I, and a mythic hero for me. He had not lived at home much in the years we had lived in the Islands, and I called upon his faraway power for support when I thought life was unjust.

We never heard his name read from lists of survivors, nor did we hear Marie Smith's name. She had gone to get Christmas presents in Manila, and her three children were here with us and their father, Larry. It was worse for Mr. Smith, I thought, because we all knew Marie couldn't swim. My wonderful brother could swim like a flying fish. There were others from mines nearby in Manila, but they weren't listed, either.

Everyone had disappeared into the war.

For something to do while she waited for the war to takes its course, my mother began a nervous sorting of the household. Cartons containing essentials for an evacuation were stored by now in the *bodega* near the mine office; her sorting at this point was a different thing—a farewell. Her collection of native hats didn't seem worth dealing with. Today anthropological museums display hats like hers, but then they were simply decorations on the walls of a graceless house in a mining camp. She could have packed the two sets of Rose Medallion china, perhaps, but where would the packed boxes go that would be any safer than the cabinets they were in? Evening dresses and white Saigon-linen suits were frivolous now, not worth saving.

In the end she packed one carved Chinese chest with family pictures and old letters. She put in cutwork linen tablecloths that she had bought from a Chinese peddler who traveled from mining camp to mining camp. My father, disapproving of excesses and my mother's spendthrift ways, had forbidden the peddler to come into Mindanao Mother Lode, but he came anyway, tempting and delighting the women who gathered on our porch. He carried huge soft bundles tied in large cotton squares. He opened each bundle slowly—each piece of linen was more beautifully embroidered than the one before it. His soft voice described the fine work of the orphaned girls in China, tempting, coaxing the women to buy. At the very center of each bundle, he packed jade and ivory carvings. I longed for an ivory pleasure boat. I loved the way their miniature shuttered windows opened to reveal tiny passengers. The peddler tempted us to buy ornate carved ivory balls with portholes revealing freely moving balls inside, one within the other. I could not imagine how they could be carved so marvelously. The peddler cast his spell on me, as well, but I had no money to buy his treasures.

After my mother packed the chest with linens and a few trinkets, she found room for a few of her unframed watercolors.

"Dionisio, do you think you could look after this chest for me during the Emergency?"

"Ma'am, your chest will be safe with me."

We didn't see much of my father those days; closing down a mine is complicated. The crease between his brows deepened, he spoke even less than usual; tension came with him when he was home, waned when he left. Acid water made our mine difficult to operate; only a Worthington pump made in England could pump underground water out of the mine shafts without being destroyed by the very water it pumped. The men decided to hide valuables in the mine, then dismantle the pumps at the last minute, leaving the Japanese to deal with the acid water.

I couldn't overhear all the whispered conversations about the pumps, but one morning I helped my mother choose things from her jewel box for burial in the mine shaft. The best things, my mother told me, would be the safest: Daddy was going to hide them in the mine shaft.

"Daddy gave me this lapis ring"—it was a rectangular block of stone in a silver setting—"for my birthday. These amber beads—see the fly caught in this bead?—come from Russia. These are your grandmother's silver forks—your uncle Cameron has the spoons. Oh, and here is your baby book. How dear you were, but we can't look at it now. We have to get this packed for Dionisio to take to Daddy to put in the mine shaft."

"I need a good luck charm," she said, "so I'll keep this five-dollar gold piece with us." She tucked the golden coin, so heavy for its size, into a deerskin pouch, and sent the package of family papers and valuables off with the houseboy.

That night, Daddy came home with a bronze fire extinguisher with a screw cap. He put his Leica camera in it, along with other things less precious than the ones hidden in the mine shaft, and buried it in our garden. I watched him pacing, measuring, taking angles in the dim light from his flashlight. Americans in the Philippines, like the Spanish before them, had learned to maintain their dignity by doing no manual labor. It amazed me that he could dig a hole with a shovel.

After the valuables were hidden and the favorite things given to Dionisio, who took them to his village, the house remained much as it had always been—rattan furniture and thick Chinese rugs on the shining floors, dishes in the cabinets and pots in the kitchen. It was impossible to believe that the United States couldn't protect her possessions or that we would leave our house.

———⟫◆⟪———

When a cable finally came from Manila reporting that no one from Surigao was on the *Corregidor*, a great tension left our family. At least we knew Bob hadn't drowned in Manila Bay. He might still be in Baguio, but that offered little comfort because the Japanese had bombed Baguio the first day of the war. He might already have been rounded up for prison camp.

Disaster retreated, but only for a little while. Twelve days after Pearl Harbor, on December 20, 1941, Davao, the biggest city on Mindanao, fell without a battle.

I was learning what "falling" means.

Once Davao fell, our situation became more serious. It seemed likely that the Japanese would move quickly, as their momentum carried them, and that they would come in on both sides of our peninsula at Placer—a beautiful black-sand beach where people from the different mines in northern Mindanao met on Sunday afternoons—and Surigao, leaving only the dark jungle behind our mine for an escape.

The men were meeting to discuss the new situation when Major Graves of USAFFE happened by. When he learned that there were five women and five children in the camp, he ordered us all to leave immediately. He called it a "temporary precaution."

After all the planning and preparation, it seemed nothing was organized after all. No one had planned for a hasty flight, and few overnight bags or containers of food were ready to go. We grabbed a few things, said good-bye to the servants, went down the long wooden steps to the road, and crossed the bridge for the last time.

"We'll be back in a few days, Dionisio!" my mother called.

I leaned down to pet my black-and-white cat. She purred and sat calmly on the wooden steps to watch us walk away.

It was all over in fifteen minutes. We never saw our house, or anything in it, again.

Our own car, now an official USAFFE vehicle, was waiting to take us to the little town of Timamana where we spent the night. Families from other mines nearby joined us, and soon we were gathered around a campfire in the churchyard of the village.

Mother made canned-salmon sandwiches for dinner. Larry Smith made coffee the way cowboys did, he said—boiling the grounds and water in a pot. It smelled wonderful, but we children got powdered milk instead.

The Filipino priest welcomed us to Timamana, saying that his humble mission was a good place for an evacuation. His accent made "evacuation" sound like "vacation," and I had to agree. If this is a war, I thought, wars are fun!

I fell asleep on the ground beside the car, watching first a bright star and then the moon move past the cross on the tower of the little mission church. It had been a long, long time since I had slept without a mosquito net.

———◆———

"Any day, now," the grown-ups kept saying, "any day, the Air Force will be here. We'll show 'em!"

But no planes came. Where could we go? Mr. Plowman had not found a sailboat by the time we left Mother Lode, but there was another waterway open to us: the Agusan River and its tributaries. It flows through swamps and jungle from the southeastern part of Mindanao and empties at Butuan into the Mindanao Sea. Up four more rivers, high in the Diuata Mountains, was Gomoco Goldfields. The mine had shut down a few months before for auditing, but it was fully equipped with houses, power, and freshwater. There would be no malaria at such a high elevation. Our hope was that it would be far enough from the coasts that the Japanese would not have time to take us before the American Navy steamed in from Hawaii.

A message came to us by runner at our campsite in Timamana that the *Gomoco Chief*, a river launch that carried supplies to Gomoco, was in Butuan. The skipper, Nelson Kellogg (a scraggly man who had done the unforgivable and "gone native" by marrying a Filipina) would take the Surigao Americans to Gomoco if we wanted to go.

We went by car to Butuan to meet him. The Japanese had not landed yet, so my father went back to our mine to get as many supplies as he could gather while we waited for the rest of our group to assemble. Any thought of hesitating about our new plan vanished at the radio report of 110 Japanese ships sighted off Lingayen Gulf near Luzon.

My mother and I went shopping again, this time accompanied by Helen Welbon, whose husband ran a sawmill in Butuan in partnership with Mr. Kellogg, owner of the *Gomoco Chief*. Helen was a large woman, a teacher, whose size fascinated the Filipinos. "When will you be delivered, ma'am?" they asked her all the time. Any woman that big, the Filipinos reasoned, had to be pregnant. She was planning to come with us to Gomoco on the riverboat.

My mother decided that I would need shoes. Everyone had been shopping before us, and I ended up with a strange pair of pointy beige-and-white wing tips and two pairs of Japanese tennis shoes, far too large. It doesn't really matter, I thought, being barefoot is best anyway.

As we went around the town, a small Japanese observation plane buzzed over us. The Filipinos stood in the doorways of the shops watching us as we made our rounds, preparing for our escape inland. We had planned to leave the next morning on the *Gomoco Chief*, but when my father arrived with the truckload of supplies, we loaded and left. The Japanese plane was unnerving. It seemed better to get away quickly.

The townspeople followed us to the dock where the *Chief* waited for us. We were the best entertainment they had had in years. Spare mattresses from the mine's bachelors' quarters were spread over the deck alongside cases of canned food and piles of fresh bananas. Fifteen adults, five children, Mrs. Feigel's enormous German shepherd, Pat, and a raggedy little dog, Toto, who belonged to my favorite grown-up, Mrs. Plowman, all joined Mr. Kellogg's family who were on their way upriver to their *kaingin*, where they would farm while they waited for the Emergency to end. They seemed happy to have us join them on their trip up the rivers.

We pulled away from the town with its Spanish plaza and regular street plan and were immediately in a tropical wilderness. Long grass leaning over the riverbank replaced the palm trees of the coastland. We found places to nestle into on deck and settled into the monotonous landscape and the hypnotic throb of the boat engine. Mother put me on top of a pillowcase full of stuffed toys and towels and a large part of the Mother Lode's payroll that had arrived by miracle just as we left home. Sometime after dark, she handed me a spoon and a can of cold beans.

I woke to a foggy morning at the junction of the Agusan and the Gibong Rivers—the Land of the Floating Houses. The houses sat on the land in the dry season, but in the rainy season, when the waters were high, the houses were tethered to sturdy trees and left to float on the river. A wet season when the houses floated freely all year was better than a dry year because the mud flats of less rainy years were inconvenient to live on.

The launch stayed on the Gibong for only a few kilometers, then we turned into the Sulibau. Each river was smaller than the last, and shallower. The banks closed in on us, the channels meandered through swamps clogged with floating hyacinths. A thick growth of trees and bamboo, entangled with vines, some bearing large white waxy flowers, others carrying huge brown pods longer than my father's arm, lined the edge of the river.

Mr. Kellogg, calmly steering his launch through the waters he knew well, hailed some hill people coming down the river in their dugout *baroto*.

"Cay-o! Cay-o!" he called and then in the soft hill dialect of the boatmen, he asked them to turn back upstream, with a message asking for a smaller launch with less draft, to keep from running aground.

We children were allowed to swim in the river while the boat tied up to wait for the smaller boat. Silence closed in on us, the sounds of the water riffling past the launch and the calling of birds mixed with rare bits of conversation as we dozed in the hot afternoon. Late in the day, we heard the launch in the distance, now loud, then farther away, as it turned with the river's lazy course.

The smaller launch carried us up the shallow river, but soon sandbars blocked the way of the smaller boat, too. The adults pushed while we children and the cargo rode. Sometimes the boat could go on its own. Then the grown-ups waded in the shallows, laughing and talking to one another. Larry Smith was always good company—even when he had three small children to care for alone. I thought then that the grown-ups were having fun wading in the river and chatting, but the diary my mother began almost the minute she heard of the bombing of Pearl Harbor reads:

We arrived, wet and exhausted, at Krieckenbeek's landing by the Sulibau long after dark. We carried the sleeping children in and laid them on the damp mattresses we hauled in from the boat. Krik is a small wiry Dutchman, burnt brown as a Malay by the sun. He trades with the Chinese along the river and lives with a native woman who has borne him many children. He smiled a white smile and offered us tea. How grateful I was for his welcome.

Pale rafters reflected light from kerosene lamps as I lay on a damp mattress. The building was filled with the smells of barrels filled with raw sugar, of dried fish, of reels of hemp rope, and of dry goods that Mr. Kreickenbeek sold to merchants up and down the rivers of interior Mindanao. Voices, both familiar and unfamiliar, mixed with the sounds of the jungle night, and I fell asleep.

Mother had carried eggs from Butuan in a little basket, and there was bread left from our kitchen, which now seemed so far away that I might only be imagining it. A breakfast of scrambled eggs cooked on an alcohol stove was a big improvement over the cold beans of the night before.

———————

At dawn, Charlie Martin, the caretaker at Gomoco Goldfields, walked seven kilometers down the mine road to welcome us. Big and comfortable and Texan, he was unfailingly cheerful—a man of infinite optimism and generosity. He was missing a few teeth here and there, and his bent gold-rimmed glasses glinted cockeyed in the light.

Charlie had been alone at Gomoco for several months and was happy to have company at last.

"Glad to see ya! Lots of room for you at Gomoco! It's a great little place—I think you'll like it!

"We got a truck up at the mine. Let me try to get it going so you ladies won't have to walk all the way to Gomoco with the children. Seven kilometers is hard going for women in this climate."

We heard Charlie's truck coming toward us long before it crashed through the grassy opening to Krik's boatyard. The engine's roar broke the jungle silence the way the launches had ripped the rivers' quiet the day before. Charlie was driving, and Julio, a houseboy, was there to help us load.

Huddled under umbrellas protecting us from the sun, we sat in the back of the truck and waved good-bye to the river. The road led through tall grasses in the lowlands and then climbed into the mountains.

We had always lived in clearings at the edge of the jungle, but this was the first time I had been in it. Giant trees, hung with vines, edged the road. Darkness was just behind them and all around us, though the sun pounded on the road and through the umbrellas.

Charlie announced that we were almost at Gomoco when we passed through a village in the jungle. It had been only a few months since the mine's workers had left, yet already the *nipa*-grass roofs were fallen and vines invaded the open windows. A few more turns in the road brought us to a shallow crossing of a clear creek and our refuge.

Gomoco was perfect for us. In an opening in the jungle at the edge of Kagomay Creek, it was a good place to build a community. The mess house and kitchen included, beyond all expectations, an electric stove and a refrigerator! There was even a Singer sewing machine powered by a treadle. Two staff houses built on stilts each contained three rooms. These three buildings all faced Kagomay Creek, which babbled cheerfully below the porches. The dark jungle began on the other side of the creek. Another larger building, with a long veranda, faced the white-gravel "common."

The mill was equipped with many meters of khaki filter cloth; there was plenty of diesel oil to run the generator in the powerhouse, and supplies in the assay office would be valuable to us for trading. There was a blacksmith shop and a *bodega* for storing supplies.

While the truck went back for the rest of the people and for supplies, we chose our rooms. My parents chose the room at the farthest end of the row of staff houses. The room overlooked the creek, which filled our ears with its comforting babble. Perhaps fifteen feet square, it was utterly bare. Rough-sawn boards were both inner and outer walls, and we came to use the horizontal two-by-fours as shelves.

I was happy when Beth Plowman chose the room next to ours. She was in her late twenties and was the youngest grown-up I knew. She came from Texas. I had never been there, but I knew it was a wonderful place because Beth—and now my new friend, Charlie—came from there. She had dark curly hair and blue eyes and the patience to spend time with an adoring child.

Jean Feigel chose the third room in the little house and moved in with Pat, the big dog. Her husband, Fred, was a friendly man and a good friend of my father's. He had chosen not to come to Gomoco with Jean, hoping to help defend the island. Jean was a private person both before the war and at Gomoco. We saw little of her, except at meals. My mother was somewhat in awe of Jean because she had gone to Wellesley College.

Beth asked me to help her scrub the slatted floor of the tiny room that connected our rooms. Bath facilities at Gomoco were simple: a bucket of water, a bar of soap, and a slatted floor. It had been a convenient home for a young pig being fattened for Charlie's Christmas dinner, but now he, too, had to evacuate and move to new quarters. Beth and I carried him, squealing and struggling, to a pen near the kitchen building, and then we hauled water from the river to wash the floor. Never before, in my protected life as a white child in the Philippines, had I been asked to work. We scrubbed the slats with yellow laundry soap and native fiber brushes. Beth probably did most of the hard work, but I was proud to be included and not left at the fringes of activity. When the floor was clean and the wood dried white, I had learned another new thing from the war: anyone could work hard, not just natives. I was proud of that primitive bathroom.

December 23, 1941. We three will live in this small bare room. I'll try to be cheerful and brave, but my throat aches at the thought of our comfortable home at Mother Lode. I must remember this is only for a few weeks at most; and when it's over, we'll pretend it was all a lark.

Supplies took days to arrive at the camp because the truck never again made the trip without breaking down. The men labored in the heat to load it, repair it, unload it. It brought bedding, clothing, and food, and it came to its final resting place at the edge of the clearing where it sank toward entropy and formlessness.

Moving to Gomoco and settling in was the easy part. Now we had to learn to live together.

Except for the Welbons, who had lived in Butuan, all of us came from Mindanao Mother Lode, and we knew each other well. Our past had not prepared us, however, for giving up our independent lives and cooperating in close quarters.

December 25th. It isn't easy living like this. I brought little Christmas gifts for the children and think that we cannot let

Christmas go even though our world is turned upside down.
Jean's argument prevailed, and now we have to wait until all of
us—and all of our supplies—are here for our celebration. She
thinks we ought to combine Christmas and New Year's! How sad
to limit our good times.

There were five of us children. Larry Smith's three—Roxanne,
who was five; her sister, Shelley Lou, who was three; and their
six-month-old brother, Rusty. They all had red hair like their
mother's. Hazel Crenshaw was about six. I was nearly eight.

My parents had always kept me close to home, and though
we all lived in a mining camp, I hadn't seen the other children
much. My companions had usually been adults.

New Year's came with a great show of jollity, with toothpaste, soap, and cigarettes being exchanged by the adults. We
children got our presents at last. In my collection of presents
was a pair of yarn lovebirds in a hoop that I had longed for in
Manila the previous September. The word "war" did not have
much meaning for me if something I had wanted so much so
long ago and so far away could appear again in Gomoco. We
might have left our homes, but our lives were not so changed
that things I wanted could not still come to me.

In reality, New Year's was a grim time. Hong Kong had
fallen. Manila radio signed off after the news broadcast on December 31. The Japanese were everywhere in the Far East, con-
quering everything, with no resistance at all.

The rains arrived in January. It seemed as though it would
rain forever. Sheets and clothing hung indoors from every available spot, so that moving around our tiny room involved duck-
ing under and around sagging wet things. More sheets hung in
the *bodega* where my father oversaw the counting and listing of

the canned goods. Lists were updated as more supplies were brought up the rivers with the rest of the staff at Mother Lode.

A plan for living began to develop. My mother's diary calls it a "socialistic plan."

January 15, 1942. At a meeting today we voted to pool every-thing—now, as it happens in socialist societies, the ants will feed the grasshoppers.

Rationing was the first big issue. There was a contingent that was sure that the war could not last long, that the Filipinos would be able to bring in food. They thought that we could live off the land if we had to and that we could use the canned goods and powdered milk and coffee as we needed it. There were the pessimists—my father on that side, with my mother supporting his point of view, even though by nature she was a grasshopper—who were not so sure of the Filipinos' or the land's ability to support us. They wanted to begin rationing right away and to save the food while trading with the Filipinos as long as possible.

The pessimists won:

January 20, 1942. Here at our camp of refuge, we are hungry and we eat stringent rations in order to economize. We have begun gingerly to try native food—camotes, kangkong, ubod—which gradually, very gradually, we accept as a part of our meals in order to save the canned goods. Two meals a day is the rule, coffee early, if you want it, then breakfast at 10:30 and dinner at five. No milk or sugar in coffee. We feel hungry most of the time, but we are not starving. Two squares of toilet paper are allowed per visit to La Casa that hangs out over the creek below our house. We are on our honor to observe that, and I wonder who's obeying besides me.

At this point, the Japanese had not taken more than Davao in the southern part of Mindanao, and Americans could still move freely around the island. No one knew just when the Japanese would close down travel on the rivers and the coastline. In the middle of January, when the camp was functioning well, the single men left Gomoco to volunteer to fight the Japanese. Some of the married men left, too.

Beth's husband, Red, young and in the mood for adventure even though his wife was expecting a baby, also left for the coast. He still wanted to get away by boat and planned to buy a two-masted *lorcha* large enough for all of us to sail to safety in Borneo.

The idea that we would scramble down limestone cliffs on the west coast to get on a boat to travel through dangerous waters was, to my mother, preposterous. Once she found a nest, she never wanted to move; Gomoco was to her a fine place to wait. My father, on the other hand, was willing to consider any plan to get his family to safety.

The plan frightened my mother, who distrusted boats, but it delighted me. I had loved the Sundays we spent on sailing boats. Filipino sailors knew how to whistle for the wind with a long, slow "oooooooo, oooooooo" when our sails flapped on quiet afternoons. Their song always brought up a breeze, and I thought the plan of going to sea was splendid.

Beth stayed with us at Gomoco while her husband went off to find a sailboat. Her baby was expected in June, and she joined us children at our table for the extra rations of milk and protein that we were given. She ate with us, I suppose, partly to keep us in line, but also partly because it might have been hard for the rest of the adults to watch her eat so well.

Then, my father, too, went to offer his services and his World War I experience to Colonel Chastaine of the U.S. Army at Anakan on the west coast. He came back in a week with orders from the colonel to take charge of the camp and to be responsible for the refugees at Gomoco. He wasn't happy with his order; he wanted something more heroic than shepherding women and children at a hideout in the mountains. I think he was more in mind of a charge up San Juan Hill like Teddy Roosevelt.

The bamboo telegraph kept us informed.

"Somewhere in this rumor, there's a grain of truth," my mother said. "We just have to figure out what it is." And then she told me about a game called Telephone that children played at birthday parties. I had never been to a birthday party, so we tried playing it at dinner one night, and I understood about the grain of truth on the bamboo telegraph.

<hr />

There was no hard news about the Philippines now that Manila belonged to the Japanese; no one knew what had happened to the Americans and British on Luzon, though they were assumed to be interned. The agony was in not knowing what had become of my brother. We did know what was happening in the world beyond the Philippine Islands because every evening Peter Kurtzweill, the Danish mechanic, turned on the generator to bring in KGEI from Treasure Island in San Francisco Bay.

February 6, 1942. The Agusan River we came up is beginning to have importance to the army. It may be the Japanese route of advance from Davao. Perhaps the home we left is to be unmolested

*and this "safe" place will be in the middle of the conflict. I try not
to waken in the night because that's when worries become un-
manageable.*

The only person in all the jumble of characters assembled at
Gomoco who was happier than he had been two months before
was Charlie Martin. Alone at Gomoco as caretaker for six
months, tended by a few Filipinos who scarcely spoke English,
he was suddenly host to a gathering of people from mines
around Mindanao.

"Don't you be blue, Harriet," he said to my mother, "this war
isn't going to last forever, and this is the best place to spend a war
you could find! Who else in the Far East has everything they
need? It's gonna be fine! I know it. I know it." He bustled about,
his long shorts hanging below his belly.

He was everywhere, offering advice, getting things for people, borrowing a mattress from someone, giving a mosquito net
in exchange. He knew the Agusan river basin and everyone in
it. Using the bamboo telegraph, he could find almost anything
that anyone needed.

Because of Charlie, refugee Americans had servants to take
care of them through most of the war. Lacking anything else to
do, the staff he had assembled while the mine was working
stayed on in hopes that the mine would open again. Instead of
working for gold miners, they got an expanding and contract-
ing group of refugees.

Julio, whom I first met when he rode in the truck to Krik's
Landing and helped us come to Gomoco, was a tall strong boy
who didn't know a word of English. His face lit up when someone thanked him in his language. *"Salamat po"* coming from us
was a great delight to him. He carried water to our rooms and

firewood to the kitchen. Juanito, our cook, could deal with the native foods we were eating. He worked long hours for us, using the wood-burning stove. He used the electric stove as a countertop, because diesel oil was too precious to use to generate electricity for anything but the radio.

Philomena, our new *lavandera,* washed all our clothes on the river rocks. She had three children about my age: Opron, whose charm soon made him the business manager for his family; his shy older brother, Opren; and a little girl named Ameliana, who lusted after my dolls.

Just as I had before the war, I spent a lot of time with the servants. I was a novelty to Philomena's children. Opren and Opron showed me swimming holes in the creek above the camp that no grown-up ever knew about. We talked pidgin and played counting games with pebbles as we passed the steamy midday hours under their *nipa* house.

My new life was more interesting than my old one. I could play in the rocky little creek just below our room with the Smith girls whom I had known at Mindanao Mother Lode. Both of them were younger than I, and being with them could pall quickly. Hazel Crenshaw was a little more than a year younger than I. She came with us from our mine, but I knew I shouldn't play with her. My mother never said so, but she disapproved of my playing with Hazel. In the rarefied class system of the Colonial Philippines, it was better to be all Filipino than part Filipino, and I suppose that's why my mother let me play with the servants' children but discouraged my spending time with a mixed-blood *mestiza* like Hazel.

In the long, hot hours of siesta, Beth Plowman played her violin for me. Her hand quivering to make a *vibrato* embarrassed me; I was uncomfortable when her concentration turned inward to a place I didn't understand. Beth was supposed to pay attention to *me*, not to music; but I stayed to listen because I loved her, and the pull of the music held me, even though I didn't understand it.

After siesta, I could watch the grown-ups counting, making lists and categories in the *bodega.*

When that became boring, I explored the mill building where there were enormous tanks of freshwater left from the filtration process. The tanks—there were perhaps six of them—were twelve feet across and enormously deep. The creek below the houses, where I loved to play, was too shallow for adults to enjoy, and the tanks in the mill became a meeting place in the late afternoons when the chores of the day were finished. The tanks both fascinated me and frightened me. There seemed to be no bottom to the dark, still water, but the water was cool. I clung to the edges of the wooden tank as I eavesdropped.

The adults talked lightly about the war—not wanting to admit to fear. Their faith in the American Navy might have been faltering, but optimists still hoped for a quick end to the Emergency. Even my father, who was never an optimist, had no doubt that we would win the war. Listening to the grown-ups' conversations, I learned that Americans win; other people lose.

January 1942 passed into February with all of us hovering over the radio at five, hoping that Singapore would not fall. If Singapore fell, our time at Gomoco would extend into the unknown future. "Falling" was no longer a mysterious word to me; everything was falling.

Then our group expanded. In the first days of the war, when the Japanese bombed Davao, the important city of southern Mindanao, four women and their four children left their homes and went to safety at a sugar plantation inland; their husbands stayed with their businesses in Davao. When Davao suddenly fell to the Japanese, their husbands were trapped. Their little band grew to fourteen, and they began to move north, away from the invaders. By February they were in Veruela, a village on the Agusan where the river passes through swamps. Mosquitoes and malaria made life in the lowlands nearly as dangerous for them as meeting Japanese soldiers would be, and they asked to join us at Gomoco.

Tuesday, February 10, 1942. The Davao refugees came to stay with us at Gomoco yesterday. We were greatly relieved to have them all here safely, for the night before they were to arrive, we heard wild sounds like human voices crying in distress somewhere in the jungle. Alex, our Russian Mill Boss from Mother Lode, came down from his new quarters in the mill, where he had moved to make room for the new people, to help Douglass find the source of the spine-chilling sounds. Mary and I waited in my bed, gooseflesh rising, but they found nothing anywhere. Finally the cries died away in the moonlight. Perhaps it was a band of ground apes—no one will ever know—but it was a frightening thing to hear, knowing that people were coming to us from across the mountains the next day.

The people from Davao wanted to have a separate kitchen and to keep to themselves, but we had so much more of everything and the clearing in the jungle was so small that the two camps were soon joined. It meant that thirty-eight people had to depend on what was in the *bodega* at Gomoco.

My father took the commission from Colonel Chastaine to care for and to lead the group of refugees at Gomoco seriously, even though he would have preferred another commission. As general manager of Mother Lode, my father controlled the December payroll and felt responsible for it. Complications soon arose because many of the men who had worked at the mine felt that they deserved some of the money for their private use. Nor did they regard Colonel Chastaine's commission as sacred as my father did.

Into this web of dissension came fourteen new people who had no loyalties to any of us. They did not want my father's leadership and did not feel that the charge given my father by Colonel Chastaine applied to them.

My father was too serious and too much a Scot to be able to retreat from a position he thought right. He quickly became unpopular and was regarded as a rigid authoritarian. The ill feelings of the first weeks never healed.

At first, supplies brought up the road from Krik's Landing on the Sulibau River were unreliable, and there was great pressure to use the food in the *bodega*. My father would not back away from the decision to keep the preserved food unused until there was nothing coming from the lowlands. There was a need to make sure that as much food as possible could come up from the river lands so that pressure to use the canned food in the *bodega* would ease.

Charlie hired Maximino Perez to be our procurement officer. Maximino was a Manobo, a tribe with a head-hunting reputation in the rest of the Islands. That reputation was hundreds of years out-of-date—Spanish priests had been in Mindanao for more than four hundred years. Maximino had been to Mission School in the Agusan valley, and he was proud of his good English.

"Provisions, Sir! I will be The One to bring your Provisions!"

His handsome face and smooth manners disguised a bit of larceny. He was the kind of liar who charms as he spins tales. He promised his undying faithfulness and untiring efforts to supply us with food—for just a little extra pay for himself.

Eventually, he brought us chickens to raise, two goats to milk, a tiny billy goat, and a couple of pigs to fatten. Philomena's cats were keeping the rat population down, but an army of cats would have been needed to protect all our food from the rats.

We ate BB-size *mongo* beans that I hated, but which I am sure are the mung beans we now use for bean sprouts. I also hated *camotes,* a stringy kind of sweet potato. There was *opo,* a cucumber that Juanito cubed and cooked to such transparency that I called it "boiled ice," but the worst of all was *kangkong,* a swamp cabbage that looks like a potato vine. Juanito overcooked the "slippery greens" every night until the slime oozed out to contaminate everything on my plate—even the rice that I loved.

We used nail kegs with boards fastened across the tops for stools. They were open at the bottom, making them perfect dark homes for colonies of cockroaches. No one could quite bear to eat knowing the two-inch-long tropical cockroaches were so close, and a ritual banging of the nail kegs began every meal. The roaches left their havens in a great clicking scatter, but they always returned to the nail kegs in time for the next meal and the banging.

In time, the rhythm of the ritual accompanied the motto "Gomoco still stands!" Once Singapore fell, as it did on February 15, 1942, Gomoco had to stand; there was not much hope of the war being over very soon.

Tamara Vigliada came to Gomoco with the group from Davao. She was Russian, married to an Italian. In the evenings, she and Alex Goodkoff, who had come with us from Mindanao Mother Lode, often sang together. Alex had trained in a cathedral choir in Siberia, and when their Russian voices blended in minor harmonies, the sound floated off into the dark jungle night. In the lamplight, they sang "Ochi Chornya" and "Volga Boatmen," of course, but there were other nameless songs that knit us together as a community.

The formal meetings meant to set up a system for managing our exile often set us apart in dissension. The Russians' singing brought us together.

———※◆※———

The Japanese were slow to occupy Mindanao. Bataan and Corregidor were still holding on, but the loss of Singapore on February 15 was devastating. Sure that we were in for a long siege, my father decided to go back to our mine and close it down completely by flooding the tunnels. He would hide the gold concentrate that was still there and bring back to Gomoco all the supplies he could carry.

Yesterday, February 15, Douglass left for the down-river trip to Butuan and thence to Surigao. It will be fine to have him bring us news from home. That seems so important to us shut in here. Maybe he will bring my big dictionary and my suitcase full of linens and small ivories.

Did they worry about separating when their world was in such flux? Did they know it was possible that he might not be able to make it back? Did she have a list of specific things she wanted, or did she just hope he'd know to bring what she wanted? Why linens and ivories? Why not thermometers and medicines? He went around the turn on the trail and vanished for three weeks, leaving us with only the bamboo telegraph, which we were beginning to trust, for communication.

He must have passed Father Abbitt on the trail. An Episcopal missionary from Dansalan, Father Abbitt was an emissary from the husband of one of the Davao women. As word of his arrival flew around the camp, we all came out of our rooms and gathered around him. Even Jean Feigel, who kept company only with her big dog as she always had at Mother Lode, came out to hear what might be happening outside Gomoco.

"Giving you news isn't why I'm here," he said. "I'm here to talk to Mrs. Lane."

Helen Lane, one of the women in the Davao party, announced at lunch that she and her three-year-old son, John, would be leaving that afternoon with Father Abbitt to go to a refugee camp at Dansalan where she would be nearer where she thought her husband might be.

"It's where Americans from the Del Monte pineapple plantation have gone. There's quite a large group there," Father Abbitt said. "I'm able to ask anyone who wants to go with us to join us. There might not be another chance to make a move, the way things are going."

Suddenly, white-faced, Beth Plowman said she'd go. There was a hospital at Dansalan, and Army nurses. It would be a much better place for her to have her baby than Gomoco, and it was nearer her husband on the coast. We helped her pack, and then she, her violin, and raggedy little Toto were gone.

I will miss Beth, but I am very happy that she will have her baby in Dansalan with the Army nurses in attendance. I know I was the one destined to be midwife in June when her baby comes, and I was frightened of it. Father Abbitt said that Baguio was taken by the Japs earlier even than Manila. Bob could be interned already. Oh, I hope not. I hope he's out free with the rest of the boys in his school. I can't bear to think of him being a prisoner.

———⟫·◆·⟪———

And then—wonder of wonders—a few days later, my mother and I left Gomoco, too! The bamboo telegraph was saying that the Chinese merchants in the barrios on the rivers were rapidly running out of things to sell.

"Daddy's away, and I want to get some cloth before it's all gone. I want to have material ready to make you clothes if we're here long enough for you to outgrow what you have, and wouldn't it be lovely to have curtains on our windows? I think you should come with me to Rosario. It will be a long day, but you could stay here with Mr. Smith if you want to."

Stay at Gomoco when I could go somewhere with my mother?

We left on our shopping trip early one morning. Juanito abandoned his post at the kitchen stove to be our guide and bearer. He led us down the narrowing path and then to a short-cut toward the river. As my mother later recorded in her journal:

Juanito reminded me of Robin Hood as he went ahead of us through the dappled glade.

It was a long walk for me, but the path was well beaten by the *cargadores* who brought our provisions. The high shrill song of the cicadas and the calls of birds beyond our sight in the tall trees kept us company. White dendrobium orchids grew far beyond our reach in trees so tall they seemed to me to be only tree trunks, not trees. The leaves were so far up that I imagined they were green clouds instead of treetops. As we neared the river, bamboo and *cogon* grass, with its razor-sharp leaves, gradually replaced the jungle.

We were probably the first white women ever to visit Juanito's tiny barrio, and we were soon surrounded by curious villagers. I had grown up being encircled by enchanted people telling each other that surely this child with the golden braids must be an angel. "An-hel, an-hel," they said in the Spanish pronunciation. The Manobos of the interior had the same reaction to me that the Visayans on the coasts had had. I had found it profoundly annoying when I was three or four, but not on this day in this village—the people were too delighted to see us and to help us for me to feel invaded by their interest.

Juanito's uncle Juan, host to strangers, offered green coconuts for our refreshment. He slashed the top off each coconut with his *bolo* and ceremoniously gave us the green goblets.

"For you, I give you from the coconut!" We drank the sweet, clear water inside.

Juanito hired a *carabao* from his uncle for us to ride. Uncle Juan pulled the water buffalo from its midday rest in a mud wallow and scraped off as much mud as he could reach, and we set off for Rosario on the broad black back—Juanito in front, my mother behind, and me in the middle.

Juanito's uncle put the end of the *carabao*'s tail in my mother's hand. When she looked puzzled, Juanito said, "You must pull on the tail if you want to go more fast!"

Once she felt we had the rhythm of the animal's gait, she gave the tail a tug, and he lumbered along the heavy trail, making it even harder for us to ride him. I had never been near a *carabao* before, though they are in nearly every picture memory I have of the Islands. After their work pulling plows and working in the rice paddies, *carabao* spend hours up to their necks wallowing in water and mud. Three or four of them together in a pond, only their noses and long curving horns out of the water, say much about contentment and escape from heat: they define the Philippines.

At first I was delighted to be riding one; but staying on our dusty steed wasn't easy, even though I had Juanito to hold on to.

We found the shelves in the *tienda* bare.

"Juanito! Where is everything? Are we too late? I need cloth!"

"No, ma'am. Everything put upstairs. We afraid for Japanese steal everything."

The simple things my mother bought—lipstick, buttons, safety pins, a hand mirror, notebooks, and pencils—had a magical quality for me because I knew there would be no more until the war was over. After only two months at Gomoco, the glitter of new things and the act of buying something had a new importance. A few months before I might have waited outside in a hot car while my mother shopped, but now I watched every transaction and listened to Juanito and my mother bargain with the storekeeper.

My mother found ten meters of unbleached muslin and a couple of *patadiongs* to use for trimming. On washday, native women wore brightly colored *patadiongs* when they walked to the rivers with their children and their laundry. Hand-woven plaid cotton, sewn into wide tubes, the *patadiongs* opened so that the women could bathe modestly in public. Their laundry clean and ready to be spread in the sun, the women wrapped their vivid sarongs around them, gathered their clean children, and walked home together, their wet black hair dripping down their backs.

The wife of one of the merchants brought us hot rice, boiled eggs, and tea. The food was truly a gift because the Filipinos were facing the same uncertainty about supplies that we were and rice was precious. Such an act of generosity deserved ceremony, and we spent a long time over our meal, Juanito interpreting the small talk.

The inevitable question came: "How old are you, ma'am?" My mother believed that a lady never tells her age, and she couldn't answer. She knew that the Filipinos had no idea how to judge us and that, for them, it was not a rude question. She knew, too, that our life expectancy was much longer than theirs and that they would be amazed at her great age and that that would make her uncomfortable. It wouldn't have hurt her to say "Forty-five," but she couldn't do it.

At the last moment, a boy offered to sell us a young cat. I held my breath until my mother bought her for me. Miss Puss rode home, yowling, in a sack that I insisted upon carrying.

We found a *baroto* and floated downriver to the clearing where the trail to Gomoco began. Floating down the winding river by the feathery bamboo and bending grasses on the shore was much better than bouncing along on the *carabao*. I watched my hand make ripples in the water as Juanito guided the dugout. Bright blue dragonflies hovered above eddies at the edge of the river, and white cockatoos flashed through the trees.

We started up the trail to Gomoco as the daily afternoon rain began. Juanito cut large banana leaves for us to carry as umbrellas. We hurried up the trail with our purchases because dark falls quickly in the tropics. Juanito's uncle came along with us; he had to be sure we would pay him for the rental of his *carabao*. As dark fell, Juanito carried me, exhausted, into camp.

My mother paid Juan with two shotgun shells. Wreathed in smiles, he said, "Now I can shoot the wild pig!" and went back to his *kaingin* by the Sulibau.

———⟫◆⟪———

My mother had the curtains up in time for my father's return from "home" early in March. Trimmed with bias bands from the red-and-white plaid patadiongs, they hung on bamboo rods and made the primitive room cozier.

"Very nice," he said when she proudly showed them off. He didn't have much to say about "home."

He borrowed back the diesel trucks the Army had commandeered and took the gold concentrate back to the mine from Surigao where it had been stored for shipping. The gold is now in solution in one of the mill tanks. He pulled the mine pumps from the lower levels of the mine and left them to flood.

"The jungle's already moving into our clearing and vines are all over your gardenia bush. Dr. Abdon has moved into our house, but he's not interested in your garden. He has enough to do trying to help people without any medicines."

"What about the servants?" my mother wanted to know.

"I sent Dionisio and Consuelo home to their village, and I let Enriquita go. We don't need houseboys and maids anymore."

I was happy to see my schoolbooks, and my mother was delighted with more things to read, but my father had no more news of the rest of the Philippines than we did.

He was grim. He had believed General MacArthur's bland assurances about the power of the United States, and now his family was separated—his son missing, and his wife and daughter in danger. The gold mine he had so passionately managed was closed down. All of this was happening in a war that looked endless. He wasn't sure his wife could stand the hardships she faced, and added to all this was the humiliating commission of looking after a group of women and children behind enemy lines.

He had made a bigger, and more dangerous, mistake than he had in taking his young family to the coast of Washington. I don't think my mother blamed him for their predicament, but he felt the responsibility deeply. He had to come through this crisis with his self-respect, and, as a result, he took command of Gomoco in an even more authoritarian way.

I think it was then that he moved into Beth Plowman's empty room, leaving my mother and me to sleep in the small room the three of us had shared. Perhaps they felt their bed was too small to share in the heat under a mosquito net or that I was too young to be the one moved. Whatever the reason, he stayed alone in that larger room for the rest of our time at Gomoco.

—————————

During the night of March 15, planes flew over us. They flew from west to east with the sound of war. The roar of many warplanes flying low after so many weeks of silence was chilling. They passed out of our hearing and were gone without our knowing whose they were.

The next news broadcast from San Francisco announced the arrival of Douglas MacArthur and his staff in Australia. Then we knew what those planes had carried—the whole High Command! A week later, the radio told us that Admiral Hart, commander of the Pacific Fleet, and High Commissioner Sayre were both in Washington.

The news meant two things: that there had been indeed a way out of the Philippines and that Charlie Martin's dream of flying out was possible, but it also meant that the Islands were being abandoned to the Japanese.

March 17, 1942. The days have strung themselves together with links of darkness studded with stars, and of sunlight accented with shadow. Perhaps there is peace here in the dreaming jungle and in the speech of streams. The warp of my days is thought of Bob and the weft is thinking of home while I play a part not of my choosing; the pattern shows confusion and fear.

Our room, at the end of the row of staff houses, looked onto the river and the opening of the path leading out. We had the first view of exciting events in the camp. The arrival of Maximino's *cargadores* plodding up the trail pulled us out of the house nearly every day to see what was for sale. Usually the same greens, *camotes,* and rice came up from the river, but one enterprising man brought fresh fish all the way from the Agusan River in a sloshing tank strapped to his back. The price was high, and the haggling was fierce, but the need for fresh fish won out, for our little Kagomay Creek provided only minnows. We paid the price for fresh fish, and soon it arrived quite often. Always we succumbed to temptation, even though we were learning to eat the dried and salted fish that had offended our noses in the native shops before the war.

In March, a family reunion took place under our window. Hazel Crenshaw's brother Warren, aged eight, had been at boarding school on the island of Leyte when the war began. His parents, even before we left Mindanao Mother Lode, had sent a trusted employee to find him and to bring him home. One day, accompanied proudly by Ramon Noriega, Warren arrived in camp. He was a tired, filthy, pale little boy who accepted his parents' tearful hugs almost impassively. I knew he wondered where he was and felt that even his parents were unfamiliar after such a long separation. I saw them take him to their room. After a few days, though, he was sitting at the children's table and playing happily in the river with the rest of us.

Seeing little Warren arrive, so tired and sad, set my heart to aching with the need to have Bob with us. Who is helping him? His allowance has stopped now, and how is he living? Is he a prisoner, or is he trying to find us? It's harder for me now than it was before I saw Carlota splashing across the creek to her son.

My father summoned Ramon Noriega to our room one evening to ask him to do us a great service. Lantern light picked out Ramon's features as he waited to accept his mission. A thick letter lay on the table addressed to my brother, wherever he might be.

"Ramon, I am sending you on a great mission. You have brought Warren Crenshaw here unharmed, and I know you can do many more brave things. This letter to my son in Baguio contains an important message and five hundred pesos so that he can eat. He is a student and has no money now. If you can find him and help him, I will be indebted to you," said my father.

"Yes, sir. I will try. It is the best I can do. I am not afraid, and I have many friends in Luzon who know many things," Ramon replied. "I am proud to carry your message."

As he turned to go down the trail the next morning, he said, "I will be The One to help you, Sir! This is the Message to Garcia! If I am not back by July One, I am dead!"

———<>———

Planes flew over again on the night of March 26, and then we learned that Philippine President Quezon was in Australia, too. Over the radio, MacArthur promised to return and to retake the Philippines.

March 25, 1942. MacArthur says he'll take the Islands back? Those of us who were offered no escape hadn't yet known we were lost!

Charlie Martin steadfastly held to optimism. "MacArthur just went out to get reinforcements. You'll see. Bataan will hold, and the Japs'll never take the Rock!"

Someone at dinner growled, "Yeah, Charlie, you said Manila wouldn't fall, either."

"And what about Singapore?" another voice asked.

"Sneer if you want to, I'm telling you, those Japs'll never take the Philippines!" Charlie was undaunted.

The noose tightened again when Bataan fell on April 9. On April 13, the Japanese entered Cebu, and put an end to the Voice of Cebu, which had been broadcasting what little news of the Philippines they knew; now we would have to rely on KGEI, the Voice of America's short-wave station in San Francisco. Beamed at the whole Far East, the broadcasts came with heavy static and were hard to hear.

"They'll never take the Rock!" said Charlie, optimistic still.

———⊰◆⊱———

Evelyn Burchfield had a painful tooth and Carlota Crenshaw an infected arm. There seemed still to be time for a last run down the river before northern Mindanao fell to the Japanese, so Charlie and my father took the women to Butuan.

One morning after they left, when the dry season should have started, daylight never came. The wind lifted our *nipa* roof, laid it back, and then lifted it again. The wind felt evil; there was no air to breathe, and it was raining hard. The clear little river below our window rose yellow with silt. Each minute it ran faster, carrying larger and larger debris in its current.

My mother and I leaned out our window watching it, and I asked, "Could the water ever come as high as that rock?" I pointed at a rock high above the brook.

"No, never," my mother said, and turned to move her bed away from a leak in the roof.

Our roof leaked more and more as the *nipa* lifted off the rafters and then flopped down again. I helped move our things away from one leak, only to find a new one heavier than the first. We ran to help Jean Feigel with her leaks at the other end of the house, but we abandoned the idea when the roof flew away altogether.

As the wind increased, our little house began to shiver. A tree fell parallel to our front porch—its branches rested uneasily on our veranda. On the ridge, the tops of giant trees snapped off, flew into the raging river, and were carried away. I saw my rock disappear under the roaring river our creek had become. The tar-paper roof of the kitchen building peeled up and sailed away like a witch's skirt.

Everyone clustered in our room because it was on the far side of the wind and the tree closest to the house had already fallen. Soon they decided that we would be safer under the house. The floorboards were nailed down too well to be moved, and we ran across the porch and then to a bomb shelter the men had dug under the house. The hole filled with water around our feet, and the wind screamed.

We were cold and wet and hungry. I could no longer remember what the world had been like before this typhoon. In my panic, I vomited down poor Warren Crenshaw's back. My mother had given me a cod-liver-oil capsule early in the morning and the taste and smell of fish oil and vomit made me even more nauseated.

The river continued to rise and our little house to shake. The river swelled, its sweet babble now a slapping, sucking roar. Either the river would take us, or the house would crush us. We decided to make a run for the powerhouse where we could hide beside the diesel engine, even though we ran the risk of being killed by corrugated iron sheets flying off the mill roof.

Julio was there to carry me. Philomena and her children joined us, and we all huddled next to the huge blue-black engine. Not one thread of clothing was dry; no one had eaten since the night before.

In midafternoon, after the eye had passed over us and the storm had retreated, a bottle of gin appeared from someone's private stock. The grown-ups got giddy. They sobered up quickly, though, when Peter Kurtzweill, the Danish mechanic, went stiff and passed out, his glasses glinting crazily on his nose. They thought he might be dying—so much alcohol on an empty stomach unused to liquor—but in time he came around.

The wreckage was shocking when we emerged late in the day. Roofs were gone; the bamboo irrigation system that carried water to camp from higher up the river was blown apart. An enormous tree had fallen on the assay office where our supply of rice was stored, reducing the precious stuff to wet pulp. Torn bits of green leaves plastered the windward sides of the buildings and reminded me of native women who stuck green leaves to their temples as a cure for headache. The protecting walls of jungle were stripped to matchsticks. Our three radios were water-soaked.

More devastating, though we didn't know it yet, was the damage in the lowlands. Rice paddies were destroyed; coconut and avocado trees, which take years to grow, were uprooted. All of us in northern Mindanao faced famine.

⇒·◆·⇐

We had no idea where my father and Charlie and their charges were. Even the bamboo telegraph seemed blown out of commission, because there was no news of any of them.

Then, three days after the typhoon, my father came up the trail alone.

"We were on the way home on the river when the typhoon kicked up," he said. "We spent the night with Cajada in his floating house. The river started to go crazy, and we really thought we'd get blown away from the shore and blown apart. We had a good rope that the Army left around, and Charlie and I tied that house together with a Spanish windlass. It was a wild night, I'll tell you!"

"Charlie's with Evelyn and Carlota at Talacogon. I'll go back now to get them, now that we know you're all okay here."

He said that the seven-kilometer trail from Kellogg's was almost impassable because of fallen trees.

"That storm has given us more protection from the Japanese than we ever thought of having!" he said.

"I guess the red truck won't ever leave Gomoco now," my mother said.

A couple of days later, Charlie and my father returned with Evelyn and Carlota and a family they had met in Talacogon. The Jarvises had lived before the war in a small logging camp on the west coast of Mindanao. They had left that coastal spot in search of safety inland. The welcome that met them was meager, and they moved quietly into the room Helen Lane and Johnny had left empty. They had a son, Neil, who was fourteen.

More interesting for me were the things the travelers had been able to buy on their way up and down the rivers: kerosene lamps and glass chimneys and even red lipsticks for my mother—her red badge of courage. The lamps and breakable chimneys were rare now and important because the generator ran only for radio broadcasts.

My mother chose a little red kerosene lamp made in China labeled Blizzard Brand, because it reminded her of winters in North Dakota. She thought it must have been designed to light a farmhouse on the prairie; now it would light a rough little room in a jungle camp.

Fortunately, on the heels of the typhoon, the rainy season relented a little, though in our part of Mindanao there is no reliable dry season. The dry weather gave us a chance to dry the wet rice that had been in the ruined assay office. The adults let us children help spread it on straw mats in the sun and turn it in the welcome heat. Hard work saved most of it, and we lost only a little to mold.

The hot season, which usually began in April and lasted through August, was hotter in our stripped jungle than it would have been without the typhoon. Clothes dried nearly as soon as they went on the clothesline—not like January when they had hung so dankly in our rooms. The dry weather gave us a chance, too, to repair most of the damage to the buildings.

Then one day we smelled smoke coming in from the higher mountains. It drifted into camp, then drifted away as the wind changed. For a few days, there was no smoke; then it was back, heavier. Forest fires were feeding on the dry, fallen leaves. We looked anxiously over our shoulders, wondering when it might come our way, wondering how to evade it, hoping our little (once again) river could protect us. The sun set red and fiery in a heavy sky.

In all the time of war, this was the most frightened I had been. I lay in my bed at night smelling the smoke, imagining the fire coming closer. For the week that the fire flirted with us, the smoke would lift in the morning breeze, giving me hope; but the wind shifted in midday, and the haze returned with the afternoon heat to bring back my dread.

I knew there was no escape: the fire would come and smother us. The river seemed too small to me to be a haven in a forest fire. Other dangers, like the arrival of the Japanese, were only possibilities. The jungle fire was real, uncontrollable and menacing. I could smell it. I relied on the adults to take care of danger, but they did nothing. Their idle waiting terrified me. If they wouldn't stop the fire, then what would?

Then a hard rain fell, and the danger went away. It was another of the miracles that were part of our lives in the war. We took it calmly and went on with our quiet lives in the jungle.

———⟫⟫◆⟪⟪———

The jungle was unknowing of the world outside. The days fell one after the other evenly and unchanging: the sun rose over one green bank of trees and set behind the other. Sometimes there was a moon, and sometimes there was not. Always the cicadas sang, often the hornbill called to his mate his mournful "callao, callao," and sometimes monkeys passed through the trees noisily. The most difficult thing was filling the hours.

The ebon velvet plush of the black, black jungle night curtains my rough windows, which are closed from rain and wind by sliding panels of rough-hewn shutters. Out of this black fabric, the flame of our lamp lures strange winged moths, insects and beetles. The wings of some are mother-of-pearl, others are patterned with fine lacings and patterns of gold. Great, gold beetles with hard wings bumble in throngs around the lamp. Poor moths in the flame, they are no different from us caught in our destiny.

Charlie had had some chickens when we arrived in December; now, in May, the flock was bigger and was providing a few eggs each day. It was my job, in the morning, to put my hand under the warm soft hens and to take the eggs to the kitchen. I loved the hens and named each one. I cried when my father said at dinner one night, "Henny Penny was tasty, wasn't she?"

He thought he was being funny, but he broke my heart.

We dried our precious reading material as carefully as we dried the rice. Books helped quell the uneasiness: Pearl Buck's *The Good Earth* was one; another was Thomas Hardy's *The Return of the Native*. There were some magazines, most of which belonged to Helen Welbon. She handed them around carefully; I was allowed to read them in her room only "under supervision." I resented not being trusted by her, but I needed to read them. One frustrating thing about the *Ladies' Home Journal* was that Daphne du Maurier's new novel, *Frenchman's Creek*, was running as a serial, and the end of the story was lost to us. Dona, Lady St. Columb, "tired of the artificiality of court life, the intrigues and silly escapades of London society," at the end of the second installment, had just agreed to spend days with the dashing pirate on his ship as he marauded the coast of Cornwall. As they set to their tasks of helping Juanito prepare vegetables or picking bits of stone out of the rice, the women speculated about how the story might continue.

Charlie and my father got involved in trying to determine the exact time by using information in one of the men's magazines. It was essential to know the time so that we could tune in to the news with the least expenditure of diesel oil. The system used string, a protractor, a simple formula, and a certain star. It was just the kind of problem that delighted my dad. There was not quite enough information in the magazine, and he had to call on all his engineering and reasoning skills to figure out the angles he needed to use near the equator. He and Charlie—and my mother—craned their necks at night looking for the particular star. The problem took my father's mind off his predicament for a little while, at least.

Carlota Crenshaw, who had gone to school with the nuns, taught Hazel and Roxanne Smith and me—the older girls—to embroider. I enjoyed the handwork, learning French knots and hemstitching. She taught us how to make a strong seam by hand, and it was years later that I learned it was the "back stitch," not the "box stitch." In that way I learned Carlota had a Filipino accent, though I never heard it then. We made samplers of our work on bits of filter cloth left from the women's sewing and mending. We were constantly reminded how rare the needles were and had to return them for counting at the end of each session.

One of the women of the Davao group taught reading. My mother took the youngest children for kindergarten. I went to Mrs. Welbon for arithmetic; and there, one day, I took my revenge for the supervision of the *Ladies' Home Journals*.

"Do you understand the word 'respectively,' Mary?"

"No, Mrs. Welbon."

"The problem says that John and Fred are ten and eleven years old respectively. That means that John is ten and Fred is eleven. 'Respectively' means that the two pieces of information are in the same order. Do you understand?"

I understood instantly.

"No, Mrs. Welbon. Tell me again."

"Well, if the problem tells you that the two boys are named John and Fred, and then it says that they are ten and eleven respectively, it means that you're to apply two pieces of information in the same order. See?"

"No, Mrs. Welbon."

Mrs. Welbon sighed and started again. "I suppose the problem could have said that John was ten and Fred was eleven. But another way is to use the word 'respectively.'"

"I can understand you when you tell me that John is ten and Fred is eleven, but I don't understand why they had to use respectively. Respectively is silly."

"Let's try again. Fred and John are two brothers. They are eleven and ten respectively. What does that mean to you?"

"It means that you are still using respectively and you haven't explained it to me."

I was having fun and was learning what the Filipinos were learning in the lowlands. You can win against stronger forces by pretending to be stupid.

She was saved only by the triangle being beaten to call us to an early dinner.

———⟫•◇•⟪———

Meals were planned, prepared, and eaten. The men turned the rice; we became accustomed to eating some weevils in the starchy foods and spent companionable hours over the task of getting as many out of the food as we could before Juanito cooked it. The women taught the children in the mornings, and we took siestas in the heat of the day.

As we came to life again in the afternoon, we could hear the rhythmic thud of Julio pounding the rice. We bought unhusked rice, called *palay*, because it was cheaper than white rice. Julio could remove the husks in a wooden mortar with a long, heavy pole as pestle. After he beat the soft husks from the hard kernels of rice, he winnowed it in a flat basket. *Swish, swish, swish*, rest, he threw the contents of his winnowing tray into the air. *Swish, swish, swish*, rest; *swish, swish*, rest—the husk blew off into the air as Julio moved the tray full of heavy rice kernels away from the path of the flying husks. Rice pounding and winnowing were sounds of the afternoon in the Philippines; it meant that siesta was over and the afternoon's preparation of the evening meal was under way.

In villages, women usually pounded the rice. Three women could coordinate the fall of their long poles into one wooden bowl by singing. I loved to listen. I wish I could remember the songs.

———◆———

Dinner on the porch was the one time that the whole camp assembled. Conversation combined anxiety and gallows humor with requests for another serving of camotes.

Perhaps the dinner-table attempts to be funny frightened Juanito, the cook, and the two *amahs* who looked after the two babies; but more likely they understood the situation better than we did.

"The Hapons will kill us all, sir. I am very afraid, and I will take the *amahs* to my village. I am sorry, sir, but we must go tomorrow."

Casamera had wept softly on the trip upriver in December. She missed her family, but she loved redheaded Rusty Smith, who was now a year old and whose mother had been in Manila when the war began. I saw Casamera cry many times at Gomoco; she used to tell me about her village by the sea on the island of Leyte, and she sang sad, minor-key songs about families and sisters. Her job with Larry Smith had allowed her to have a gold front tooth, but the job was no longer enough; she was frightened and far from home.

Fanny, the other *amah*, surprised me when she left with Juanito. She was *amah* to Stevie Crytser, who had come in the party from Davao. She was formal and cool for a Filipina. I was disdainful when she decided to leave because I thought her running away was cowardly. She knew her situation better than I did: she was from another island and did not know the local dialects. She was wise to leave. She needed to get back to her own people before it was too late.

After Juanito left the kitchen, the women took turns cooking meals for everyone. Carlota Crenshaw, who was half Filipina, taught my mother how to find wild ginger and lemongrass at the jungle's edge. These were new flavors to my mother, a North Dakotan, who favored sweet accents in her cooking.

In a few weeks, the women gave up cooking and Ah Hing came to take over the kitchen. Before the war changed everyone's lives, he had worked for Mr. Kellogg, the owner of the *Gomoco Chief*, in Butuan. My mother was happy to turn the cleaning of the rice pots over to him when he came from his *kaingin* by the river, but he wasn't much of a cook. In a few weeks, her diary reads:

April 1942. We eat overdone greens and rice and raisin pie that Ah Hing does his best to make unpalatable. The raisins brought in from army supplies are "inhabited" and we have them every day to use them up before they are too far gone even for us. Ah Hing's individual turnovers with armor-plate crusts sit like small forts in a moat of pallid juice, but we eat them anyway, for now we eat to live and not for enjoyment. Still, we women are glad to give up the cooking, though we still spend mornings pushing weevils out of the hollow stems of spaghetti. Struggling with the rice pots and the greens was arduous.

Colonel Chastaine, when he commissioned my father to look after the band of refugees at Gomoco, had sent a shipment of Army supplies to us. Canned meats and vegetables came in on bearers' backs to line the shelves in the *bodega*. Included was an astounding amount of raisins and maraschino cherries. Ah Hing had to be asked not to decorate the rice bowls with the cherries.

Ah Hing's bad cooking didn't bother me, even the runny raisin pies that ended each meal. There were bad jokes every night about the raisin pies and how they would frighten away the Japanese army if it came up the trail. Someone suggested using them as catapults; someone else suggested building a raisin-tart wall across the trail.

———⊰◈⊱———

I liked Ah Hing anyway, and he liked me. He had time after making pies to spend long hours doing complicated cat's cradles and folding intricate origami toys; he taught me to count to a thousand in Cantonese. He must have missed the family he left at his kaingin in the lowlands because he always had time for me.

I needed Ah Hing, just as he needed me, but for quite different reasons. He was neutral and nonjudgmental, and he helped me swim through dangerous waters of my childhood simply by liking me. He came just at the right time—at a point when I was suffering all alone.

There were several children at Gomoco, all but two younger than I was, and both of them were boys. All my life I had been the oldest—or the only—child in a mining camp, except for the rare times when my brother was home from school. A brother ten years older, who was home only sometimes, was not enough to fill my aching need for company. I longed for a twin sister, and I filled my life with imaginary friends.

"What did Mrs. Dyer and Mrs. Inkso do today, Mary?" my mother would ask me.

I dutifully filled her in on events in the beauty parlor that the two imaginary ladies ran. I held my mouth in a certain way when I was Mrs. Inkso, the terrible gossip, and repeated every intimate detail her clients shared with her. Sometimes I heard my mother retelling my stories with wonder: how could I possibly imagine such domestic crises in an entirely different world than the one in which I lived? Did my mother know how lonely I was? Could she have done anything about it? My stories simply amused her; she never thought about the loneliness they must have represented.

Jim Burchfield was thirteen and had come to Gomoco from Davao with his mother, Evelyn. Mrs. Burchfield had found the trip north through the swamps taxing, and Jim usually stayed with her in their quarters. The other boy, Neil Jarvis, the newcomer, was alone like me. I didn't know why his family was left aside in the life of the camp, but he was restless and unable to stay with his parents in their room.

Neil began to spend more time with me than with anyone else. He told me about the big house perched above the sea, about his sailboat, about how he had spent hours skin-diving and spearfishing in the sea before he and his parents had run from the Japanese. He knew all kinds of things that I didn't, and he wanted to spend time with me; I was ecstatic to have—at last—someone interesting to be with.

For the first few weeks after Neil's arrival, I was deliriously happy. I didn't need to spend time with the younger children; the grown-ups could be busy with survival. I could go to school in the morning with Mrs. Welbon and my mother and then be free to play with Neil all afternoon.

We went down the trail a little way toward the river landing and explored the workers' quarters as they fell into ruin among jungle vines. The roofs were down, but the rooms and the fire pits were still there. Abandoned only months before, the village had magical properties of another time. The vanished people who had lived there so recently were as mysterious as the knights of Camelot.

We ran up the trail into camp one afternoon, breathless with the discovery of an enormous mushroom we had found. I pulled at my mother's skirt, begging her to "Come see, come see!" but she was too busy. The next morning, when there was time, and we all went back, it had collapsed into its fading yellow veil. Philomena crossed herself when she saw it. "Oh, very bad, very bad. Devil's Basket. Never eat. Not good luck to find," and hurried us back to the safety of camp.

Neil and I explored the river, walking farther up than I ever had before, even with Opron and Opren, my native friends. We looked for fish and pretty rocks. After the typhoon, Neil and I climbed on the log jam that formed around the boulders that had rumbled downstream in the yellow torrent.

There were endless things to do for two children left to run wild because their parents were preoccupied with a world collapsing around them. One day, Neil and I climbed up on the rafters of our three-room house and ran along the tops of the walls. Houses in the tropics then had no ceilings—walls only ran up to eight feet so that air could circulate under the almost free-floating roofs.

Squealing with joy, having more fun than I had ever had in my life, I pretended to lose my balance. My mind was on my father's grim fear that someone at Gomoco would be hurt and have no doctor. I knew better; I was never going to be hurt!

Rocking my pelvis back and forth, I squealed, "I'm falling, I'm falling!"

"That's what they do," Neil said.

A shadow fell.

"What do who do?"

"They do that. What you're doing." He pushed his pelvis in and out, too. "What I told you about. About grown-ups. I told you I'd show you."

A lump of fear rose in my throat. I climbed down from the wall and said, "I'm going to find my mother."

But I didn't know what to tell her. How could I tell her I was afraid when I didn't understand what I was afraid of? I hung around her a little while, watching her make a dress for Roxy Smith, and then the day was over.

For a while, my days spent playing with Neil were placid again. I hoped the frightening thing he knew wouldn't be mentioned again. Of course it was.

We went down the trail again to see if there were any more Devil's Baskets. I went even though Philomena's warning voice ("Bad luck! Bad luck!") was with me as we disappeared around the bend. I went with Neil even though I was becoming afraid of him. I didn't want to be alone with him because I didn't want to know more about his secret. I didn't know what the secret was, but I knew I didn't want to know it. Maybe, I thought, maybe we really are going only to look for Devil's Baskets, maybe, maybe. I hope. And so we went to the abandoned houses down the trail.

I had seen hundreds of penises. Filipino children wore only shirts in those days, and little brown penises were in full view; it was how you knew boys from girls. Neil's was appalling. He made it bigger and bigger, and then it squirted.

Then he told me that men put their penises into ladies and that he wanted to try it, too. With me.

"No, no. You can't. Not now."

"When, then?"

I cast about, looking for an escape but could find nothing. Finally, I thought of a date so far in the future that I might be safe.

"The second of May."

"Okay, the second of May."

We headed home to the cluster of houses in the clearing. Utterly alone, with a problem bigger than my abilities to articulate, I was completely miserable.

"Don't you dare tell what I showed you," Neil said.

I didn't tell; I couldn't tell. I had seen something that I knew no one would believe. I somehow knew that if my parents did by any chance believe me, they would punish me.

My days were filled with dread, "the sikenamay, the sikenamay, the sikenamay" ran through my mind like a *mea culpa*, and I didn't know how to get help.

In eight years of living with my father, I had learned that compliance and docility brought the best rewards. I had no knowledge of my self, and so I continued to play with Neil because I didn't know that I could do anything else.

Neil remembered the second of May, too, as we wandered up the river and through the camp and April ticked away.

One afternoon we waded around the bend of the river above the camp, and Neil could no longer wait for the second of May. He pushed me against a huge boulder the typhoon's flood had rolled down the river, and found that I was too small for his obsession.

"Please wait for the second of May, please wait for the second of May."

I could hardly talk. My throat ached from the need to cry and the need not to cry. I pushed him away, but he was too strong for me.

"Please, Neil, I'm afraid. Please, I don't want to."

Neil showed no signs of hearing me. He was in his own world of confusion and need.

And then, Opren and Opron and Ameliana stepped out of the jungle, and it was over. They danced around us, laughing: "Ha ha, Neil! Ha ha, Neil! What you do to Mary? You like goat; you think make a baby! You funny boy. Ha ha, Neil!"

I hadn't known all this was about babies. How could babies come from all the dread I lived with? I stood by the rock in the jungle with my friends and watched Neil run for home.

For a little while that afternoon I was happy, and soon I was splashing and playing in the cool creek in the green jungle with my rescuers. I laid down my burden until I came back to camp and found it all the same. Nothing had changed; the second of May was a deal I could not escape.

One evening, before the mosquitoes came on too thickly, and while the adults could sit together at the table after their meal in the mess house, Neil told me he had something to show me in the room where he and his mother lived. We slipped away from the table and crossed the gravel yard between the buildings. Evening was falling fast, and my heart beat quickly from fear. Still innocent and hopeful, I prayed a simple prayer that Neil had something to show me that I would like, something that would make me happy, though the dread I was now used to was with me again.

As soon as we got to his room, Neil could wait no longer. He pulled down his pants and mine. He was nervous and breathing hard. I felt wooden and unable to move in their bare room. At the river, before Opren and Opron had burst out of the jungle, I had had the energy to struggle against Neil, but now I was paralyzed. He pushed himself on me; I turned my head away from him as far as I could and shut my eyes and I waited.

Then I heard my mother's quick steps on the porch—my heart leaped: another miracle?—and she burst into the room.

"I thought so!" she said, and grabbed me by the arm. For a wild moment I thought I was safe and that the nightmare might be ending, but she was angrier than I had ever seen her before. She dragged me by the arm home to our cabin—the gravel grinding under her heels and past my sandaled feet.

"You get into bed and think about this!" And she left me alone without even the lantern lit in the blackness of the jungle night.

In a while, I heard my parents in my father's room next to my bed—their voices rising and falling. My mother's voice was shrill and angry, and my father seemed to be trying to calm her. I could not catch more than a word or two, and eventually I heard my mother come to her bed, climb into it, and tuck in the mosquito net.

I had no tears, only a terrible sadness, and at last I fell asleep, only to awaken in the morning with a new kind of dread. There was silence—just silence—from my parents toward me and between them.

The long day of abandonment lasted until siesta, when there was time in the camp routine for my mother to deal with me. I thought about my big brother, Bob, and how he surely would not have left me alone all day. I remembered how tall he was and how he looked down at me when he held my hand; how he smiled at me and called me "Peek" from our old baby game, Peek-a-boo. He was so far away.

After she had finished her tasks of cleaning the rice for lunch and her turn at supervising as Ah Hing stored any leftovers, Mother finally returned to me.

"Mary, you disappoint me. Why didn't you tell me this was going on?"

I hung my head. I couldn't talk around the bones in my throat. It was too hard to explain. "I don't know," I said.

"You don't know? I'm your mother; you can tell me anything! You should have told me the minute this thing started."

"I couldn't tell you. I thought you'd be angry with me."

"Angry with you? Angry with you?" There was a tiny white string holding her lips tight across her perfect white teeth. I wondered where the knot might be that held the string so tight. "How could I be angry with you? I'm your mother!"

I hung my head.

"Well, now I have to tell you things that I should never have to talk about with you so soon. But now you have learned some things you have to know the truth about."

I looked at the wall behind her, the raw boards ran up and down; with my eyes, I traced the cracks between them.

"Look at me! You have to listen!"

"I don't want to hear anything," I said in a low voice. "I want to go outside."

"Don't sass me! You have to learn what it is you have been playing at. Men and women, when they are grown up and married, make babies in a special, sacred way when they love each other."

That I heard, but the rest, as my mind wandered away from her voice, only partly filtered through the veils of feelings I was dealing with. I heard "penis" and "vagina," and then she began to tell me about menstruation and bleeding once a month. I knew about that from seeing a bucket she used to soak her rags once a month, but now I was learning why that happened, and that it would happen to me one day.

I could stand no more and put my hands over my ears.

"I don't want to hear this, Mommy."

"Well, you must hear it. It's my duty to tell you these things. It seems that I waited too long to tell you this." She sighed, rubbing her hands as she did when she was anguished.

"Your father and I have talked about this, of course, and he's going to have a talk with you, too. As of this minute, you are forbidden to talk to Neil. His parents agree with this decision, and he will be punished. He won't bother you again, I can promise you."

Days later, my father and I were together at siesta time. We lay on my mother's bed in the hot afternoon, as we often did.

Usually he told me stories, or we read together, but today there was a deep silence from him. Every so often he would take a deep breath as if to speak, but no words came. I knew what he was going to talk about, and I could easily have gotten up and scampered away. Something in me, though, needed to make him suffer, and so I waited.

At last he said, "I hear you got into some trouble."

I was only eight years old, but I knew that what he said was crude.

I turned off my mind and let him talk, and I don't remember what he said.

As long as my parents lived, no one ever mentioned my troubles again. I have no idea what my father said or did to Neil. He needed much more sympathy than he got. My father was hard enough to live with when he loved you; to be shunned by him must have been hell.

My parents had always kept me close to them, but now I was rarely unsupervised. I have no memories of Neil at Gomoco after this, and very few of Jim Burchfield.

My parents must have trusted Ah Hing, because they let me talk to him in the lonely hours between meals. He either didn't know about my sordid past, or he didn't care; but he was there when my parents didn't know I was suffering.

I have forgotten how to count in Cantonese, but I can fold an amazing origami tea cart.

———⟩◆⟨———

"Well, I'll tell you one thing—they'll never take Gomoco!" Charlie said after the first news broadcast in the month since the typhoon.

KGEI, the short-wave station in San Francisco Bay, came in without static for once with the devastating news that Corregidor had fallen on May 6.

The Japanese now controlled the Philippines.

Now we had one radio made from the three ruined by the typhoon. I liked it better when the radio didn't work because now the grown-ups looked solemn. They gathered in groups and shooed me away from their conversations.

May 12, 1942. On May 6, after 300 air raids and countless shore bombardments, The Rock fell to the invaders. I felt a raging gorge of resentment when an arrogant Oriental voice announced, with much hissing of the s's, "The last stronghold of the American Military Force in the Far East has fallen." There is no asylum anywhere to offer us peace and safety. The future is difficult to visualize, but long, dark shadows are being cast farther and farther in our direction. It is a new feeling to realize that nothing we have can be replenished. Every match used means that we are one more nearer none. Every quinine tablet, roll of bandage, drop of antiseptic used is gone and not to be replaced until after this is over.

If only Noriega would come back with news from Luzon. It's eight months since Bob left for school. . . . I can still see him leaning out of the train window calling, "See you at Christmas!"

Japanese began to occupy Mindanao, marching into Dansalan, where Beth had gone to have her baby, and to the Del Monte pineapple plantation's airfield, where my mother had dreamed we would be whisked away by miraculous American airplanes. I worried about Beth and wondered if she was a prisoner. Maybe her baby was a prisoner, too. Would the Japanese let her keep her violin?

May 15, 1942. Some days it seems that every step taken and every fork chosen in the path of life was wrong, for they have led up the blind alley to this blank wall with no way out except at the orders of the Imperial Japanese government. Will we all be taken to Japan and concentrated in their industrial cities to be targets for our own bombs when they fall? Will they really pen up women and children and keep them with no diversions and little food? Or will they just kill us instead? What will all this do to Mary? I worry so about Bob. Who is he with? What is happening to his health, his mind? Does he worry about us? Where is he? Where? Where? Where?

My father called a general meeting after supper. Unnoticed, I slipped under the veranda to my favorite listening place.

"As I see it, with Corregidor gone, everything has changed. We aren't waiting anymore. The Japs are in control now. That's the main problem. We don't know what they'll do with us, but I'm in favor of holding out here as long as we can. They might be glad to leave us here to look after ourselves. They know we can't get out. I'll tell you, though, what worries me almost as much as the Japs is the natives. They know we have money and guns, and without the Americans to keep order, God knows who's going to come up that trail!"

My mother's voice, "Oh, surely, Douglass, the Filipinos will stay loyal!"

"Don't kid yourself, Harriet! A lot of them have just been waiting to get rid of us Americans, and they want our guns. They know about the Army food we've got from all the *cargadores* who carried it in! We're in deep trouble." That was Jean Feigel.

"And I disagree with you, Mac, I think the Japs will be here soon. They can hardly wait to lord it over us."

"Without the U.S. Army, let me tell you, the Moros and the Christians are going to erupt, and we'll be in the middle of it!" Mrs. Burchfield had lived in Davao for many years, and she thought she knew the Filipino mind.

"Well, either the Japs or renegade Filipinos would be bad, but we have to be ready for either one." My father's voice: "We better get some of the food and valuables hidden. We shouldn't hide it all, so they won't suspect we've hidden it."

Larry Smith, always calm, always helpful: "When do we get started?"

"There's no moonlight this week, and we can get started right away moving things and getting ready to bury it without the Filipinos here knowing about it," said my father.

They began making plans, but I needed my mother, and I crept out from under the mess house and approached her from another direction so they wouldn't know I had been listening. I crawled into her lap and said, "I'm scared!"

"It's all right, dear, we're making plans now and everything is going to be fine! Really."

I was comforted because I needed to be.

Plans were made to bury cans of food at the edge of the clearing in two fifty-five-gallon oil barrels—the jungle would quickly hide the digging scars with vines. First, however, the cans had to be greased so that moisture wouldn't cause them to rust. We children were given that task, and the women checked the lists while the men sauntered out, casually, they hoped, to dig the rocky soil. All this took place at night with a minimum of light. I began to pretend that I was watching the pirates in *Treasure Island,* and that I was Jim behind the barrels on the deck of a pirate ship, but I think I really knew it wasn't pretending. The adults were frightened.

They thought all this could happen without the servants knowing, but I remembered that Opren and Opron had soundlessly followed Neil and me through the jungle. The Filipinos who shared our camp knew everything.

At night, in the steady light of the carbide lamps, and in private after the others had gone to bed, my father counted the payroll money we had brought in the pillowcase. Money lay in piles on the bed and desk in his room until it was sealed in pipes taken from the mill where gold had once been refined. It was to be buried, also, but in a place known only to my parents and to Larry Smith.

This time, because danger seemed more real than before, my mother allowed the lucky five-dollar gold piece and her diamond ring to be buried. She loved that ring and looked at its Greek-cross, diamond-and-sapphire setting as she slowly slipped it off her finger. She wrote her last thoughts in her diary so desperately that I imagined I could see a line down the page left by her pencil when my father took the notebook from her for burial.

Tension released a little when the big job of hiding supplies was done. In the middle of May, the Japanese declared an armistice until May 31. By that date all American soldiers were to surrender themselves and their equipment to the Imperial Military Command of the Japanese Army. There were no messages for American civilians in the jungles.

At dinner, Jean Feigel became more insistent in her predictions that the Japanese would come up the trail any day now. "Any minute! They'll be here, and no Filipino will come to warn us!"

Charlie thought they would never come for us.

"Mac's right. Why should they come get us when they know we're here and can't get out? They don't want to look after us in camps when we're doing that ourselves up here. We'll be here for the duration!"

My father began, each afternoon after siesta, to slip into the jungle. My mother said little about it at first, but she finally told me that he was building us a little house to escape to if we needed it. Once I knew about La Casita, I stopped worrying about bandits and Japanese soldiers. I was sure the *cargadores* would warn us and that we could run to La Casita. I could run forever, I thought, and showed my mother how I could leap over fallen trees. No Jap can catch me, I thought proudly.

My mind wouldn't let me imagine Japanese soldiers crossing our river and telling us what to do. I remember knowing, deep down, that if they came up the trail after us, they would not be kind; but I had faith in my parents and in the Filipinos, and I played happily with my friends in the pool at the bend of the creek below our house and went to the makeshift school that the women kept for us.

May 20, 1942. I can't help it; I've started a new diary. I'll keep it well hidden. We buried the first little school copybooks I am using as diaries with the money and valuables. I memorized the coordinates of the three places we buried things—the pipe with the small bills is near us, so if necessary we can pay the cargadores *who bring us food. So far they are happy with the trading, but the big bills are getting hard to use without small bills in circulation.*

Colonel Chastaine, commander of the American/ Philippine forces in the area, came into camp to raise our flagging spirits and give us the firm conviction of final victory. He gave Douglass a letter of commendation: "In organizing this group of men, women,

and children and looking after their welfare, you have relieved me
of a great responsibility for which I could ill spare any time. . . .
You have served your country and its interests in a time of great
danger." Then he went to Butuan to surrender his men, his equipment and himself to the Japanese. I can't bear to think if it.

There were different faces at the dinner table every day.
Peter, the Danish mechanic who had drunk too much the day of
the typhoon, now had a neutral passport, and he left us.

In the middle of May, George and Tamara Vigliada went
away, too. George was an Italian citizen, and now that the
Japanese were in control, George thought they should not stay
with us any longer. Tamara did not want to go; her tears fell like
rain, my mother's diary says.

There were no more Russian songs after dinner.

Men without families to protect had so far been able to live
freely on Mindanao, but now they came to join us at Gomoco;
others, like Fred Feigel and Roy Welbon, came back to wait with
us for word from the Japanese.

Many young American soldiers who refused to be in Japanese prison camps drifted through the jungle in the aftermath of
the surrender. I remember them arriving, silent as Indians, not up
the trail that everyone used but from the opposite direction
where there were no trails. Perhaps it was their anger and sadness at being defeated that makes me think of Indians. More than
twenty stopped with us; we fed them, let them rest and heal; and,
when they were ready to move on, we filled their packs with
canned goods from the Army stores brought up the rivers before
the surrender. They hoped to live off the land and to elude the
Japanese; but they were not prepared, many of them, for life on
the run in a tropical jungle, and they faced death in many forms.

My mother thought of them all the time, trudging from barrio to barrio, risking instant death if they met Japanese patrols.

If they were not so young, I could bear it . . . and if one of them had not had a quick laugh and glance like Bob's, I could forget him and be at peace.

Those "unsurrendered" soldiers joined guerrilla cadres that carried on behind-the-lines action against the Japanese all through the war. The wandering boys were insubordinate in 1942 for not following orders to surrender, but they were heroes later. They built radios and made contact with Australia, bringing "The Aid" (the phrase we all used now) to the Philippines much sooner than had been planned.

I remember one of them well, for he nearly killed me. My mother decided that I had intestinal worms and was looking for a remedy. One of the soldiers, his accent heavy with Appalachia, told my mother that his mother used to dose all the kids with a spoonful of sugar melted in turpentine. My mother prepared the dose and I dutifully swallowed it. In the night I woke with my throat and stomach on fire. In the dim light of the kerosene lantern, I lay in her arms, crying in pain and panic all night. Not for a minute did the burning let me free; the smell of the turpentine on my breath reminded me of the cause of my agony and made my nausea more severe. My mother held me calmly, her faith in the home remedy so complete that she was not afraid for me. I don't think she ever wished for a doctor during that long night.

In the morning, I was still alive. I presume the remedy killed the worms.

PART
2

WAITING AND LIVING

June 19, 1942. The days seem fruitless and misspent, no matter what I do. Bob's nineteenth birthday was yesterday, and my earliest waking thought and my last at night were of him. The rains, famous for heaviness and duration, are beginning now in Luzon. Has he shelter? Is he well, and has he enough to eat? When will I know? How will I know?

June 24 marked six months at Gomoco. The Japanese had sent no messages to tell us what they wanted us to do, or where they wanted us to go. We had heard only the general requirement for the military to surrender by May 31. The waiting went on.

The spluttering radio told us that Tobruk fell to the Germans in North Africa, and Sebastopol was tottering in Russia. The Germans and the Japanese were pushing the Allies back everywhere. There hadn't been any good news since Jimmy Doolittle's raid on Tokyo in the middle of April.

Food was becoming an obsession. People passed around for discussion recipes they had copied out of Helen Welbon's *Ladies' Home Journals*.

One night at dinner, Glenda pushed a rice weevil to the edge of her plate and put down her fork. "I know that weevil won't hurt me, and that he's probably even good for me, but I just can't eat him." Tears came. "The only way I can eat cracked corn and slippery greens day after day is to pretend there's a Baked Alaska waiting for me in my room!"

Larry Smith wanted a peach more than anything.

"What's a peach taste like?" I asked him.

"Oh, they're juicy and sweet, and if you get a really good one, the juice will run down your hand and you have to lick the heel of your hand so you won't waste any of the goodness. And the best part is, you can only get a really good peach in the middle of summer!"

"But we can get mangos here all the time. They're juicy and sweet and the juice runs down your arm," I said. "Why is a peach better?" Larry couldn't answer me.

People waited all day for dinner, the highlight of the day, but Ah Hing's meals were always a disappointment. Sometimes cracked corn replaced the rice, but always we faced *kangkong* (slippery greens) or "boiled ice," that almost translucent squash called *opo*. Sometimes we had chicken, more often dried fish. We watched the growing pigs with real anticipation.

We even ate "puffed cans." Botulism growing inside a tin can causes it to swell, but throwing away precious canned food was not to be considered. My mother boiled the tins for three hours, and we were never poisoned. No one dared to taste the food until after we gave a large sample to the pigs and they asked for more.

The *bodega*, however, was full of food. I have my father's meticulous six-page inventory on accounting paper showing that on July 1, 1942, we had pressed meat, corned beef, hams, bacon, pigs' feet, sliced beef, frankfurters, Vienna sausages, sardines, salmon, oysters (seven tall cans), tuna fish, crab, clams. There were rows and rows of canned fruits and vegetables, barrels of raw sugar with heavy syrup forming at the bottoms, and boxes of macaroni. There were eighty-four bars of toilet soap and sixty-two bars of laundry soap. We had seventy-six flashlight batteries and nine small cans of mushrooms . . . and the maraschino cherries.

Some were obsessed by food; my father was obsessed by the *bodega*. He counted and recorded the supplies with the help of Larry Smith and Fred Feigel. We had greased the other cans before burying them. Now the humidity was causing the cans on the shelves to rust; and the men began the job of greasing all the cans to keep them from rusting.

My father felt that as long as we could subsist on food brought in by the natives, the food in the *bodega* was insurance against the long war we seemed to be facing. He was convinced that wasting some food from spoilage was better than consuming it when other food was available. He would listen to no argument.

My mother begged him, in the privacy of our quarters, to relax his rules and to share more with everyone—even the money. He would not give Mindanao Mother Lode money to anyone. My mother argued that it would be paid back one day, and that if we all were lost somehow, the debts wouldn't matter.

He couldn't be moved, and she supported him publicly, only to suffer the consequences of being despised as well.

His complete power over the *bodega* and over his company's payroll made him thoroughly unpopular. Hunger and fear, coupled with the suspicion that he was depriving the others while taking good care of my mother and me, made mealtimes silent and hostile.

When insurrection came, it came, surprisingly, from the Feigels. They had seemed to me to be allies of my father's. Fred had spent the morning with my dad in the *bodega;* Jean had spent the morning, as usual, alone in her room. Bowls of food came to the table from Ah Hing's kitchen: boiled rice—again, slippery greens—and again, stringy, partially cooked *camotes.* Ah Hing had forgotten to take the heads and tails off the dried fish, and their blind silver eyes stared up from the plate as they floated in the vegetables' green juices.

Jean threw her plate into the brush below the porch.

"Goddamn it, Mac, I can't eat this swill one more time!" she said to my father. "Are you going to sit on the food in the *bodega* like a big toad forever? When we leave this place, are we going to leave the food to rot? Is that your plan?"

I was stunned. No one ever talked to my father like that.

"Chastaine commissioned me to look after the people in this—," he began.

"Chastaine's in a Jap prison camp by now! What he said three months ago is worthless! There's food going to waste, and you're too damn stubborn to give up one can of beans. I saw you leave the *bodega* last Sunday with a can of something under your shirt. What were you and Harriet and Mary eating in your room, anyway? Something that belonged to all of us?"

It was true. He had brought a can of Argentine corned beef home. We ate it with our fingers, the fat running down our chins, and I had never tasted anything so good in my life. Daddy said it was part of the cache he was taking to La Casita.

"Jean, we all have emergency rations. You know that, because you helped divide it up when we buried the food. That can of corned beef was ours, and if we chose to eat it in private before an emergency, that's our business!"

"Well, you sure looked like you were sneaking it!"

"Look, no one is sick here; the children are growing. This war could last years, and I am going to continue to hold that food—hoard it, if you prefer—until things turn bad. Next rainy season, when the crops are done and the trail's slippery, you might be pretty happy for a can of maraschino cherries!"

Jean left the mess house, and lunch continued without her. She showed up for dinner but was silent. There were many who sided with her, but for the moment they said nothing.

———————

Toward the end of June, Waldo Neveling, whom we had last seen in early December waving cheerfully as he went off to internment camp as a German national, arrived in camp from Davao. I was happy to see he still had his silver tooth. It seemed a long time since I had seen him, and I had wondered if he still looked the same. The silver tooth interested me because Filipinos bought gold ones when they were rich enough to afford them. I never asked him why his was only silver, but I wanted to.

He was a free agent in the Islands, now that the Japanese had released the prisoners held by the Americans. The Japanese asked him to find, please, all the Americans in the jungle and tell them to come to Japanese headquarters for "beneficial concentration." Waldo heard about us through the bamboo telegraph and came to find us.

"The word I carry is from the commandant in Davao. You are in an area controlled by the Surigao Japanese. I think you could stay here and delay until you hear from the Japs in Butuan or Surigao. It's not too bad for the Americans in the camp in Davao, but it's much better here on your own," Waldo said.

He didn't know for sure if the husbands of the women from Davao who were with us were in the internment camp in Davao, but he thought they were.

"I wish I'd known about you; I would have made sure to learn about your men."

He had seen Japanese film of the attack on Pearl Harbor and said, "If smoke means destruction, then there's nothing left of the American Navy in the Pacific. We'll be waiting here a long time."

June 30, 1942. Waldo's report of the destruction of Pearl Harbor is truly bad news. Here we have been waiting for the Navy to bring us freedom, and there is no Navy! Why hasn't the radio told us this? We listen often enough. I wonder if we, forgotten here in the jungles, know more than they do at home?

Waldo rested with us a few days and then left to deal with the Japanese in Surigao.

"I'll be back with more news when I can. I'm going to play both sides as long as I can, and I can be useful to you! Stay out of the Japs' hands till you hear from me!"

He waved good-bye and was gone.

We returned to our routines of turning the rice to keep it from molding and of drying the fish in the sun so that it wouldn't rehydrate and rot.

In the blacksmith shop near the powerhouse, using some of the springs on the red truck, Charlie and my dad made a horseshoe game they played after dinner. *Clang, clang,* sounded the hammer on the anvil; the conversational on-the-spot planning of the projects in the shop was companionable and happy.

They let me stoke the fire, and I loved watching the coals burn redder after I blew air onto them with the bellows. When the red-hot steel came from the coals, it began to cool on the surface, turning gray. As the hammers struck, gray flakes flew off to reveal the red metal. Over and over the steel submitted to the hammers, and soon the horseshoe game was made.

July 1, 1942. Last night the near-round moon of high summer reached through the widening cracks in the rough board walls and laid silver bands of moonlight on the floor. I slipped from under my mosquito netting and went to the window where I stood spellbound at the beauty of the jungle, moon-drowned and dreaming.

By day the sun shines through the cracks and glints through the colored bottles we have set on the two-by-four that runs like a plate rail around the room. The amber beer bottles, the dark green Spanish frasco—full of bubbles and swirled like Mexican ware— and the blue and brown bottles make a kind of necklace for our room. Today is the day that Ramon Noriega promised to return with news of Bob. I still hear him say with the drama that only a Filipino can assume, "If I am not back by July One, ma'am, I am Dead!" He is not back with his Message to Garcia and we still know nothing about our loved ones. I was so sure of Noriega when we sent him off to Luzon, and now he, too, has vanished into the darkness of his war. I am losing courage. I want my son.

Morale was low by the beginning of July. The Japanese had neither come nor sent a stronger message than the one that had come up the trail secondhand in May. We watched the opening in the jungle where the trail crossed the river. A Japanese search party could arrive at any time, though we hoped a loyal Filipino would run ahead of them. The food issue was still volatile, with my father holding firm control of the supplies in the *bodega*. People were hungry, frightened, and surly.

Larry Smith, always the mediator and nominally second-in-command, convinced my father that the Fourth of July would be a good time for a celebration and feast.

"Mary, come look!" I followed my father that morning to see an American flag hanging from the roof of the powerhouse. I didn't know where it had come from. I couldn't imagine who had kept it hidden. I knew that an American flag, if found by the Japanese, would be even more infuriating to them than a radio. None of this mattered to me in the face of the miraculous flag; it mattered only that it was there. The flag at Gomoco the morning of July 4, 1942, proved to me that one day we would walk free out of the jungle and that we Americans could do anything.

Preparations for our feast took most of the day. Maximino Perez came proudly up the trail with two *cargadores* carrying a large pig on a pole.

"I am The One, sir, to bring the *lechon!* This is the pig of my brother-in-law. He is proud to present you with his pig. It is a fine pig, sir. I will give my brother-in-law ten pesos for you, sir?"

"Ten pesos! That is very much money, Maximino. You must take the pig back to your brother-in-law."

"But, sir, he will be ashamed you did not like his pig. Eight pesos!"

Seven pesos and sharing the meal with Maximino and the two *cargadores* made the deal.

Ah Hing dug a pit and built a fire under a turning spit. The pig, stuffed with rice and wild ginger, turned slowly, all of us taking turns at the crank. The smells from the fire pit wafted all over camp, driving us fat-starved children to a frenzy of anticipation.

My father opened the *bodega* and we children danced along beside the tins of sweet southern yams, pickled beets, and string beans as we helped carry them to the kitchen. We saw that the treasured American food was accompanied by the inevitable *kangkong*, native squash, and *camotes*, but it didn't matter. Dessert was going to be fruit salad—we could see the cans waiting in the kitchen for Ah Hing to open them!

The children ate first, getting a plate of mouth-watering meat along with crisp, roasted skin. Charlie served us "all the fixin's" and piled our plates high. We ate—and were even offered seconds—then were turned loose to play while the grown-ups ate.

We were too full to run; we just sat and watched the adults enjoy their dinner. After we were in bed, the adults listened to the news and played poker. The news was no better than it had been recently, but it didn't seem to matter so much on that glorious Fourth—not, at least, with a full stomach.

—————⊰◆⊱—————

A festive Fourth of July wasn't enough to make us a cohesive group, for right after lunch on July 19, the Feigels left camp. They waved cheerfully and were gone to a new life near the east coast. *Cargadores* laden with their belongings followed them down the trail. Pat, their big German shepherd, ran up and down the trail in a demented, joyful freedom; he, too, had spent a great deal of time alone.

July 21, 1942. Living in a confined group causes tension. Large disputes and small hurts become equal. Much as we respected the Feigels and wished they would remain with us, the bowstring snapped when they left and we all felt easier. I remembered, as they disappeared into the green jungle, when, just before the war, Jean found a pretty bush in the jungle and transplanted it to her garden. Enday, her lavandera, *saw the plant's tall yellow flowers and pleaded with Jean not to plant it. "Oh, please, Ma'am, do not grow this flower. It is the Typhoon Bush. Something terrible will happen. You will be very unlucky. Please, oh, please, Ma'am, you do not know what you do!" Jean laughed at her fears; I wonder if she'll ever think of Enday's prediction.*

Then, just a month after he left the first time, Waldo Neveling returned from Surigao with news from the Japanese that threw the whole camp into panic.

"The Japs know you're here, and they're planning to come and get you. They're forming a search party right now!"

Since the fall of Corregidor, the Japanese had had two months to cement their control of the Philippines. New, rougher occupying troops were arriving in the Islands, and they turned to eradicating resistance.

"They're angry that you didn't respond to the first directives, and they won't be kind when they get here! They say you didn't respect the words of the Imperial Japanese Army, and you must pay. Leave. Just get out of here! Maybe you can come back after they leave, but you don't want to be here when they get here."

"The Americans in the camp in Surigao are doing okay," Waldo said. "They're living in the upstairs of the Chinese grocery store and can get deliveries of food from the natives. It would be better to be in a camp like that than be caught here by a search party. They're angry, those Japs!"

He told us that the Japanese and some Filipinos had looted our houses at Mother Lode and that everything we had left there was gone.

The most devastating news, because it involved a betrayal, was that Ernst Heidepreim, the German master mechanic who had helped my father hide the mine records and our valuables, had led the Japanese to the cache. Everything was gone: the household goods and collections as well as the family pictures and jewelry.

My father had vouched for the wrong German.

⊰•◦•⊱

My mother sat in her room at Gomoco and listed in her diary the vanished things she had loved:

> *My Philippine hat collection; the ceremonial hat of the Manobos; the soapstone-inlaid Chinese chest. My old, old ivory snuff bottles, my sterling. Nothing is left but the shreds of dreams and a picture of my husband slashed across the surface by a bayonet. Now, though I can't bear to think of it, we might face the same fate. . . .*

Listing her vanished belongings was a way of avoiding, for a few minutes, the terrible decision that was before all of us at Gomoco: Trust Waldo or not? After all, he was German, too, like Heidepreim, who had betrayed everyone who worked for the mine. Stay or turn in?

Gomoco suddenly looked like Eden, but it all could end violently any time the Japanese chose to arrive with their bayonets—or a band of outlaws decided to kill us for our assets.

"I simply cannot live behind barbed wire! I grew up running on the prairie. Prison isn't possible!" my mother said wildly at one meeting. I crept closer to her as I realized that the safety of Gomoco might be disappearing; I would miss my native friends and protectors, Opren and Opron. All my pets—the cats and the goats and the chickens—suddenly became more precious that I had imagined.

On July 26, the group met to give their decisions. One by one, the decisions made in private became public.

"I can't risk being on the run with three little children," Larry Smith said. "Rusty is just learning to walk, and he already doesn't remember his mother. I'll be taking a chance either way, but it seems safer to get to an internment camp now. We'll take our share and hire a *baroto* and go downriver to Surigao as soon as we can."

My heart sank. Larry was always cheerful. Even though his two daughters were younger than I, they were playmates whom I had known for most of my life.

The Jarvises also decided to leave us. Never truly welcomed, they had been shunned by everyone in the camp after Neil had been caught with me. There are no secrets for long in a tiny community.

The Crenshaws were turning in, too. The three families with the most children were leaving, taking six children and five adults from Gomoco.

"I'm staying out because I'm not putting my Jim near any Japanese!" Mrs. Burchfield, I think, surprised us all. She was still weak and sickly, but she was staying.

Glenda Crytser said she would stay, too. "At first I thought I would turn in with Stevie so I could find Bob in prison camp.

But they're going to Surigao, and I think Bob is in Davao. I'll stay because I can't get to Davao by myself."

Alberta Stumbaugh, one of the four women who had come from Davao, quietly said she felt safer at Gomoco than she would anywhere else. That meant I still had one playmate, Helen Louise, and someone to go to school with.

July 26, 1942. The Welbons are staying and so are we. Somehow Douglass' mouth opened and "no" came out, even though I thought we had decided to turn in. I am afraid to be staying out, but I can't bear the idea of prison, either. Perhaps we three are a small enough unit to hide at La Casita and elude our would-be captors. Eleven are leaving; fourteen are staying, including Charlie.

In a few days they were ready to leave. My parents let me walk the seven kilometers to Krik's Landing to say good-bye. *Cargadores* carried pots and bedding and bags of clothing for the three families as our party started out for the *bodega* on the river. Huge trees had fallen in the typhoon, and sometimes we walked the length of them where they had fallen along the road. Other times we climbed over them, using steps the traders had cut into them with their *bolos.*

It was my first excursion to Krik's since our arrival in December, but the heat of the jungle and the somberness of the party soon faded my excitement. Carlota Crenshaw did not want in the least to leave the hiding place in the mountains; she had deep misgivings about the decision to go to the Japanese, and she wept as she turned for a last look at the little camp where she had spent almost eight months.

Larry Smith was quiet. There was no way of knowing what kind of greeting the Japanese in Surigao would give them, nor any assurance that they would reach Surigao at all, even though he was armed with a .38-caliber revolver.

From the shore, we watched the three *barotos*—two loaded with supplies, and the other, larger, carrying the three families—slip away. The boatmen pulled swiftly at the water, and they were gone.

> *We walked home silently together. Only our feet, and the clicking of great fans of black locusts that spread away at every step, made sound. I was glad to reach Gomoco's little clearing again, and thankful to be with Douglass and Mary. We have weathered an upsetting time and have stayed where we are. My mind circles around Larry and those little children—over and over I think of their scared little faces in the baroto as they went down the river. What will they find with the Japanese? Then I ask, what will find us here? Oh, this dreadful, dreadful war!*

All through the packing and loading and saying good-bye, no one knew who had made the right decision.

———◆———

La Casita kept us from turning in. The bamboo house was taking shape nearby in a small canyon fed by swift little Kamaginking Creek.

For one of the walls, my father chose the flat side of a giant boulder that perched a few feet above the creek. He cut and skinned small trees and bound them with thongs cut from rattan vines that grew looping through the jungle. To make the other three walls, my mother helped him weave lengths of rattan through the skinned poles. They made the floor of rattan instead of bamboo, which is usually used in Philippine huts, because bamboo is a lowland plant and wasn't available.

Somehow they carried three sheets of galvanized iron from the closest corner of the mill building over the trail and made a roof of them. Once the roof was in place, they realized that it could be seen from the air, and they covered it with branches and then trained vines to grow across it.

The jungle was thick near the river; the typhoon's winds had not reached to the bottom of the ravine. My father hoped we would be safe there if the Japanese decided to come to Gomoco for us. They hid a cache of food as well as a few utensils for cooking.

Jungle trees are shallow-rooted compared to their height. In order to anchor themselves more securely, many form high, wall-like roots that curve outward from their trunks. It is as though roofless rooms nestle next to trees where falling leaves make a soft humus floor. At the base of a giant tree just opposite La Casita, the sun shone through the narrow slit in the jungle made by the river's path. Sunlight lay in a warm golden pool there for a little while each day. In that sun-filled tree room, we started a small vegetable garden and made a little world where domesticated plants lived for a while by a giant tree, festooned with rattan vines, that was more naturally host to orchids, air plants, and stag horn ferns.

Though La Casita was built in fear, it was a happy place for us—a refuge from the closeness of living in a group of people. We left the others at Gomoco behind when we went through the jungle to La Casita, and it became a weekend cabin in the wilderness where we cooked our meals on fires set between stones and I scrubbed the pots with sand in the clear water of our creek.

The trail from the main camp to the hideout was easy to disguise because we could walk along the tops of the fallen logs along the ridge and then walk up the river to the shelter. My parents hoped that it was secret, and they hoped it would save us if the Japanese decided to round us up, but I knew that the children, Opren and Opron, often followed us through the jungle and that we had no secrets at all.

La Casita was a counterpoint to this:

August 8, 1942. Eight months since the bombing at Pearl Harbor . . . Each day here is a golden arc of sunlight in a gold and green world. Near the zenith now, the sun is strong and glares from the heavens with a hot white eye. Banana leaves glance in the sun with the shine of a bayonet on their waxy green. The cargadores yesterday told of a Japanese search party on the way to us. After so many rumors, I can't believe anything one way or the other. Douglass assures me we will hear from Maximino first, but I know that Maximino could be dead!

School went on for us children; Carlota kept us to our sewing lessons. We met for meals, but over it all was silence and a suspension of time.

August 12, 1942. We have no radio now and are cut off completely from the world. The radio has been hidden now that the Japs may come at any time. Listening to The Voice of America from San Francisco is punishable by death, it is said; it is better not to have them find one. Roy Welbon walked down to see Mr. Kellogg, and we learned that a major offensive has begun. I believe Guadalcanal

is the name of the island where American troops have landed. We
have one map book, an advertisement for a business in Manila
named "Tabacalera." It is small and inaccurate, but we are thank-
ful to have it.

Though we begged for news from the traders, nothing more
was heard of the Japanese search party. Charlie Martin volunteered to find out what had happened to them and set off on a
fact-finding trip. He planned to walk about twenty miles
through the jungle to Prosperidad, a trading town on the Gibong River. The Gibong roughly parallels the Agusan until it
flows into the larger river. Charlie could be quite close to the
Japanese, whom Waldo had last seen on the Agusan, but be protected by the mountains between the rivers.

The thought of capture was so strange to us that the trip to
Prosperidad was a shopping trip as well. If the Japanese decided to leave us alone, we would need any useful or valuable
trinkets that the Chinese merchants might still have. We were
being careful with things like needles and lamp chimneys now
that we could see no end to the war.

My mother took Charlie aside and begged him to buy as
many lipsticks as he could. She couldn't bear to be without her
red badge of courage—especially if she had to face Japanese
soldiers.

"I know, Harriet. The redder the better!"

Our group was joined by two men whom we had known from
the mining community before the war began. Bill Gorler was
alone because his wife and baby daughter had been in Manila and
had possibly been on the sunken *Corregidor*. No word from them
had ever come to us. Like my brother, they were lost in the war.

Bill's constant worrying sent him pacing the length of the mess house porch; sometimes that pacing turned into longer walks down the trails and rivers of Mindanao. He and his wife were Australians, and I liked the fact that he, born in 1900, would always be the age of the century.

Bob Crump was a young geologist who had worked for the Philippine Bureau of Mines. We had known him before the war because he surveyed the mines and their ore bodies for the government.

Money was running short for Evelyn and Glenda, and Bill and Bob agreed to assume responsibility for the two women. Bob had a paycheck he had been unable to cash in the confused first days of the war. The two men decided to try to get as near to Surigao as possible and to find someone who might lend him money against the check. They also meant to find out as much as they could about the situation outside Gomoco. They were free and could move easily.

The first news came from Charlie by runner: "Leave Gomoco at once! Two to three hundred Japs are in Talacogon [on the Agusan] and are on the way to you. They know you are there, and they are angry."

We held a meeting.

"Harriet, Mary, and I will hide in the jungle," my father announced. "I have hidden our cache of food, and we'll take our chances there."

The three women with children and the Welbons had no choice but to stay and meet the Japanese.

Glenda said, "I can't run with Stevie, and I have to take my chances here at Gomoco. There's a chance they'll get me to Bob. If not . . ." she didn't finish the sentence. Evelyn, Alberta and their two children will stay with her. Oh, God, what will happen to us? It's funny how the worst you can imagine cannot be applied to yourself. I just can't help thinking that we'll live through this, and yet I'm filled with terror.

I had a little pack to carry containing a change of clothes, including the Japanese tennis shoes we had bought in Butuan. They were beginning to fit me now. My mother packed a few cans of milk for me to carry, and then put more in her heavier pack.

August 15, 1942. Douglass has tried to think of every possibility. We live each day, poised for change, knap-sacks ready, waiting for Maximino to warn us. We sent him to Krik's on the Sulibau to watch for Charlie's search party. I think I can't be a fugitive! I'd rather meet what is in store for us here with everyone else, but Douglass thinks the Casita is a refuge safe enough for us. He fears the Japs will not simply take us prisoner. Horror stories of their atrocities and cruelty to the gentle Filipinos they came to "liberate from Western oppression" filter up here to us. Many of the stories are unbearable and unrepeatable. They maim and torture and then they kill. They force-feed their victims with salt, then bury them to the neck and leave them in the sun without water. I try not to think about it—maybe I can't think about it.

After a week of suspense, Maximino ran up the trail to report that the Japanese had gone past the Gibong River because it was too low in the dry season for their launches and, staying on the Agusan, were in Bunawan on the other side of the swamps to the west of us. Fear abated somewhat. At least we had a few days. It was possible they could come through the swamps to us, but floating water hyacinths that fouled boats' propellers choked the waters in the swamp. It would be difficult for the Japanese to come from Bunawan in their launches.

Our position at the end of a river system with no place to go except into the jungle was more frightening now than comforting. The fact that the Japanese had come to the interior of Mindanao made us realize that we were trapped rather than hidden.

It was finally too much for Alberta Stumbaugh, one of the women from Davao. When an American, Swede Swanson, paid a surprise visit to us and offered to help her move, she decided to go to the east coast of Mindanao with Helen Louise. She thought she could keep moving more easily on the coast, and she hoped that two people could hide more easily than a group. Her money was slipping away too quickly on high-priced food carried into Gomoco by *cargadores*. Perhaps she could have a small garden and raise food herself or perhaps the sisters in a convent would take them in.

So, once more, the *cargadores* were hired, loaded with mattresses and mosquito nets. We shared our food, and each of us offered what we could to make her new life possible. A washcloth from one person, a pair of socks from another, a frying pan from the kitchen. Helen Louise was younger than I, and a dress that I was outgrowing went with her.

We all gathered at the edge of the river to say good-bye, and just as they turned to leave, Swede said to my father, "I'm glad I'm not you, Mac, because when the Japs come up this trail, you're going to have to shoot all the women and children first!" Everyone but my father laughed, even though they all suddenly realized it was true.

Standing near my mother, I was suddenly grateful that I had grown tall enough to nestle under her arm and against the soft curve of her breast. I looked up at her, hoping for a comforting squeeze and a calm gaze from her gray eyes, but she was looking at Swede in shock.

I thought about the Luger my dad kept nearby most of the time—its black heaviness no longer meant safety to me. Could my father truly turn it on us? Somehow, I knew that Swede meant it was better to die quickly than to be tortured, but being killed by my father was a reality I had never allowed into my mind.

I turned to him for comfort, but there was none: I could see that he had always known what he would have to do—kill cleanly the ones he loved in order to save them from a terrible death.

I looked then to my mother, but she couldn't see me. It was the worst of news for me. I learned then that there are situations that no one has the power to change. My parents could not change their fate, nor could they change mine. Even though they loved me and would take care of me, there could be things beyond their control. I was alone with my life and could not always be safe.

———➤◆◆◀———

Nine people at Gomoco waited for the Japanese, and three men were away on search parties. Part of our minds watched for men with bayonets; another part listened to the news, plotted the progress of the Allies, slow as it was, and waited for The Aid.

My parents and I were the last of the original refugees from Mindanao Mother Lode. The Feigels were living a day's walk from us, farming like *taos* now that their plans to sail to Australia had failed. I have a few transcripts of letters my father wrote to Fred Feigel as the war went on. One reads:

> August 10, 1942. At present, the family and I are the sole survivors of the "Black Gold" crowd here at the Last Resort. From the others I get no cooperation or help, and have been bearing down; so, I am now in the same category as a civet cat at a Sunday School picnic.

They had not been able to resist listening to the radio. It was hidden most of the time, but on Sundays it brought in the short-wave broadcast from San Francisco.

"We may as well listen," I heard Charlie say one night. "The Japs aren't gonna like us anyway!"

The Feigels had no radio, and another letter to them gives a summary of the war on two fronts without mentioning the source of his information. My father ends the letter:

> Personally, I do not see evidence of a collapse of either enemy as imminent, and although it all looks better, I feel we still have a lot of work cut out for us on both sides of the world. Hence I am disposed to hitch up the old belt another notch or two and make such physical and mental preparations as I can to stick it out another year. I admit mine is a minority opinion here locally.

The hot season was upon us.

Throughout August, the grown-ups were stupefied in the molten days of Mindanao's hot season. Perhaps that lethargy made them less susceptible to fear. Perhaps it is impossible to remain frightened for long periods of time. When the bamboo telegraph told us that the Japanese would not come so far inland, that they would send the Philippine constabulary instead, we waited for warnings from Maximino. None came. His vendors came instead, carrying vegetables and an inflated vision of our wealth.

The Filipinos believed that we had unlimited amounts of money and were hurt when the prices they quoted were higher than we wanted to pay.

"Only pity me, sir. I have many children, and because of typhoon, I have no growings. I come to you for a long way with my *camotes*. Only pity me, sir. I cannot give you lower price."

My father would offer half the given price.

"Oh, no, sir. You are very hard, sir. My wife is sick, and I must buy medicine, and now it is very dear."

For a while, my father could move the prices down; but in time there was no room to bargain.

Rumors came up the trail with the traders, and one day I heard my father ask, "Any rumors today?"

"No, sir, only *camotes* and eggplant." That was a good day, a day without rumors.

The Filipinos fled their farms and *kaingins* whenever the Japanese came near, knowing that torture was inevitable now that the rougher soldiers hardened by Nanking had replaced the first troops. Crops were not planted.

We became traders. Gomoco's *bodegas* were full of supplies needed for running a small gold mine: nails, tools, pieces of steel that could be made into knives in the blacksmith shop. There was diesel oil for the generator; there were chemicals in the assay office. The things that we found at Gomoco, and a few of the things we had brought with us, soon became more valuable than money. A quarter of a bottle of diesel oil plugged with a dirty rag was worth a half-dozen eggs. Two nails bought a hand of bananas. A sack of *camotes* was worth a few paper clips to be made into fishhooks. One round of ammunition bought a kilo of dried fish.

The two most valuable commodities were dynamite and cyanide. The dynamite had been used to blast tunnels in the search for gold, and the cyanide had been needed in beginning the process of refining the gold ore.

I was afraid when cyanide was traded because Daddy had told me that a tiny amount under a fingernail was enough to kill a person instantly. I hung back, listening to my father caution the traders about its dangers. They must have listened because they always came back for more and we never heard of an accident.

The Filipinos traded for cyanide because it was an easy way to fish the rivers. They poured it into the rivers and then gathered all the dead and dying fish into their nets. None escaped them, and they ate well for days after a cyanide-fishing day. The cyanide stayed in the gills of the fish, my father said, and the fish were safe enough to eat. We surely bought dried fish we had indirectly killed with our cyanide.

One afternoon, after a cyanide-trading session, I found one of the goats lying on her side in agony, her eyes glazing over. I flew to my father and panted:

"Nanny One is dying! She can't breathe! Oh, please come. Please please please."

Nanny One was the larger of the two goats Maximino had brought us at the beginning. She was smooth and serene; the horizontal pupils in her amber eyes gazed at the world with dignity. I couldn't bear that she was dying.

"Do something, Daddy! Do something!"

He calmly, maddeningly slowly, went to the assay office and mixed a solution of potassium permanganate, which we used to purify leafy vegetables. Then, with a funnel, he poured it down her throat.

"What's wrong with her? What are you doing? Will it help? Don't hurt her, please."

"I think she ate grass with cyanide on it. The permanganate might mix with the cyanide and stop the poisoning."

We sat by her for a long time, it seemed, and finally she stood. She was sick for a while, but she didn't die.

Perhaps the antidote worked because goats have compartmentalized stomachs and the poison didn't immediately enter her bloodstream; perhaps she hadn't eaten cyanide at all. Perhaps it was a miracle. I didn't wonder at those possibilities; I only knew that my father knew everything and could do anything.

He was a hard man, but he had intelligence and courage.

———⟫◆⟪———

The slow procession of days continued. Maximino sent no messages, the traders came with no new rumors. We waited for meals that disappointed us: Some people played Bridge; men whittled; the women swept their rooms and mended clothes.

Every day the jungle sang with cicadas and calls of unseen animals. When my morning classes were over, I followed Opren and Opron as they hunted for freshwater shrimp in the river, now running cool and clear again below our house. My bare legs wavered below the water's green reflections as I waded barefoot over the smooth stones. My hands were as fast as theirs, of course; and soon I learned to catch the shrimp, too. It is simply a matter of coming from behind and being quick.

I learned from them that the sun and the moon were once married and had children. The sun, angry at their son's disobedience, turned him to ashes. The moon, even angrier, chopped their daughter to pieces and scattered them to make the stars. Since that terrible quarrel, the sun and the moon have stayed apart.

The boys knew that *busaws* and *diwatas* lived in the bushes along the river and under the stones. They asked pardon of the *busaws* whenever they turned over a rock in the river and were careful not to offend the bad-luck spirits at any time. If you could be sure of having a *diwata* with you, then the powers of a *busaw* were useless. *Diwatas* are shy and capricious and only their joints have skin. The rest of their bodies are protected with a covering like fingernails. You cannot be sure they will use their powers to bring good luck. It is better not to offend a *busaw*; it is necessary to beg their pardon for being intrusive.

From deep in the jungle a call often came: *Buu-saaw, buu-saaw*, a mournful descending minor third. *Buu-saaw, buu-saaw.* I had heard it all my life. I was learning that the earth is full of spirits. When the *busaw* called to me from the darkness behind the trees, I reminded myself that we were living in the Diuata Mountains. If the mountains were named for the good-luck spirits, then surely their shy powers would defeat the chilly call of the *busaw*.

Other afternoons, usually on Sunday—it is strange that weekends still existed in a life outside of time—my father would take my mother and me out into the jungle to show us what he had found on his explorations. He couldn't break a lifetime's habit of prospecting for gold, and often, if there were no traders to bargain with or cans of food to count, he took the trail behind the mill building into the jungle to follow the creeks and rivers near us. Gold washes out of the rocks and settles at the edges of mountain rivers, sometimes giving a clue to a rich vein of ore nearby. He had roamed the Sierra Nevada in California during the Depression when he had no work; it was the same in the Diuata Mountains. When the war finally ended, a new claim of undiscovered gold wouldn't hurt!

The jungle usually hid its treasures behind a green wall, but the typhoon had opened ways through that wall. The undergrowth was returning, but we could still walk along the fallen trees. My father went first, hacking at the vines with his *bolo*, and we followed behind, my mother looking up to see the orchids—white, yellow, or pink—high above us. Birds flew there, red and blue, and the *busaw* called from far away.

The *busaws'* power diminished when I was with my parents, but I was careful of them nonetheless. I watched my father's *bolo* swing against the brush and kept Opren's invocation in my mind. I knew that my parents didn't believe that good and bad spirits were everywhere; but I did, and I protected them as much as I could.

My father had something special to show us one day, and we went farther from La Casita than we had ever gone before. The sound of water pounding on rock joined the other sounds of the jungle and the *chop-chop* of the *bolo*. We came to the top of a ridge and looked down onto a waterfall dropping into swaying, pale-green ferns. A rainbow shone in the spray.

In the black lava, the river had carved deep pools linked by white water racing over the rock. We followed the water higher, farther than my father had yet been, and found a deep chasm carved in the dark stone where the water flowed quietly in blackness.

We turned back to the waterfall, caught in sunlight, to stand in the pool below it where we had seen the rainbow. The water pounded on our backs so heavily that it was hard to stand. We shouted at each other in the roar.

"Oh, Douglass," my mother said, "this is worth facing the nettles and the leeches! It's hydrotherapy!"

"Hydrotherapy." Another new word for me.

Then we followed the path of the water past Gomoco to the abandoned barrio down the trail. We came back to the camp the usual way across the creek below our window. We lifted the leeches off our bodies by touching them with an ember burning at the end of a stick. Matches were too precious now to use for leech removal.

September 13, 1942. And now at night the music of the waterfalls lulls me to sleep, and my dreams are bright with the beauty of their plunging flumes hanging like great white tassels against the jungle green.

⇒◆⇐

We came home from one of our adventures under the waterfall to find that Bill Gorler had returned to camp with the news that the Japanese had indeed gone back to Butuan and had passed us by. Perhaps they would be back when the rivers were flooded again after the rains. Maybe Charlie was right, after all.

He had always said, "The Japs'll never come up after us. We'd be too much trouble for them."

We couldn't celebrate Bill's good news because almost as soon as he arrived in camp, he collapsed from sunstroke. He had not worn a hat or carried enough water with him as he hurried back to us. His fever was high, and he raved loudly. People took turns trying to help, but there was little they knew to do.

Bill's fever lasted for nearly a week, despite the best efforts of everyone. To break the fever, my mother wrapped him in blankets with hot stones, a treatment she learned from the doctor at Mother Lode when I had had pneumonia. We killed chickens to make broth and gave him special rations, but it was more than two weeks before he tottered up to the mess house table. There was no longer a children's table; I was now among the adults.

September 20, 1942. I am living in peace again, now that I know the enemy is not nearby. Bill is healing after his heroic walk to bring the good news. Now the hot season is fading. Rains come at night again, and wild winds rush like rivers of sound through the trees. The stream rises swiftly and talks loudly in tones to match the wind. Night in the jungle is full of sound; and now, at the autumnal equinox, lightning splits the dark starless sky and thunder rolls almost constantly. But, oh! the silence of a jungle noon! No winds stir, the stream slips silently over the stones. Palm fronds are interstices of silence; liana and rattan are syllables of silence written in scrolls and loops.

The days now are glorious. The water sings, the sun shines, and it is hard to believe we are hemmed in by Jap garrisons. It is a year today—one whole year—since we last saw Bob. I see him still, swinging onto the train, bound for his senior year and waving good-bye. I know he's all right. I just know he is.

Planes flew over Gomoco, singly and in groups, during September. At first we hoped that they were American planes on bombing raids, but the radio news did not support that dream. The Aid was still far in the future, and we knew the planes were Japanese.

From time to time, a small plane flew over us—the rising sun painted on its fuselage. We all ran out to watch it, my parents, the Welbons, and weak Bill Gorler. I heard my mother say, "You yellow, murdering Jap! Leave us alone!"

The plane flew over us again one morning as Mrs. Welbon and I were having arithmetic class. We went outside to watch it fly over us, as we always did, and I said to the plane, "You yellow, murdering Jap! Leave us alone!"

Mrs. Welbon was shocked and told me *never* to talk like that.

"It's awful to hear language like that, Mary!"

I learned about a double standard that day: grown-ups could shout insults at distant Japanese, but children couldn't.

———◆———

Miss Puss, the cat my mother and I had bought when we walked to Rosario, had a litter of five kittens under my bed, just where I had carefully made her a nest. Sweet, little, furry, blind things, they were my great happiness. There was something wrong with the home I chose, though; and Miss Puss tried to move her babies to a higher spot in the clothespress. We moved the kittens back to the place we preferred; she moved them again. We put the kittens back.

I woke one night to find my mother on her hands and knees talking to the yowling mother under the table. Her flashlight sent long, confusing shadows across the floor. "You can't move now, Kitty. Not at this time of night. Here, let me take your baby home." She reached for the kitten and a dark shape behind the kitten slid toward her.

Snake!

My mother tried to scream, but no sound came. She ran to wake my father, finally managing to scream just by his ear.

"Douglass! Help! There's a snake under the table! He's after a kitten!"

"Will you ever learn not to scream at little things?"

I curled up in the corner of my bed, as far as I could get from the snake, and watched it carry the kitten across the floor and under my mother's bed.

Immobilized, Miss Puss watched him, too.

My father was deliberately, infuriatingly, calm, just the way he had been when Nanny One was dying of cyanide poisoning. He was so calm that by the time he got to our room the snake was slithering through a hole in the wall. One heavy chop of my father's *bolo* stopped the snake. Two more finished it. My father picked the snake up on the point of the blade and dropped the six feet of limp darkness over the sill to the ground below. Then he went back to sleep, saying, "Harriet, I thought I'd trained you not to scream at things like that. It was only a python; they're not dangerous."

Bill Gorler, recuperating in our end of the house, woke enough to say, "Python, harmless." The Welbons, from their end of the building, called to ask what was going on. My father assured them that the fracas was all over and that there was nothing to worry about.

My mother and I returned the wounded kitten to its nest, but Miss Puss couldn't accept it. It smelled of other powers.

I spent the rest of the night in my mother's bed, tucking the mosquito net under the mattress as tightly as I could. The snake had, after all, been under the bed, and I couldn't forget that.

The kitten died during the night.

In the morning we found that the snake wasn't a python, marked in bargello designs of beiges and browns, but was gunmetal gray with a yellowish belly. Charlie declared it to be an unusually large cobra.

We scrubbed the snake blood from the floor, but the three chop marks on the stained floorboards remained. They reminded me that horror can come at any time in any form.

Miss Puss moved out of the building to the *bodega,* her head held high as she carried each kitten across the clearing. We let her go; she knew best.

———⟫•◇•⟪———

"MacArthur is coming, tra la, tra la!" Bill Gorler and Bob Crump sang each evening on the way from their rooms in the mill to the mess house. They followed the line by deeper notes like drumbeats, "I shall return!"

Once the arrival of the Japanese Army no longer seemed imminent, the radio had come out of hiding. Every other night for fifteen minutes during dinner, we listened to the news from Treasure Island in San Francisco Bay. Names of places where the Allies were fighting rang in my mind: Stalingrad, Buna, Piatagorsk, Guadalcanal, the Coral Sea, El Alamein. The places were scattered across the world, and they were all very, very far from us.

The fighting in the Pacific was on the other side of New Guinea, in the Solomon Islands, and I wondered if anyone at all remembered the Philippines. The Filipinos who came to Gomoco told tales of the terrible Japanese who burned their barrios after they stole their food and who tortured them for pleasure. The bamboo telegraph reported that the Japanese had arrested a whole town during a fiesta and beaten many of the men because they heard the Spanish priest say "Luzbel" many times during the church services. "Luzbel" is Spanish for "Lucifer," not "Roosevelt."

We heard that on the Fourth of July the Japanese shamed U.S. military prisoners of war in Dansalan and Iligan by parading them, hungry and dirty, through the streets. The Japanese thought they would gain respect as the Americans lost face, but the shaming of American soldiers backfired. The Filipinos hated the Hapons even more.

From the local jails, they said, screams of their friends taken prisoner kept them awake at night. They knew it was better to die than to be taken prisoner by the Japanese. They were sure that The Aid would soon come and bring freedom. Their faith gave my mother hope, and so I, too, believed that the fighting would someday get me to the States.

Whenever the Japanese came to a village, the townspeople killed any livestock they thought the Japanese would take and then scattered to hide in the jungle. To keep the Japanese from getting their rice, they stopped planting. The typhoon had destroyed banana and papaya trees, and it looked as though we were facing a hard rainy season. Even if food were plentiful in the lowlands, the trails would be difficult during the rains. We began to plan for a long, dark future.

The men built a grinding mill from two slabs cut from an enormous fallen tree. They salvaged more steel from that handy red truck, and cut it into rectangles to drive into the inside faces of the grinding "stones." They drilled a hole in the top one and turned it by hand, then spent long hours sifting the corn they ground. We had a good supply of corn and *mongo* beans, but we still preferred rice.

Charlie could remember his mother in Texas making hominy by soaking yellow corn kernels in lye. First he had to make lye, and that took some experimentation. Lye is made by soaking wood ashes in water and then removing the ashes. We had plenty of wood ashes and plenty of water. There was filter cloth in the mill that had been needed to refine gold. All the ingredients were there, but it took many tries to get the right proportions.

Charlie and my mother set up a systematic process for re-learning the ancient art, and after a week or two, they finally were happy with their lye. Then they began on the hominy project. They soaked the hard corn and boiled it in lye, then rinsed it in the river. They rinsed away the hulls, and finally hominy appeared at the table to shouts of praise. As far as I was concerned, rice had it all over hominy, and I didn't have to listen to Charlie give us every detail of the process of making rice the way I did with the hominy.

At last, one of the pigs was big enough to be butchered. I heard the dreadful squeal as they cut its throat. My mother tried to distract me from the event, but I escaped from her.

The pig hung upside down, the last of its blood draining into a bucket. Once again, it was Charlie who knew how to do things. He and my dad dragged the carcass to the riverbank and slit its belly. Out rolled a pile of insides, iridescent, beautiful, and efficient. I had known that there were things inside us doing things to the food we ate, but I had never thought to ask what they looked like.

"What's that?" I asked, as they cut away a large, dark-red, shiny, double handful. It was heavy and rich looking, with scalloped edges.

"His liver."

"What does it do?"

"It purifies his blood."

"Oh. Are we going to eat it?"

"Yes, tonight for dinner."

"Will I like it?"

"You probably will; it's very good for you."

"Oh, now what's that?" I was spellbound at the whole new world I'd discovered.

Charlie said, "That's his bread basket."

"What's a bread basket in a pig?"

I guess I was a pest, for Charlie said, "It's just his bread basket!"

"Well, what does a bread basket do?" The straight answers I got from my father; Charlie was teasing me. I persisted, "But I want to know, why does a pig have a bread basket?"

My father stood up from his labors, knee-deep in the river, and said to Charlie, "I guess I'm going to have to pay for a medical education for this girl!"

I withered when I heard the sarcasm and the intimation that a girl learning medicine was an outlandish idea. I didn't ask any more questions. I didn't even watch any more of the butchering. I went up to the kitchen where the women were preparing to take care of the meat.

The women shooed me away when they scalded the pig's skin to loosen the hair so it could be scraped off. The skin and fat boiled in pots while the pig was cut into pieces. Shining white joints that slipped by each other easily where the legs joined the body appeared under the sharp knives. Those flashing knives formed chops that were cooked and dropped into rendered fat. Charlie said that in Texas that's how they preserved food—by putting cooked meat into congealed fat.

Crisp bits left over from the rendering were cracklins, Charlie said, and they tasted wonderful.

My mother's diary doesn't mention the pig, or even the rich meals that followed his demise. Instead she wrote,

> *October 1, 1942. When the natives from the river valley brought eggs and green corn yesterday, one of them carried a large goldfish all the way up here in a glass jar. Mary and I bought it for fifty centavos; but, on claiming our prize, we found we had purchased "the fish only, ma'am." In order to find suitable lodging for it, I had to get Ah Hing's salt jar, and now the fish ogles horribly at me through the glass, curved in too small a space. In a day or two we'll let him go, too, as we have other captured things we've tried to keep as pets.*

We were saving tiny bits of soap now, dissolving them in jars of water to make shampoo. As soon as the lye was made, my mother began a soap-making project, boiling the pig fat with lye. She gave the soap to Philomena to use in washing our clothes in the river, even though Philomena, who had grown up without soap, knew that the only way to get clothes really clean was to beat them on rocks. She was the one who wore out our clothing and kept my mother busy patching with the treadle sewing machine. Patches appeared on patches, as Philomena worked her magic on our clothes.

As we wore things out or used them up, we had to reinvent them. My mother made wicks for the lamps by folding canvas over strips of asbestos from the mine supplies and stitching them on the machine. They made a steady, bright light.

Our deceptively peaceful days were shattered again by the arrival of a runner warning us that the Japanese were on the way to Gomoco once more. We three still planned to melt into the jungle if the Japanese came. (At La Casita, our onions and peanuts were growing feebly by the giant tree.) The others would meet the Japanese at Gomoco, hoping only to be taken prisoner. We didn't talk about the possibility of murder.

I tried to comfort my mother. "Look, Mommy, look how fast I can run and how high I can jump!" I hurled my little body over a log. "I can beat any old Jap any old day!" She didn't smile a big smile.

Maximino came into camp. His wide smile set our minds at ease, as he said, "I am The One to tell you that the Hapons will not come to you this day!"

He told us that this time the Japanese brought larger launches than before, not knowing that the rivers were much lower at the end of dry season. They came closer on this trip than the first time, but ran aground in the shallow, winding Sulibau.

October 2, 1942. Such a weight of foreboding lies within my heart that I cannot breathe freely and my breast is bound with bands of fear. Twice, now, Nature has turned them back, but this third time Nature was helped by that wily Syrian, Khalil Khodr, on the Sulibau: He swore to the Jap Commander that his shallow-

draft boat was sinking in a town not far from them for want of caulk. Maybe now they will not ever come for us. As a precaution, we have hidden the radio again and now we have to live without news—good or bad—of the outside world. Perhaps we could chart our fortunes by the presence and absence of the radio!

It was not only the Japanese that kept us uneasy; there was real reason to fear the Filipinos as well. There was talk about a *mestizo* named Sam Goode who commanded a marauding group of bandits in the vicinity.

Every time natives come from the Pacific coast to bring us fish, sugar or coconut oil, they also bring disturbing tales of plans to rob the people at Gomoco of the fabulous sums of money they think we possess. We have buried what we have and go furtively at night to the hiding place to retrieve a few more pesos to keep us going. What if bandits replace the gentle traders who need our diesel oil and dynamite?

My father slept with his loaded rifle by his bed, and we hoped for warning from people who were loyal to us.

We could do nothing to prevent the arrival of search parties, bandit or Japanese. We could only hope for a warning giving us enough time to melt into the jungle. We kept to our routines.

October 10, 1942. Mary and I let the fish go. I'm afraid I forgot him in these last days of worry. When the river was pale amber in the early evening we carried the not-quite-big-enough square glass jar to the riverbank. We made a rite of it, paused on the bank to take off our shoes, and then waded into the current. Freedom was so strange to the poor captive that he didn't respond— just stayed in the confines of the submerged jar and let fresh water stream in around him. At last we poured him out of his prison, but still he swam carefully in the same dimensions, finding his former existence strange. Perhaps we'll be the same when we can go out again to live lives of our own choosing.

———◆———

Our water supply came from a spring high on the hill across the creek from our house. Spilt bamboo troughs carried water down the hill to us. Once in a while, my mother and I would make an expedition to drink the water at its source while it was still cold from the earth. When we crossed the river and climbed up to the spring, we could look down on our settlement in the jungle.

Gomoco looked homey and sufficient to me, and I didn't want to leave it, even if the Japanese came. The clearing in the jungle lay next to the cheerful brook rushing over its mossy stones. Our three-room house with its thatched roof sheltering the long porch looked onto the river. I could see the white curtains at the windows of our room and the empty houses where the people who had been with us at the beginning had lived. Now the chickens roosted under the eaves at night and we used the buildings for storage of anything extra we had. The mess house, not so different from the three staff houses, was the farthest up the row of buildings. A gravel "plaza" ran parallel to the houses; it separated the houses from the workings of the mine—the *bodega*, the mill, and the powerhouse with our precious generator. The tiny blacksmith shop where my father and Charlie so happily had made the horseshoe set for after-dinner games was the last building before our tiny, faint trail led to the spring.

I knew Gomoco as only a child can know a place, and I
loved it. My mother looked at the same scene, but saw it as a
prison. She sighed and tried to be thankful for her cold drink
fresh from the mountain.

After supper, when the conversations about the war news
ended among the grown-ups, my parents and I would return to
our room and the little red Blizzard lamp. We climbed into my
mother's large bed and tucked the mosquito net in tightly. In
that cozy nest, the three of us played cards. I learned to add by
playing Cribbage and I learned strategy and revenge by playing
Hearts. I loved the hours of closeness in the lamplight. I had to
concentrate on the game and remember at the same time to keep
my body from touching the net that separated me from the mosquitoes swarming outside, hungry for warm flesh.

When the game was over, my father and I would leave for
our own beds, and my mother would try to rid her net of the
mosquitoes that got in as we untucked it. Then she blew out the
lamp and another day would end.

———⟫•◆•⟪———

I never questioned why my parents slept in separate rooms
during the war. In the tropics, sleeping in separate beds was
cooler than sharing a double one; my parents had had twin beds
at home before the war. My bamboo bed was in a corner of my
mother's room; her bed was across the room between two windows. My father slept just the other side of the partition from
me in the next room where Beth Plowman had lived in the first
months of the war.

One morning I woke early and, in the pale dawn, saw my father rising and falling slowly and quietly over my mother in her
bed. The knowledge I had learned after the Neil episode a few

months before told me that there would be a new baby in nine months.

Now I had another secret I could never betray. I could never talk about Neil, and I could never talk about what I had seen. Such a secret was too big to hold inside me, and busy with an importance born of secrets and stealth, I wrote a note on a small piece of paper, "Mother and Daddy conceived today. October 17, 1942."

I folded it tightly and crawled deep under the house where the goats were living. I told the goats my secret and wedged the note between the floorboards and the beam under Glenda and Stevie's room. The goats looked at me with their horizontal pupils and chewed, their jaws moving sideways rhythmically. My secret was safe, but it wasn't quite a secret anymore. The goats knew, and the secret wasn't just a thing in my head. It existed as a note that I could read when I needed to. That was important.

My secret and my anticipation occupied my mind until one day, in the little slatted-floor bathroom, I once again saw the bucket where my mother soaked her muslin cloths before washing them in the brook. The water was red with blood, and I knew my secret was nothing.

—————◆—————

Just as life settled into calm again after Maximino walked through the jungle to tell us the Japanese had called off their search for us, a message came up from the Sulibau that set us off balance again.

The message said: "Important events in the Agusan valley will be reported to you by trusted runner in the next few days."

We waited two days, three days, then four days. My father packed up another extremely heavy box of supplies to carry to

La Casita and stored it under my bed. Mother made a felt pad for his shoulders because she couldn't bear the thought of his carrying so heavy a load through the jungle, and she wanted to help, at least a little.

When Corporal Pritz, an American soldier who had not obeyed the orders to surrender, arrived at noon on the sixth day of suspense, he held us in his power still longer by delaying the announcement until after lunch was over. We ate silently, wondering if what he had to say would instantly change our lives.

Finally, when he was sure that no one could overhear, he told us that guerrilla activity was beginning on Mindanao, that a small army of Filipinos and Americans was forming to harass the Japanese.

After nearly a week of thinking that a Japanese party was on the way to kill us, the news of organized resistance was a letdown. Charlie wasn't impressed because he knew Pritz pretty well from his recent visits up and down the rivers.

"Pritz wouldn't tell the truth if he could think of a lie instead," said Charlie.

Still, my father was hopeful. If the news were true, the guerrilla army could keep the Japanese too busy to think about us. He was afraid, though, that a network of warlords fighting among themselves would put us in a different kind of danger. He hoped for an army unified by a strong leader.

The news made little difference to us, and after Corporal Pritz left Gomoco, our lives continued as they had.

⟫◆⟪

One day Florencio Gelacio, the schoolteacher from Rosario, stepped out of the jungle dressed in a fine *piña camisa* and immaculate white trousers. A teacher could never carry anything or appear in clothing that did not maintain his dignity. He had washed quickly in the stream and put on his wonderful clothes just before the trail turned toward Gomoco. His brown skin shone through the transparent embroidered shirt made from pineapple fibers, and we were honored by his respect for us. I had not seen a *piña camisa* since before the war, when wealthy Filipinos wore them to banquets in the Manila Hotel.

His *cargadores* carried beef! For a few days we ate beef at every meal until we couldn't preserve it anymore. Then we cut it into strips and dried it in the sun to make *tapa*.

A few days later, the grown-ups learned that the beef had really been *carabao*. No one explained to me why *carabao* wasn't as good as beef, but I went around saying, "Ugh, *carabao*," too.

The Japanese occupation had closed the schools in Rosario. Mr. Gelacio brought from the school books that smelled dusty and damp instead of crisp and new, as I had hoped when I first saw them. He brought pencils and notebooks with blue lines and smooth paper that I loved.

I drew lines halfway between the lines in the notebooks with my ruler and practiced my longhand when my father wasn't around. He seemed to think that I had deliberately chosen to be left-handed to annoy him, and he hated to watch me write.

"Just use your right hand, will you? You look awful writing like that!"

My left hand was agile and made the even letters I wanted to fill the lined notebooks with. I tried to write with my other hand, but it wasn't the same; it was jerky and awkward. It was best to practice alone.

One night, while I was practicing my writing by the lantern light, I invented what I later learned had already been invented: a palimpsest. 1 wrote one direction on a page and then turned it and wrote across the first lines. The paper had been erased a few times and had a worn fuzzy surface.

"Mommy, do you think that if the Japs find this paper they'll feel sorry for us and not kill us? I wonder if they'll feel sad that we're running out of things here at Gomoco."

She looked at me for a long moment without any expression and then went back to her mending. I went back to my palimpsest without really knowing what I had done.

October 27, 1942. Finding a radio enrages the Sons of Samurai, but they have to catch us first, as Charlie says, and we listen because we must. The news tonight cast me down. The same reports come again and again about the Solomon Islands. The enemy has landed troops and heavy equipment and are attacking positions the Marines have held since early August. Stalingrad still stands, but is in ruins. We listen each evening, even though running the power plant draws heavily on our diesel oil.

We have magazines, but they are re-read and old. Fortunately, we all brought books. The Romance of Leonardo daVinci *is going the rounds. I have just finished* The Education of Henry Adams, *and after that heavy fare, I am enjoying a book of Li Po's poems, which Roy Welbon happened to bring. It is enchanting with swift brush strokes of color and imagery. When I watch the pair of lovely white cranes that hunt our stretch of the brook, I think of his imagery. Mary is reading Pearl Buck's* The Good Earth. *She needs very little help with it. I guess I won't have to worry about her starting school when this is over. She*

asked me today what "whore" means and I wished we had more
suitable reading material for her.

———⊰•◆•⊱———

Native women from higher in the Diuata Mountains came
one day to sell us gold. They brought an interpreter to help with
the trading.

"These women," he said, "come from far in the Diuata. They
have traveled many days to sell you gold. They have many *col-*
intasin of gold, and from you they want to buy *crudo*. You have
much *crudo*, they have many *colintasin* of gold. I will be The One
to talk for you."

The women stood, heads held high. They had left their babies at home; their hands hung free at their sides. I suddenly realized that we rarely saw native women without babies. They
had walked a long distance on mountain trails on their hard
bare feet. They came from the south and they dressed in dark
plaids; perhaps they were Moras, Muslim women. It didn't matter who they were; the issue was how to convert *colintasin* of
gold into diesel oil.

We learned that a *colintasin* (I immediately loved the word; it
slid so easily into my mind and around my tongue) is a grain of
a cereal grass a little smaller than a millet seed and is the measure for gold in the interior of Mindanao.

My father, one of the women, and the interpreter went to the
assay office and measured the gold. He paid them seventy prewar pesos an ounce, and then they bargained with their money
for the *crudo*.

One woman rubbed the hem of my dress between her
thumb and finger and offered me a tiny bottle of gold plugged

with a wad of cotton. We squatted together while the *crudo* was measured. I couldn't trade this dress for her gold, I told her with the pidgin I used with Opren and Opron, but I had another one I had outgrown. I showed her that one—it had been my favorite, a pale blue sailor dress printed with little white stars. Soon I had a little bottle of gold, which I still have, and she had my dress.

When the women left us, we all were happy. My father said that one day money might be meaningless and the gold would come in handy, but I had no intention of parting with my gold. Ever!

October 29, 1942. Mary has a squash and is cutting a sorrowful face in its green sides for Hallowe'en. No pumpkins grow here, so a squash will have to do for a jack-o'lantern to carry the eeriness of the season around our small stony street and to peer into the few windows of rooms still occupied. I wish she had carved a cheerful face, but the whole world now seems a tragedy and perhaps the face she carved on her own impulse is appropriate.

Mr. Kellogg had good flour in his *bodega* but no baking powder. We, on the other hand, had many cans of the U.S. Army's baking powder, but our flour was heavily infested with weevils. Bartering was becoming the system of commerce. We traded flour for baking powder with Mr. Kellogg, and salt and diesel oil for vegetables and bananas with the Filipinos.

At the beginning of November, the accounts showed that we had been using what my father called our "iron rations" in the *bodega* too quickly. We had opened each can my father allowed us reverently because each one taken left an empty spot on the shelf. Reverence was not enough; from now on there would be no sugar at meals, except for dessert every other day. Black coffee would get weaker each time Ah Hing boiled the grounds.

The children were allowed three tablespoons of sugar a day. I had a week's ration in a jar in our room. The amount of rice and corn allowed a day for all of us was cut from three *gantas* (twelve cups) a day to two and a half and *camotes* could not be served with either rice or corn.

November 2, 1942. Lunch today was an ordeal of eating to live— boiled camotes, boiled eggplant, boiled greens, salt and tuba vinegar. No spark of interest anywhere. I wonder if we are too saving of our canned food. It is like saving all our money for our old age and never enjoying it while we can. It would be easier for me to want something that I did not possess than to want something in the bodega that's denied me.

My father imposed the austerity program because the procurement officer, Maximino, was having difficulties. Rice was a difficult problem because it was grown farther away and had to be carried from the lowlands near the coasts. It was in short supply everywhere.

Maximino said he must have the money in advance so he could bargain in the markets on the east coast of the island. He had to be able to take possession of the rice when he found it; no merchant would wait until he came back with the money; prices were rising too fast.

My father counted out one hundred pesos.

I sent for shoes for Mary, ping-pong balls, lipsticks, pencils and Ace combs for the men for Christmas, and gave him twelve precious prewar pesos to pay wartime prices for the trinkets and for cargadores to carry them over the trail back to me.

When Maximino came back from Hinatuan, there was only one *cargador* instead of the many there should have been. One man carried a single bag of *palay*. Rice was what we needed, many bags of it, before the rainy season. One sack of palay, after being pounded in the mortar to remove the husk, yielded only a half a sack of rice—enough to last only a little over a week.

Our procurement officer was not the proud man he usually was. He didn't look at my mother or me as we stood to the side while the discussion of rice and *palay* was going on. He said the rest of the *palay* was at the entrance to the Sulibau and would be here when the river rose after a few rains. He said it would cost too much to bring it so far on men's backs. The river was faster and easier, and they would carry the rice from Rosario. I remembered Rosario, where Juanito had taken Mother and me on a shopping trip, and I knew it wasn't too far away.

At last, when the heavy discussion between the men was over, my mother said, "You will bring the pack to my room, Maximino?" She wanted her trinkets. I wanted my shoes.

"I do not have your things, ma'am. They were taken from my *cargador* at the house of a Moro where we slept. He is very bad man, that Moro. I am very sorry, ma'am, but they are lost."

The trinkets were so important to her that she gave him twelve more pesos, even though she was sure Maximino had gambled away her money and that the "bad Moro" was a story. He swore he would pay her back over the next few months.

"You don't worry, ma'am. I am faithful to you; your money safe with me. I have said to you that I will bring provisions. I will bring you provisions!"

The mood at dinner was sour. The Welbons were sure that all of our money had disappeared at a cockfight and that we would never see any of the rice.

They teased my mother for trusting Maximino with more money. No one understood her need for lipstick, though they would enjoy the Ping-Pong balls if they ever arrived. Bill and Bob had a table set up in the mill near their rooms and their never-ending and violent competition was entertainment for everyone. When the Ping-Pong balls split in half under constant battering, they could be glued together in the assay office, but new ones were best.

Bill says that gossip on the river is that Maximino's wife is a domineering scold, and for respite from her tongue, he has found solace in philandering. It could be that he has spent our money impressing his ladyloves, and now is desperately gambling to make up his losses to us.

———◆———

Helen Welbon was the one who argued for the rationing of sugar, but she couldn't stand black coffee. When she appeared at breakfast with a supply of saccharin, there was trouble.

My mother picked up her dish and her cup and left the table. "I cannot watch this, Helen. It makes me sick!"

Back in our room, she was storming.

"This is just too much! All these months when the rest of us had black coffee, that fat woman said she just couldn't drink black coffee, and she bargained with Glenda for a tablespoon of Stevie's milk every day. I've never said a word. I watched her stir milk into her coffee, and I never said a word. Not one word. Of all of us here, she could the best do without milk and sugar! Saccharin! She shows up with saccharin after she campaigned for 'stringent rationing'! Now she shows up with saccharin! I can't stand it! I want to kill her. I want to run away. I want out of here. I can't stay in this camp with that greedy fat woman!"

The Welbons lived in the room at the other end of our little house. My mother's storm lasted a long time. There was silence from the other end of the house.

At the next meal, the table was silent. My mother came to the dinner table, but she didn't speak.

Glenda tried to mediate. Helen said she had the right to her saccharin; my mother held that there was nothing to keep people from having special treats of their own, but that flaunting those treats at mealtime was not right. She said Helen had been a hypocrite to argue for sugarless meals when she knew she herself didn't have to drink bitter coffee.

The feud looked as though it might last the duration of the war.

Birthdays and anniversaries gave an excuse to feast at Gomoco. Roy Welbon, who was a gentle man, suggested that the feuding women could make peace over a rich meal.

He invited everyone to come to a feast celebrating my mother's birthday. Helen would cook. In the interest of peace, my father released some "iron rations."

At four forty-five on November 6, 1942, tomato-juice-and-*tuba* cocktails were served during the news broadcast, and then, at a table covered with a muslin cloth left from the fabric my mother bought to make curtains, the feast began:

Virginia Baked Ham
Decorated with Mustard,
Brown Sugar, Chopped Cherries and Walnuts
Rings of Pineapple Slices Centered with Cherries
Artichoke Salad with Pickled Beet Centers

Lima Bean and Niblet Corn Succotash
Candied Camotes
Baked Gold Squash
Corn Bread and Canned Butter
Pickles
Lady Baltimore Chocolate Nut Cake
Thrice-cooked Coffee

Helen lent her silver tray, which we piled with handmade gifts from everyone. On fat knitting needles my father made for me, I made washcloths from string meant to tie up the sacks of gold concentrate. All the carefully made and touching gifts have disappeared now, except a carved letter opener, beautifully balanced, a tiny model of a *bolo* made from ebony and *kolepapa* wood, carved by Bob Crump. It sits on my bookcase today.

Helen was exhausted by her efforts in the kitchen, and my mother tearfully thanked her. The feud ended, but my mother was still not welcomed to spend much time with the three other women in camp. She was seldom asked to play Bridge as she had been earlier in the war. Her watercolors were almost gone, and she took to drawing on mapping paper from the assay office.

⟷

November 14, 1942. Lunch this noon wasn't very good—only rice and mongo beans, and greens with gravy thickened with old flour full of wild life that has multiplied unto the seventh and eighth generations. We had dried fish last night and will have dried beef tonight. I come home from a meal like that and dream of last week's birthday dinner Helen cooked for me.

My father paced the porch, trying to reinvent the loom. It rankled that he could not figure out how a primitive invention like the loom raised alternate sets of threads so the shuttle could run between them. He knew there was a treadle, but he could not visualize the method that moved the bottom thread to the top. It was a theoretical problem, I think, because there were no raw materials to weave on a loom.

My mother's problem was simpler, but equally vexing. She could not remember how to turn the heel of a sock. My father made sock needles for her from the spokes of a broken umbrella. She cast on stitches and knit a tube with coarse thread used to sew filter cloth in the mill, and then she sat looking at her work, puzzling.

"I knit a thousand socks in the last war! I was so good at it that I read aloud to the other girls at university while we all knit for the soldiers in France. Why can't I remember how to turn this heel?"

In the end, she finished a pair of socks, but they were useless because the thread was too coarse to walk on. I didn't see the reason for socks, anyway. Unless it was raining, we all were beginning to run barefoot.

December 7, 1942. I wake early and open my windows to the dawn to watch the sky pale and brighten behind the black wood-cut of the trees. From the top-most branches, long vines hang across the morning sky like ropes from the masts of anchored ships. One year of war for the United States. Last night's news finally told the extent of the damage at Pearl Harbor. So Waldo was right when he told us he saw those films of smoke roiling out of our battleships. We couldn't bear to believe him then. How futile it was to hope for the fleet to come to our rescue. Have we a

This photograph was taken in our garden at Mindanao Mother Lode in 1941. Pictured second from left is Marie Smith, who was separated from her children at the beginning of the war. Fourth from left is Nelle Varney; sixth from left is Helen Welbon, and next to her is my mother.

Nov 11— Dec 31

Bureau of Education
Students
Note Book

Name .... Age ....8......

School ....

Grade ......III........ Room ....

Town .... Province ....

Teacher ....

My mother used this notebook for her diary. My writing on the front shows the isolation that I felt, which inspired this book's title.

A pen-and-ink of Gomoco done from memory. Our house sits by little Kagomay Creek. Behind it is the staff house and dining hall. The red truck is listing into entropy. The mill was much bigger than it is here, but the jungle was as dark!

A page from my father's painstakingly kept inventory of the food supplies at Gomoco.

Nanking was owned by a Chinese citizen, and was a "sister ship" to *Calape*. This photograph and the following eight were taken by Bob Crump. (Courtesy of Mrs. Robert Crump.)

Cajada's house in the Land of the Floating Houses on the Agusan.

Steven Crytser, one year old. Behind him is the kind of room we lived in at Gomoco.

Glenda and Stevie at Gomoco, 1942.

Bob Crump at Amparo. He served in the guerrillas directing the distribution of supplies brought in by the submarines. He was on Mindanao to greet the Americans in 1945.

The guerrilla hospital at Amparo on the Agusan River, where my father recovered from dysentery.

Lt. Walter Mester's house at Amparo at the edge of the Agusan.

Lt. Mester on the steps of his house.

A balete tree, where the spirits live.

Butuan, Agusan, P. I.
April 11, 1942.

General Douglas MacArthur,
Commander In Chief of Allied Forces In the Far East.
Australia.

My dear General,

A lot of things have happened since my last conversation with
you on December 5th in Manila and needless to say I have been
tremendously interested in your activities since then. And have
been thrilled beyond expression at your accomplishments and the
honors and increased responsibilities accorded you.

Notwithstanding your present responsibilities I feel that you
may still be interested in what has happened to Mindanao Mother
Lode, so I give you a thumb nail report herewith:

Operations proceeded in December at even greater than the normal
rate up to about the 20th. Due to war hysteria we were no longer
able to hold labor to continue the work and were forced to shut
down on December 21st. Pumps were pulled and the mine prepared
for an indefinite shut dhut down. Nothing was lost in the oper-
tion. Except that much of our bodega supplies has since been
taken for army use we were in shape to resume normal operation
again within sixty days. Development work was more than ordin-
arily productive of ore reserves and we set up in excess of ₱
₱15,000,000 as of January 1st, 1942. We had on hand in unshipped
products approximately ₱2,500,000 stored at three points in the
Islands.

Most all of the staff are now in the service in one way or
another, but I expect most of them to survive and be on hand
to resume operations, if and when‛‛.

I personally drew one of the least desirable jobs in that the
army placed me in charge of an evacuation camp of women and
children of this area. In that camp among others are the wives
and children of the Mother Lode staff. I am so situated that at
the same time I am able to keep in touch with the mine and to
control it's assets. My cheif interest and responsibility
at present however is in the women and children placed in my
care, and very frankly it is in their interest that I write
you at this time.

Page 2.
General MacArthur.

I hope that you will not consider me out of line when
presuming on our past cordial business and personal relations
in bringing the matter to you attention. And I do appreciate
your tremendous military responsibilities. But I feel too that
the initiative must be taken by me if anything is to be
accomplished. I have discussed the matter with Colonel Ben H.
Chastaine commanding this area, and have his permission to
write this letter.

I believe it to be feasible to evacuate the women and children
in my charge from the Philippines to Australia and thence to
the United States. Being a citizen of a democracy perhaps I
may be excused in expressing the opinion that our State Department was a bit delinquent in permitting the women and children
to be out on a limb at this time and that it should be in order
to do what is yet possible to get them off. And inasmuch as
they are in danger, and a source of concern to the local military
that it might be worth while to get them out of the way.

There are twelve women and small children in my group who could
and would go on short notice. All are Americans, and about
eight of them are of the Mother Lode staff. Others are wives
and/or children of Americans interned in Davao. All have funds
in Philippine currency sufficent so that they would not be a
charge on any community or charity organization enroute, and
would be self supporting upon their arrival in the States.
They are now close enough to the initial take-off here on
Mindanao so that there would be difficulty in making that
contact.

I need not, nor will I make this tedious by describing the
plans I have in mind as I am sure that you will anticipate them,
and if it should meet with your approval some one of your staff
would suggest the details.

If the proposition merits your interest I may be contacted
thru General Sharpe or thru Colonel Chastaine commanding this
area.

You were good enough to suggest during our last conversation
that I might be of value in the service, but then dismissed the
idea saying I was of greater service where I then was. Should I
be relieved of my present responsibility as I have suggested and
you could use an experienced soldier with organizing ability, I
at at your service and eager to serve.

Sincerely yours,

D. C. McKay.

My father's letter to General MacArthur. Note that the letter was written before the fall of Corregidor and the defeat of U.S. and Philippine forces in the Islands. My father had no thought then, I am sure, of submarines as a means of evacuation. He probably hoped for a way out by airplane.

Philippine emergency money. It was to be redeemable after the war.

Japanese occupation money— known then as "Mickey Mouse" money.

November, 1943 at Esperanza, just before our rescue. From left to right: Benny, the cook, Bill Mears, Bobbie Mears, Thelma Briggs, me, my mother, "Cap" (John) Martin, Charlotte Martin, Nelle Varney, Glenda Crytser, Helen Welbon and Senor Villareal, the Mayor of Esperanza. Note that Helen Welbon is wearing the same plaid dress she wore in the photograph taken in 1941, and that Nelle Varney has beri-beri.

Narwhal.

Hairless Joe (behind truck) and Cold Turkey, the C-47s that flew us from Darwin to Brisbane at Cloncurry, Australia. (Courtesy of Bobb Glenn.)

February 13, 1944

Commander Charles Parsons

Dear "Chick":

Individually and as a group we take this opportunity
to express to you our sincere thanks for all you have done for
us during the last few months.

We realize that our present enjoyment of freedom is
largely the result of your initiative and daring. And we
appreciate your continued interest in our welfare here in ███████.

We all hope to meet you again in the Philippines after
the war is over. In the meantime all we can say is "Mabuhay"
and "Daghan Salamat".

Sincerely yours,

[handwritten signatures]

A group thank-you letter from the survivors to Commander
Charles "Chick" Parsons. (Courtesy of Peter Parsons.)

WESTERN UNION

1201

A. N. WILLIAMS
PRESIDENT

The filing time shown in the date line on telegrams and day letters is STANDARD TIME at point of origin. Time of receipt is STANDARD TIME at point of destination

TA65 WM67

W.WMUA 195 49 GOVT= WUX WASHINGTON DC 22 204P

MRS DOUGLAS C MCKAY=
918 HILLDALE AVE BERKELEY 8 CALIF=

AM PLEASED TO INFORM YOU THAT INFORMATION RECEIVED INDICATES
THE RESCUE BY OUR FORCES OF YOUR SON ROBERT MILLS MCKAY
PHYSICAL CONDITION FAIR FORMERLY INTERNED AT SANTO TOMAS STOP
YOU MAY SEND FREE THROUGH AMERICAN PRISONER OF WAR INFORMATION
BUREAU THIS OFFICE ONE ONLY TWENTY FIVE WORD MESSAGE STOP=
LERCH PROVOSTHMARSHAL GENERAL.

The telegram bringing news of Bob.

General Yamashita declared Manila an open city and retreated to the north, but 17,000 Japanese soldiers and marines under Admiral Iwabachi swore to defend the city to the last man. As a result, 100,000 civilians died in the Battle of Manila and the city was devastated. In WWII, only Warsaw saw more ruin.

Douglass McKay in Australia in late 1943 or early 1944, dressed in the uniform he was authorized to wear while being debriefed by General MacArthur's staff.

Staff at Mindanao Mother Lode: (*l to r*) unidentified man, Larry Smith, my father, Ancel (Whitey) Crenshaw, Waldo Neveling. This photo was taken after the war.

Left to right: Mary Maynard, Steven Crytser, and William Azbell, one of the sailors on the voyage of the *Narwhal*, at a reunion in Norfolk, Virginia, in October 1994.

longer stretch ahead, or can the War be over before next Decem-
ber seventh? If I could know that Bob is well, I could be fairly
happy. We keep well enough on our plain fare, and enjoy the sun
when it shines. We do not mind the rains that are coming more
and more frequently now. By January they will have taken over
completely.

Ameliana, my little friend, knocked on our door one morning as I was filling the pages in my new notebook.

"Christmas, Mrs. McKay!"

She held an egg in her hand. I had two dolls I seldom played
with, but which Ameliana loved beyond all measuring. Her
eyes could see only the dolls sitting on a shelf above my bed.
She had brought an egg, but it was only an excuse for her to visit
the dolls. She held them for a while, crooning to them, and then
we went to play at her house where her mother, Philomena, was
pounding clothes on rocks in the river.

My mother spent the afternoon making a rag doll for
Ameliana's Christmas. She borrowed the stuffing from a corner
of my mattress. Ameliana's doll wore a green dress and a peasant apron over her stuffed body. She had yellow hair and bright
blue eyes—as bright as my stubby Crayolas could make them.

A few days later, an old man came up the trail with an interpreter who said, "Mrs. McKay, the words of this man say to me
that he wishes to Christmas you these mats and chickens."

My mother was overcome with confusion and gratitude.
Gifts were rare in wartime Philippines.

Then the interpreter said, "Mrs. McKay, you must also
Christmas him. He is wanting very much dress for his wife."

My mother had no dresses she could spare, though she very
much wanted the woven straw mats for our room.

In the end, Charlie traded a shirt for the mats, and the kitchen crew bought the chickens for our dinner. Though the man sold his mats and chickens, he was not happy; his wife would have no new dress for Christmas. It must have been a long, sad walk home.

The week before Christmas, my father began to make a Christmas tree. He said that no native tree could look like a Christmas tree, but that he could make a real one. A copper cable lay among the supplies in the mill. After cutting it to a three-foot length and making a stand for the cable to stand upright, he untwisted the strands, trimming them until he had the cone-shaped skeleton of an evergreen.

He washed the copper with sulfuric acid, and the strands turned green. As the project took shape, the crease between his eyebrows eased. It was easy to be with him when he was relaxed. Making the Christmas tree helped him forget his responsibilities for a few hours. His imagination took over and soon he was snipping *Hills Bros.* coffee cans into tree ornaments. There is a "wise man" in a yellow robe who drinks coffee on a Hills Bros. coffee can. In those days, he was drawn bigger than he is now. My father sacrificed several precious coffee cans to cut figures for our Christmas tree.

On Christmas morning, he wound twigs of hot pepper bushes into the green copper strands. Little red and green peppers and coffee-tin ornaments made the best Christmas tree I had ever seen. Before the war, we had bought trees cut in Oregon, but by the time they got to Mindanao, there were few green needles on the branches. My father's wartime tree was full and brightly green.

We had another feast for Christmas—we used the second-to-last canned ham and served it with the most wonderful miracle so far: apple pie à la mode!

We were extravagant with canned apples and canned milk and fuel oil, and turned the power plant on early to make refrigerator ice cream. We all groaned with delight and knew we must be the only Americans in the Islands eating ice cream.

My father's benign mood lasted long enough for us to leave the power plant running a half hour after the news was over. We listened to Edgar Bergen and Charlie McCarthy. In my enchantment, I laughed at everything he said, even if I didn't understand the jokes. After a year of grim news broadcasts, lighthearted sounds over the radio were so magical that laughter was the only response possible.

It was a day that stood out from all the others, because of that extra half-hour of radio from "home," even though rain fell incessantly. We had missed Christmas of 1941 running from the Japanese, and we all promised that the next one would be different.

I had to tell my mother that Ameliana didn't like her doll. She wanted one like mine, not a homemade rag doll with blond hair and blue eyes.

———◆———

December 31, 1942. The rains have come finally, after toying with us by alternating heavy rain with sparkling days. Now low clouds from which rain falls in a business-like meant-to-get-at-this manner make the shortest days of the year even shorter. The white cranes have sat for hours on the logjam, taking no joy in their swift wings. During the sunny weather they flew up and down the stream and fished in the sunny shallows. Mister sits with his beak on his vest like a statue of dejection. All his swift grace gone, he looks like any barnyard fowl. I wish he would

move around the corner out of sight. His mate has found a more
hospitable spot in a huge banana tree where she perches on one
swaying leaf taking shelter from another.

The tiny whips of rain have lashed at the stream until it is a
white foam rushing past our windows and beyond into the green
tunnel of the jungle.

On such a day, I helped my mother make a calendar for 1943
out of three old ones. The new year began on Friday, so we used
May for January. We used June from the year before for February, marking out the 29th and 30th. We cut with our precious scissors and pasted the calendar together with rice paste. Cockroaches were sure to eat the paste, leaving holes in our calendar,
but there was no other glue to use.

She was always teaching me. Working with the months and
weeks led us to talk about time and the rotation of the earth
around the sun and why days grow shorter and longer. She told
me that the days were both shorter and longer farther from the
equator, and then I learned that in the States my birthday, which
was coming soon, was a wintertime event. It was astonishing to
think of my birthday happening when trees were bare and snow
was on the ground.

Often at night we searched for constellations. The sky was
velvety black and the Milky Way was a path across it. No com-
peting lights dulled the stars, and they shone brightly enough to
make shadows on the ground. The names of the constellations
brought Greek shepherds on their hills to life for me, and I
learned their myths as though they were my own.

On moonless nights, we watch the skies and are fascinated by
their beauty. As Mary and I lean at the window, chins cupped in

our hands, we say that the Milky Way is the dust from Apollo's
chariot as it turns across the heavens. We say that the night is a
princess whose blue-black hair is braided with stars, and that she
wears too many tiaras while Andromeda weeps beside the River
of Stars because the golden hoop of the moon has rolled beyond
her reach.

On rainy afternoons we sang songs she remembered from
evenings spent around pianos. We sang "The Old Oaken
Bucket," "A Bicycle Built for Two," and "Silver Threads Among
the Gold"; but our specialty was "My Grandfather's Clock." We
sang it, our heads together, voices blending:

> "Ninety years without slumbering, tick tock
> Ninety years was it numbering, tick tock
> But it stopped! short! never to go again,
> When the old man died."

"Our voices sound good together, don't they?" she asked
my father.

My mother was tone deaf, however, and my father wasn't. I
could tell from his face that we didn't really sound wonderful,
but it didn't matter how we sounded. I liked our singing just the
way it was. Even better was when he would join us to sing "Ab-
dullah Bulbul Ameer" or "I'm a Ramblin' Wreck from Georgia
Tech" (and a heck of an engineer!).

———◆———

On a rainy morning in January, Ah Hing, who had finally
brought his family to Gomoco, came to the door.

"Ma'am, Nelson need you help."

Nelson, his one-year-old baby, was named after Mr. Kellogg, Ah Hing's former boss. He was an unusually sturdy native baby, but today his little leg was infected and swollen dark red up to the knee.

My mother didn't know at all what to do, but she bathed the leg in hot potassium permanganate and wrapped it, hoping that the disinfectant would help.

Later in the day, the whole frightened family—Ah Hing; his wife, Loling; their son Romeo, who was three; and Nelson all came again to our room. The baby and his mother were crying, and the leg was much worse than it had been in the morning.

Each time my mother reached for the baby, his older brother, Romeo, would cry out "No!" from a different spot in the room. She reached for ointment, "No!" said Romeo from under the table. She reached for water, "No!" said Romeo from behind the door.

In desperation, mother took the whole family to Mrs. Burchfield's room, hoping that the older woman would have a better idea of how to deal with this crisis. She had lived many more years in the Island than we had. They decided to send for hot water and to apply compresses to the painful little leg. Then, there on the windowsill, Ah Hing saw a butterfly orchid Jean Feigel had left when she abandoned Gomoco.

"Oh, missus, please, ma'am, I can have that leaves? When Nelson leg get bad, I look in jungle for leaf. I no find. Now you have!"

Ah Hing quickly made a poultice from the leaves, and Nelson's leg was healing by morning.

———⟫◆⟪———

January 12, 1943. Two Filipinos came from Surigao on Sunday. They had not learned much about the Americans interned there except they are all together in a house near the dock. The Japanese do not provide food. Former employees of Mother Lode cannot talk to them when they bring food. Because she is mestiza, Carlota Crenshaw and the two children live with the Sisters at the Convent. How glad I am to be here in Gomoco. We could so easily have decided to go with them all in August.

They also brought a message from Waldo Neveling, who had been working again at Mindanao Mother Lode, only this time for the Japanese. The message said that the enclosed letter had caused him to stop trying to sabotage the Japanese at the mine and to join the growing guerrilla forces. He said the enclosed message, now water-blurred and folded many times, had made his decision:

Letter to All Guerrilleros:

As senior United States officer in the Islands, Lieutenant Colonel Wendell W. Fertig, CE AUS, assumes command of the Mindanao-Visayan Force, USFIP, with the rank of brigadier general. All organized units resisting our common enemy are invited to serve under this command. Unified resistance is the key to success.

W. W. Fertig, Commanding

"Now *this* is good news!" my father said. "I know Fertig, and I think maybe he can make an army out of this rabble! If he can get them all to harass the Japs, then we won't have to worry so much about people like that warlord, Sam Goode!"

"Fertig's smart, and he's been in the Islands long enough to know the natives. This is what Pritz was talking about when he came up here in October."

My mother said, "But the truth is that, no matter what the news is—bad news that the Japs are coming, or that they're not, or that the guerrillas are harassing the Japs—all we do is wait. Wait and trade for food. Wait for dinner. Wait for MacArthur. Wait for more news. Wait. Wait. Wait. I know I ought to be grateful to be alive and healthy, but this waiting is driving me mad!"

We waited for Maximino, who was still six and a half sacks short on his contract to buy rice in Hinatuan. He said he'd been sick with malaria, but he promised that, without fail, he would produce the rice and my mother's twenty-four-peso order in time for my birthday.

January 19, 1943—my birthday—came and went without Maximino's appearance. Now that rainy season was upon me, a pair of closed shoes was my heart's desire. My father had made me sandals with soles from the tires of the truck and tops from the soft rubber of the inner tubes, but they weren't adequate in the rainy season.

It was sad that Maximino didn't come with my shoes, but my birthday feast made up for it. We used the last tins of Argentinean corned beef and made more ice cream.

The cake was three layers high and snowy white, with nine glowing candles that she blew out with one breath (her wish was to see Bob) and Oh, that cake was good! The flour was in our trail rations in a Mason jar; we had it all ready in August if the Japanese came for us, and it had kept beautifully.

My mother made me a blue sailor dress from shirting that Alex had given her when he left months before. It almost replaced the one I had traded to the Moro woman, but it didn't have stars or navy-blue piping. Glenda made me paper dolls, and Bill Gorler made a pin shaped like a boomerang out of a silver peso.

Now I was nine.

———⟫◆⟪———

January 27, 1943. The truck that brought us and our food up from the river bodega is by the road where it broke down. Now every leaf of every spring is a bolo, the rubber tires and inner tubes are slingshots or sandals. Every moveable part is gone. There is hardly a sign of it now.

The rains were heavy and unrelenting. Like the year before, wet clothing draped our rooms. Wooden matches were too wet to burn after the phosphorous tips flamed. The kitchen fire burned constantly, and one lamp was lit from it each evening. I was lamp lighter for the camp and carried my lighted lamp to each room as night fell. Each person lit a lamp from mine.

My father gave Jaime, one of our vendors, a shotgun shell. Jaime agreed to give us half of any wild pig he bagged in the jungle. A friend of Jaime's shot a pig and claimed half of it. Jaime then split the remaining half with us. His description of the pig hunt in the jungle at night was colorful enough to draw the Welbons and Glenda from their siestas.

"Oh, sir! Abundio and I hide. We make *kwan* (he waved his hands), uh, *kwan*, sir."

My father helped, "A small house? A blind?"

"Yes, sir, a small house. We hide, oh sir, we wait very long time, *Wak-wak* in jungle, no moon. We hear monkeys screaming. Mostly *wak-wak*. We afraid, but we want wild pig more. We not talking, must be ver' ver' quiet for pig. We sit long time."

"You give me bullet, sir, is mine, but gun is Abundio. He keep gun, take bullet. Then, in jungle, we hear pig. He walking, looking for food in leaves. Make noise like blowing, *ungh-ungh ungh-ungh.* We no breathe, we get cold skin. We wait, sir, he come this way, I see white teeth. Oh sir! Abundio lift gun. Pig come closer *ungh-ungh-ungh.* Maybe he smell us, lift head. Abundio shoot. I no hear, no see from noise. Pig jump, run, then walk, then fall down. Sir, I say to you, that pig heavy in jungle. Mr. McKay, sir, Christmas me bullet, I get you more pig."

Jaime left happily with another shotgun shell. Roast wild boar—even a quarter of one—was good enough for us to risk another shell. Besides, it was entertaining to listen to Jaime.

One morning we all stood stupidly looking at the beam in the kitchen. Our bag of dried fish, which we kept above the woodstove where it would stay dry, had vanished. It simply was not hanging where it should have been. The rope that tied it to the beam was gone as well, which meant that it had been untied and not chewed away by an animal. Earlier in the war, dried fish had been unappealing, but now it was a staple, an important source of protein. The loss of the fish was serious, but there was nothing to do but return from time to time to make sure it really wasn't there.

The heavy rains kept the traders from coming up the slippery trail, and we had little fresh food to eat. We drew more heavily on the supplies in the *bodega.* We were getting so used to *kangkong* and *camotes* that canned lima beans and pickled beets, while a change, were not so wonderful as we had dreamed them. It was frightening to see how quickly the shelves emptied as we used the cans. It was hard to enjoy food when we knew each can opened meant a permanently empty space on the shelf. We wanted our *camotes* and *mongo* beans back!

One night supper was late. Ah Hing was sullen and muttering. Helen sat down wearing a triumphant smile.

"Well, I got my ring back! Ah Hing stole it from Kellogg's house and gave it to Loling for an engagement ring. He says he bought it from a Moro for eight pesos, but he's lying. He took it when we were living at Kelloggs'. I bet he's got all the other stuff, too!"

Three years before, when Helen came from Cleveland to the Philippines to marry Roy, she had brought a jewelry box from home. In it was a pink emerald ring her mother had given her for graduation from high school.

When they got to Butuan after a honeymoon in Manila, they found that the house they planned to live in wasn't finished. Roy's business partner, Mr. Kellogg, invited them to stay with his family while they waited. Ah Hing was the cook. By the time they moved into their own house, the box had disappeared and Helen had never seen any of her jewelry again until she spotted the ring on Loling's finger and snatched it away.

After supper, I went to Ah Hing's quarters. Loling was crying, and Ah Hing paced their room.

"I no steal that ring! Moro sell me that ring. Eight pesos! I buy that ring from Moro! She come this place, she look and never find things she lose. No find anything! If I steal that ring, you think I let Loling wear if Mrs. Welbon can see? You crazy? Never I let her see ring if I steal. Ah Hing not robber! She bad woman, that Mrs. Welbon! I buy ring for marry Loling. Eight pesos I pay!"

I had had my troubles with Helen, too, and I believed Ah Hing bought the ring from the Moro for eight pesos.

⇒◆⇐

January 30, 1943. Squash, rice and corn are very short, as are tempers and nerves now that the rains have come again. I am not popular today. Last night, while the generator was on, I came home to iron clothes that have been wet for days. My iron shorted and blew the fuses during the first part of the broadcast. We get the news every three days now and I will have caused us to go a week between newscasts.

February 1, 1943. The men have worked hard all day to pump air by hand in order to start the compressor. I am lying low because I imagine they are muttering imprecations against me as they work.

The statement of expenses came out yesterday. The diesel oil is black gold, as we used eighty-five pesos' worth in trade. Our bills ran about eight pesos each in cash and would have been more than double that without the "crudo." Perhaps one day we will need the oil for trading for food more than we will for running the radio. Our hunger for news is very powerful, though. . . .

The armies fought grimly for Guadalcanal for nearly six months and then, suddenly, the Americans have actually occupied all of Guadalcanal and there is no longer any organized resistance there! What grand news this is.

My father wrote Fred Feigel at about this time:

No new breaks in Western Europe. Increasingly strong bombing of the Continent by the Allies. The

Russians are really going to town, and that front is the only bright spot on the world scene. The Southwest Pacific is about at a standstill. We have actually wholly taken over Guadalcanal; it took over six months to do it. It all seems most frightfully slow. I still hold the key to the food in the bodega and think we have to ration carefully.

You will conclude from the above that you should not neglect to put in your next crop.

Everyone in this camp remains well, although the morale is not what it should be. Nerves are raw, and there seems to be some discouragement. No more "arguments" so far. Evelyn [Burchfield] is steadily improving and has started coming to the table for meals.

Larzo says that Rudy did not deliver a cat on his trip over there; we sure enough sent you one.

He ends his letter to his friend:

If you have the chance to do so, come on over for another visit. I am sure you are in much better shape from hard work to negotiate these trails than I. I am very soft, and shoe leather is a prime consideration, too.

There was not enough food now in this rainy season to feed the pigs, who chased us as we left the table, begging for the squash skins that we had given them in the past. There were no table scraps now, and the pigs were starving. Jaime took two piglets and Mr. Kriekenbeek took three, but the rest of the new litter died one by one before any vendors arrived from their *kaingins.* They starved suddenly when the sow could no longer nurse them, and we could not give or trade them away in time. I was sodden with grief to watch them suffer. Their mother, now hungry, too, and used to getting our table scraps after meals, turned mean and frightening. I never turned my back on her now.

> *February 10, 1943. The rain stopped for today and the sun is glo-*
> *riously bright. A myriad of beautiful butterflies flutter about the*
> *compound. There are many varieties of great size and beauty.*
> *They look like animated flowers as they flit around the papaya*
> *trees near the mess house and delight us as we eat our frugal*
> *meal. On days like this they float in one window of my room and*
> *out the other in a bright parade of color—cerise, band black,*
> *lemon yellow and aquamarine. Helen tried to start a collection,*
> *but the ants destroyed all her specimens.*

It was glorious to see the sun, even though we knew the rains would be back before the season changed. In those few bright days, vendors managed the trails again to bring us welcome squash, *camotes,* and greens. And some dried fish.

"Only three centavos, sir, for this dried fish!" Maiximino announced.

"Where did you get this fish?" my father wanted to know. I knew he was thinking about the fish that had been stolen.

"It is the fish of my brother-in-law, sir. He is wanting to make you happy, so he ask not so big money for his fish."

"I see. It is a very low price, and I will accept this kindness."

At dinner, it was agreed that it had been our fish once, but that it was better to buy it back than to ask too many questions. It would not have been honorable to ask more for the stolen goods, neither would it have been honorable on our part to ask too many questions.

Even though nothing seemed to be happening, the days were busy. Roy Welbon, who had run the sawmill in Butuan, was writing a handbook for sawmill operators; Helen taught me math. Bob Crump carved chess sets when he had time between his job as camp tinker—beautiful ones using woods with native names like *oss* and *comogan* and *narra*.

From all over the Agusan valley, people brought broken tools, rice pots, and lamps for us to repair. There was nothing left in the Chinese stores in the riverside barrios. Bob repaired rice pots and traded his skills for supplies. He fixed our rice pot, now thin from incessant use, by riveting the lid to the bottom of the pot and making a new lid out of the leaky bottom. Whenever the rains let up, though, he panned the river for gold. He wanted enough gold to make two wedding rings—one for his girl at home in Wisconsin and one for himself.

The blacksmith shop was a great asset, and the camp often rang with the sound of hammers on the anvil. Charlie began a *bolo* factory, making the blades from the last springs of the red truck.

Joe McCarthy, a boy before the war but now a guerrilla, came to Gomoco in the middle of March.

March 16, 1943 Boys turn into men quickly in a war, it seems. He told us that Larry and the others were taken from Surigao, around Christmas-time. No one knows exactly where they are, but it might be Fort Pikit, where we once put the Axis prisoners at the beginning of this war. The rumor is that the Japanese made them walk from Cagayan to Pikit. That would be stark hardship. When I think of Larry and those three little children, I could weep. It is so sad they left this place; the children were happy here. Would Mary and I be with them if Douglass hadn't flown from Manila to Cebu and caught the earlier boat to Surigao? He got home just the afternoon before Pearl Harbor was bombed.

Joe told us that Waldo Neveling had slipped away from the Japanese after they sent him on a trip to Manila, where he had seen Marie Smith in a prison camp there and given her some of the money we had entrusted him with. It was the first news that most Americans and British were in a prison camp on the campus of Santo Tomás University in Manila.

Waldo had actually seen Mrs. Smith—it seemed impossible to me that there were people outside our clearing, and yet Waldo had talked to her. I wanted him to tell us about Bob, but he hadn't seen him—I didn't even know if Waldo had asked about him. It had been so long since Bob had gone away to school that I sometimes couldn't remember his face, though I still called out to him when I was lonely.

The end of the rainy season, toward the end of March, gave everyone new energy. Charlie Martin decided to go to Cantilan to help the guerrillas guard the rice crop from the Japanese. He set off with a load of *bolos* he had made, planning to sell them as he headed for the east coast. On the trail, he and his *cargadores* were robbed by Sam Goode and his men, the bandits the bamboo telegraph warned us of.

"Fertig had better get Sam Goode under control pretty quick," my dad said. "I guess I'd better not stop sleeping with the Enfield!"

When Charlie came home to heal after the hopeless fight to save his cargo, he was not quite the optimist he had been. By now almost all the teeth had broken off his dentures, and his glasses were turning iridescent, radiating rainbow colors in the light. The war was indeed lasting a long time.

The Welbons and Glenda had been talking about leaving Gomoco for the coast where they hoped life would be easier, but now that Sam Goode was at large and dangerous, their plans went on hold. They were restless, wanting to be anywhere else than in the green jungle under my father's rule. A town on the coast, or a clearing by a river, looked better to them than the green walls of the jungle that they had been looking at for fifteen months.

Bob Crump and Bill Gorler went downriver to get fresh news. An American, Ernest McClish, once a businessman in Manila, had formed a group in the Agusan valley that was harassing the Japanese.

Rumors have come in that McClish's guerrilla army has attacked Butuan and only a few Japs remain there hiding in the convent with one machine gun in the vantage point of the bell tower. I think Bill and Bob will want to join up with them. It's too quiet here for two young men.

My father had written Fred on March 5, 1943:

The unusually heavy rainy season here flooded the bottomlands of the Sulibau and drowned out most of the camotes, corn, squash and other garden truck. We are finding it quite difficult to secure the bulk foods that heretofore have kept our bellies full. We are also

about out of *palay*. Hence it will be necessary to draw
on our "iron rations" pretty heavily for the next two
or three months, or until the new crops now being
planted mature.

When the natives came with the little food they had to offer
at the end of the rainy season, they came with goods for us to repair, or wounds for us to treat, but they also brought encourag-
ing news about the guerrillas. They began to suggest that the
renegade, Sam Goode, had joined Wendell Fertig's army and
would now be harassing the Japanese instead of us. The fear of
sudden robbery and violence diminished a little.

We even heard, though we didn't believe it, that a submarine had landed on Mindanao, bringing help to Americans behind the lines. That was news too good to believe! It was much
easier to believe only that Fertig had radio contact with Australia.

———◆———

The Welbons and Glenda left us at the end of March 1943.
They decided to live at Prosperidad on the Gibong River, closer
to the sea, where food was more plentiful.

The *cargadores* had plenty to carry when the Welbons and
Glenda left, because Helen's home had been closer to Gomoco
than ours and she had sent for things when she could. Boxes
filled with swatches of fabric now worth a fortune in trade were
loaded on the men's backs. I knew her big silver tray was in one
of those boxes, packed with her pots and pans, and I knew our
big parties would be simpler after they were gone. To pay the
cargadores, she traded her wedding dress to Sotero Perez (Max-

imino's cousin) for three *cargadores*. They took their *Webster's Dictionary and World Almanac* with them.

After the *cargadores* came, chose their loads, and the whole party disappeared into the jungle, I wandered through the abandoned rooms, now so empty, and wished that we, too, would do something exciting. I had seen nothing but green trees for over a year, and I knew that there were towns we could live in where there would be people to be with. There were only five of us left at Gomoco: Mrs. Burchfield, who was usually sick, and her fourteen-year-old Jim, my parents, and me. When Charlie was in camp, there were six of us.

Even Ah Hing left. There were too few of us now to need a full-time cook. He and his wife took Nelson and Romeo to their *kaingin* on the Sulibau, and now Julio would look after us.

Julio pounded the *palay* until it shed its brown husks, he winnowed the rice so that the winnowing tray only held white rice. There were few pots left now that most people were gone and life grew even simpler. The tablecloth had long ago been torn up to make dishtowels.

Philomena and her family stayed to wash our clothes. It was quiet now, with five refugees where we once had thirty.

There was little to do but watch the dry season arrive with long steaming days when the sun beat down on the white gravel of our clearing. The river, so recently noisy and full, receded daily until it was a languid stream slipping over mossy rocks. Locusts and cicadas sang loudly in the afternoon heat.

April 19, 1943. The dry weather means that the cargadores can bring us dried abaca leaves again. We used up the real toilet paper months ago, and abaca has been in short supply for the last few weeks as well. Small things we never noticed before the war become issues. The Tissue Issue, we call it.

Even the news on the radio seemed to be playing from a needle stuck in a record. The armies in North Africa were in stalemate, and morale tumbled to a new low when the Allies announced that the offensive in the Pacific would happen after the Mediterranean was under their control. We had been waiting for The Aid for sixteen months; now it looked as though sixteen more months might still be ahead of us. The Japanese were threatening to invade Australia. That would make our rescue truly remote.

KGEI announced in the middle of April that the Japanese had executed eight fliers of the Doolittle raid on Tokyo a year before. It brings dark thoughts. Perhaps execution will be the fate of those interned by the Japanese. I can hardly bear to think of Bob. How is he? Where is he? Where, where, where?

April 27, 1943. Exciting news! The most wonderful news we have had since the war began. Charlie brought a letter from Walter Mester, a Lieutenant (bamboo rank, as they call the titles men assume in the new army at Battalion Headquarters), telling us that submarines have indeed landed supplies on Mindanao! He sent an empty package of Lucky Strike cigarettes in a white package. We read an ad in a Life magazine from last November that says: "Lucky Strike Green has Gone to War!" That magazine was proof to me that ships are coming to Mindanao. Before the runner left, we came to our senses enough to send letters to our families, hoping that they might possibly go out on another submarine.

My father wrote Fred:

> We got it straight from the USAFP [U.S. Armed
> Forces in the Philippines] that seven subs have re-
> cently come to Mindanao carrying all kinds of ammu-
> nition and supplies. All the guerrillas are smoking
> Camels and Luckies. There is direct radio service with
> MacArthur. We all sent letters and cables back with
> the messenger yesterday, and it would appear there is
> an excellent chance they will be delivered. You may
> take all this with a grain of salt to be conservative.
> Charlie is effusive and may have embellished it a lit-
> tle, but if anything startling should happen that might
> get us in the clear, be assured that I will pass the infor-
> mation on to you.
>
> Re typewriter ribbon: we just use "DTE—extra
> heavy" to oil the old one. We take a cloth damp with
> oil and wipe the ribbon to moisten it again.

I couldn't stop thinking about the submarine. I thought
about it, wondered about it, asked about it. Did it travel under
the water until it came to Mindanao? How had it known where
to land? Did they know we were here in Gomoco? Would they
keep coming to bring things from home? What did they eat on
submarines? Did they have hamburgers? Had our letters already arrived in the States? Would we get answers? There were
no answers to my questions. I read the *Life* magazine over and
over until I knew it by heart. Everything in the magazine, even
the ads, talked about the war. It seemed funny to me to realize
that the war meant different things in different places. Here in
the Islands, we just waited, but at home people were joining the

military or growing food for the Armed Forces or building ships.

Soon, however, like all news that came to us, the submarine faded into the sameness of time and we went on waiting.

May 6, 1943. A year ago today Corregidor fell. It is incredible that a year has somehow ground itself away since then. Time repeats itself. A new day is not a new one at all, but the old one back again for me to relive. Time has lost its ability to turn the days by.

More rumors came upriver—these told that ten American soldiers had escaped from the Japanese labor camp in Davao. They had come through the jungle and then the swamps in the center of the island and needed a place to recuperate. We hoped they would choose to stay with us, but we had to make do with secondhand stories about them. Captured when Corregidor fell, they were taken to the death camp of Cabanatuan on Luzon and then had been brought after some time to the camp on Mindanao. They reported that three-quarters of the American and Filipino prisoners had died of starvation, illness, and Japanese brutality.

Early in June, the Burchfields left. Lieutenant (bamboo grade) Mester arranged for civilians who were running out of money to receive sixty pesos a month in guerrilla money. The insurgents were printing "emergency money" now on any paper they could find. Colonel Fertig guaranteed that the Americans would honor guerrilla money when they came with The Aid, and it was accepted reluctantly. Japanese "Mickey Mouse" money was not accepted at all.

Mrs. Burchfield, who had been sick most of the time she was with us, was running out of money. It seemed better for her to be at the guerrilla headquarters in Amparo than with us. She hoped that another submarine would bring medicines to Mindanao. She and Jim left us on June 3, taking her Bible and their little monkey, Chico.

With no Bible, no dictionary or history book, we could start a culture all our own. All we have left, except a few read and re-read books, is a battered atlas that helps us believe that we are connected to the world we once knew.

Now the three of us were alone at Gomoco with Charlie. Our nearest neighbors were Mr. Krieckenbeek and his family at the *bodega* where our trail began. The Kelloggs were downriver from him a little way, ten kilometers from us. Krik and Mr. Kellogg had been feuding for years, and it took delicate tact to keep both factions friendly to us.

———⊰◈⊱———

Everything is quiet here. The sun is high and hot. The trees are still. If a breeze detaches a leaf from a tree, it falls so slowly that it seems to be let down on an invisible string.

My father was sick. At first it seemed like food poisoning, though none of the rest of us was sick. He tried not to weaken, but stayed in bed longer each siesta hour. My mother fed him extra milk and eggs, but the food did no good. He was thinner each day.

At the beginning of his illness, he was short-tempered and mean. One night in our room, he watched me writing in my notebook.

"I thought you were going to write with your right hand!"

"It's very hard for me to do that, Daddy."

"Well, lots of things are hard. You don't even try to write the right way. You're just stubborn, that's all!"

I moved the pencil over to my right hand and tried to write. The letters were large and irregular. The words wouldn't stay on the lines. He paced the room, watching me. My mother was quiet, bent over her mending.

My right hand ached. I looked at him, and moved the pencil to my left hand, the good hand.

"You little sneak!" He hit me, hard, on the side of the head, and went to his own room next door. I heard him go to bed.

Somewhere deep inside me, I knew he was sorry he had lost his temper, but I was hurt and outraged, and I wanted him to be very, very sorry. I went to bed and cried as long and as loudly as I could.

His bed was just on the other side of a thin wall of boards, and I knew my sobs were not wasted. I struggled to stay awake so I could cry just a little longer. Just one more snuffle. I took a cold-blooded, planned revenge. I know he heard every sob, and I know each one hurt him. He never, however, let me forget that he hated my being left-handed.

In the morning, my mother apologized for him. "You know your father's sick, Mary. And that's why he lost his temper last night, I'm sure. It's hard being sick here, and he just lost control. It happens to everybody, you know."

I don't think I answered her; I know I didn't forgive him.

May 20, 1943. Douglass is worse. He is down in bed now after gamely trying to dress and sit up during the day. When I see his eyes sunk in his haggard face, I feel desperately helpless. I can do nothing but bring the best food I can find and hope that he soon

rallies. I can keep busy during the day, but no one knows how I
dread the wakeful nights as the slow hours pass.

My father's fever stayed down for a few days, and Charlie
left us to go down to Kelloggs' to "grub up" and to listen to the
news.

My father's fever came back, more severely, soon after we
were alone, and though my mother continued to feed him roast
chicken and as many eggs as she could wrest from the hens, he
continued to be paler and thinner every day. She even fed him
canned milk that they had saved for me. Nothing helped. The
native cure for dysentery—burnt-rice liquid—did nothing.

"Mommy, Philomena is worried about Daddy. She says that
he is *ibaloy* because he made the spirits angry when he cut down
that *balete* tree."

"I don't think that's what happened at all. A germ causes
dysentery. He might get better on his own, but we might have to
find a way to get medicine for him."

"But, Mommy, Philomena says that when you get *ibaloy*, you
have to ask the spirits' pardon. Then you get well. *They* don't
get dysentery! She says that Daddy's soul is lost in the sun and
that a *balayan* can come to ask the sun to let his soul go. Please,
Mommy. She knows a *balayan;* he can come and have a *baliglig*.
Daddy will get well then. We don't have any medicine, but
Philomena knows a *balayan* who lives near Novele. She says
maybe he'd come for a sack of rice."

June 7, 1943. Douglass continues to look very pale and he is get-
ting even thinner. He does not gain strength at all. I spend bitter
hours in the night. If he becomes really sick, the trip out will be
impossible. I do not know whether we should conserve his

strength and remain here or to spend his last energy looking for
medical help. Mary tells me of native healers she learns about
from the servants and it frightens me that she believes them.
Then a small voice of panic says, "Perhaps she's right," and I
know we have been here too long and that I am losing my hold on
reality. Morning brings the light and I feel better, only to fall
under the spell of the dark hours again.

After three months, Bob Crump and Bill Gorler walked out
of the jungle and crossed the creek and were back in Gomoco.

"Harriet, you have to get Mac out of here while there's time.
I don't think you realize how sick he is. If you wait any longer,
he'll have to be carried out. There's a pretty good doctor at Amparo running a little hospital at the guerrilla headquarters there.
He even has a little medicine that the subs left here. The Japs in
Butuan are confined in the convent now, and Amparo ought to
be pretty safe even if it's only five miles from Butuan. It'll be less
dangerous than letting Mac stay here to get worse!"

Bob bargained for a *baroto* at Kelloggs'. We left Gomoco on
my brother's twentieth birthday, June 18. Now we were the
ones to have the *cargadores* carrying our bedding, our rice pot,
and our food away from Gomoco. I imagined Bill looking at us
vanish into the green jungle. I had watched so many people
leave that I knew just what we looked like—a last wave and
then nothing but green jungle. He stayed to watch things at the
camp, and Bob went downriver with us.

We stopped at Krik's *bodega* for a meal and then walked on
to stay overnight at Kelloggs' *kaingin*. A rooster under the
house wakened us in the morning. He was answered by another rooster nearby; the second one was answered by another

until, if I listened, I could hear the faintest crowing far in the distance. At Gomoco, we had only one rooster, and there were no others to set off an echoing morning cantata. Many families lived near the Kelloggs; I could tell by the number of roosters in the chorus.

In the morning, the *grumetes* loaded the dugouts, and we began our journey down the river. My father lay exhausted on his bedroll under the grass roof and the rest of us sat cross-legged watching the green riverbank slip by. White parrots and bright blue kingfishers broke the monotony of water, green grasses, and bamboo.

A bunch of bananas hung from the post that supported our thatched roof. The green coconuts that rolled underfoot were our canteens; with a *bolo,* we whacked a side off the coconut and drank the cool water inside. At noontime, we cooked our rice on the riverbank and then dozed in the boat as the *grumetes* poled through the shallows. The slapping sounds of water as the poles slid rhythmically into the water on that hot afternoon made sleep irresistible.

Occasionally we passed a *baroto* going upriver. Then the *grumetes* called "Cay-o!" from one boat to the other. The boatmen squatted low in their boats and smoked their strong tobacco cigars while they traded information about the river.

"No Hapons on the riber today, sir," the head *grumete* said.

We spent one night in a *nipa* hut that we shared with a family of ten and our three *grumetes. Nipa* houses are light, springy buildings made of bamboo tied together with rattan. Built on stilts so that air circulates and floodwaters pass beneath, they are like baskets. Each person's movement is answered by a corresponding sway of the house. Seventeen of us slept on the bamboo floor and were wakened by the fighting cocks under the house announcing it was morning.

The family gave us first use of their fire in the morning; and in a delicate act of hospitality the host pushed the hens, roosting on the cross beams above the cookstove, farther along the beam so they would not threaten our rice pot.

The family would not let us pay for staying with them. The solution to the problem was to buy a white rooster from them at twice the usual price. The rooster had been groomed to be a fighting cock, but he had no courage for fighting. We tied him to a heavy rock and he spent the day in the prow of our *baroto* crowing greetings to chickens on the riverbank who were not having an adventure like his. I watched him strut on his short rope. His head was small and mean looking without the comb and wattles, and he did his best to hide his lack of courage. He didn't know he would be our dinner.

We spent two more days on the rivers, now the Gibong, then the Agusan, each river wider and slower than the one before and choked with floating hyacinths. My mother and I reached out and caught the plants and decorated our boat with lavender flowers. The river was yellow ocher and as wide as the ocean as we came closer to the sea.

My father had not quite lost his sense of humor. In the middle of the third day, he suddenly came out with a line from Kipling:

> With our sick beneath the awning
> On the road to Mandalay!

Then my parents spent the next few minutes searching their memories for lines and finally patched together the last verse. Then their two voices floated across the river:

On the road to Mandalay,
Where the old Flotilla lay,
With our sick beneath the awnings when
We went to Mandalay!
On the road to Mandalay!
Where the flyin' fishes play,
And the dawn comes up like thunder
Outer China 'crost the Bay!

One of the *barotos* we met as we went along the Agusan carried our friend, Lieutenant Mester.

"Times are hard in Amparo," he told us. "I am on the way upriver to find enough food for my troops. We are down to three or four bananas a day per man. I hope you brought enough rice for yourselves. You won't find any at Amparo."

He said there was a simple hospital in Amparo, where a Filipino doctor did the best he could with almost no supplies.

"I'm sorry I won't be there to help you, but please use my house. It's by the river, and I think you'll find everything you need," he said, and was away up the river.

Amparo seemed like a city to me after living so long in the hills, but it really was only a few little huts scattered among the palm trees. Dirt paths connected the houses and the traffic consisted mainly of stray dogs and loose pigs. Chickens pecked in the dust, clucking cozily.

Lieutenant Mester's *nipa* house looked out across the wide Agusan. Palm fronds clicked in the breezes off the river, and we settled into his airy house happily.

Dr. Zapanto's hospital was a *nipa* hut with a bamboo ladder leading to a veranda where his malaria patients recuperated. He had no medicine for dysentery, and he had to send a runner eighteen kilometers to bring his partner, who agreed with the diagnosis of amoebic dysentery. His partner had only two doses of emetine left (at eight pesos a dose) and a little bismuth subnitrate.

"We have only this, Mr. McKay. We can only try. Maybe it will be enough medicine. We need luck, but you are very strong, sir, and I hope it will help you. It is good to have The Aid coming—even a little—on the submarines, but it is not enough for our people. I am helpless to do more. I am sorry."

My father had lost thirty pounds.

The first injection began the miracle, and in just a few days he was feeling well enough to begin thinking about finding Colonel McClish and volunteering to serve with the guerrillas.

While he recuperated, my mother and I foraged the local *kaingins,* looking for food. There was little available, and often we could not even fill a basket with our finds. Each time we went searching, though, we could carry home at least an eggplant or an egg to go with our rice.

After we met Fely and Meling, whose husbands were in the guerrilla army, and they adopted us, things got better. The doctors said that milk was the wrong thing for an amoebic dysentery patient, and Fely and Meling taught us how and where to trade cans of milk for food.

Fely took us to her house at the end of a grassy path beyond the barrio. Her mother and ancient grandmother gave us tea and sent food home to my father. Her family had lived in Amparo many generations, and their house had dark hardwood floors smooth as soap, which shone dark against the bright light shining in the windows.

Their famous fighting cock had won so many fights that he had earned the right to live in the house. He was tied by the leg to a table and disapproved of everyone but himself. He was a famous champion, and we were not. He was never going to be eaten the way our cowardly rooster had been—even though they looked almost exactly alike.

"Oh, yes, ma'am, we have very hard time now, but we learn to live," said Mrs. Cabodlan. "We learn to—how you say—make thread from old sock. Make enough to sew three dress!"

"You mean to ravel old socks to make thread? You teach me something," my mother said. "Now I never make mop from old sock again! Thank you!"

The Chinese merchants were charging sixty centavos for a spool of khaki thread, after unwinding several layers from the spool to sell to someone else. My mother thought that that was "highway robbery," and was happy to have a new source of thread.

The main part of Amparo was on the other side of the river. We could hitch rides across the river in *barotos* and explore the school and the marketplace.

Early on market day, we crossed the river and saw for ourselves how hard times were for Filipinos under Japanese rule. The *kaingins* were not producing enough food these days even for their owners because life was so disrupted by Japanese patrols. Before the war, a native market was a noisy place where squealing pigs and cackling chickens were almost inaudible over the din of vendors calling out their wares. Now there were only a few tiny booths in Amparo, their owners sitting listlessly behind a single pineapple or a basket of two or three small eggs.

We did find a few tomatoes to buy and some fruit that we had never sampled before. We sucked the tart juice from *guavanos'* cottony pulp, spitting out seeds as we walked through the market. We were hungry enough to try *durian*, which smells so dreadful that tasting it is a true act of faith, but it is worth the dare. We ate boiled *durian* seeds and found they tasted like potatoes.

Sweet, hot *bibinka*, made from rice flour and coconut milk, were as sweet as candy bars; but my favorite treat was *bod-bod*, sticky rolls of sweetened rice wrapped in banana leaves and baked over hot coals. I loved the smell of the food cooking in the booths in the market. I had relied on vendors coming quietly to us at Gomoco, and a market—even a pitiful one like Amparo's—delighted me. My mother's fears of native foods were finally at rest and I felt a sudden freedom that I didn't understand when she let me eat local fare.

I spent a lot of time at Amparo watching the boats come and go on the river. There I met Mercedes, a tough businesswoman whose teeth were stained dark by betel nut. Her *baroto* had been stolen a few weeks before, and she was determined to get it back. We became good friends, and I helped her scan the river as we squatted on the shore. She kept an eye on me when I swam in the yellow river.

Food was never a problem after I found Mercedes; every day she left offerings at our door—sugarcane one day; bananas, coconuts, or a basket of river prawns on another.

July 6, 1943. Douglass has much of his strength back again, and has gone to find McClish in the elusive headquarters of the 10th Military Division near Cabadbaran. I begged him not to go, because he must go near Butuan, still garrisoned by the Japs. He

would go, but I worry. Just yesterday we heard the sounds of
bombing.

Mercedes and I were talking by the river the day the bombs
fell. We stopped to watch the Japanese plane fly low over the
hills that separated us from a town called Magellanes. I saw,
and still see, three bombs fall from the plane, slowly tumbling
and then dropping, head down, toward the town. Word sped
upstream, almost as swiftly as the sound of the bombs, that the
Japanese attacked guerrillas in Magellanes near Cabadbaran.

Meling's husband, sweat washing rivulets of dust down his
face, ran into town the afternoon of the Japanese bombing attack. The bombs had been too frightening for him, and he had
fled. Meling's face was a mixture of happiness and fear. She was
happy to see him, but she knew that most deserters met execution. Luckily, Epifanio's battalion commander didn't expect
total heroism from volunteer soldiers, so Epifanio only spent a
few days locked in the schoolhouse, then was put to work in the
rice paddies. It was shame enough to be a coward, and it was
wasteful to execute a loyal guerrilla.

They should never have allowed me to swim in the muddy
river, for one morning I woke to find dark-red streamers running halfway up my leg from an infected cut. I was terrified;
all my life my mother had told me that Calvin Coolidge's son
had died of blood poisoning from an infected blister on his
heel. Mercedes came with us when my mother carried me to
Dr. Zapanto's malaria hospital. He had a tiny tube of sulfa
salve that had come in on a submarine. It was the first time I
had heard of sulfa, but I knew that anything that had been in a
submarine was miraculous. The little bit of sulfa was enough
to stop the infection. Perhaps small amounts of medicine

worked on us because for two years we had had so little. Much less than half the usual amount of antidysentery medicine had cured my father.

July 16, 1943. Douglass returned this afternoon—what a relief to see him. He's tired and pale, having walked most of the way on roads, now grassy, that we used to speed over before the war. He needed a guide on these familiar roads now because suyocs, sharp bamboo stakes that will pierce a boot, line the right-of-way. At Headquarters, he met a Captain Money, who bailed out over Luzon in the early part of the war when he was flying with Colin Kelly. McClish, the commander there, told Douglass that orders from MacArthur are not to press the Japs. Instead, they are to train troops to help in the invasion of the Islands and to send news of ship movements out to Australia by radio. The Japanese are building up their forces after harassment by the guerrillas, and have forced Fertig to move from Misamis to the Agusan Valley. Colonel McClish says the safest place for us would be Gomoco. The Colonel thinks it possible that the Japanese may well force the guerrilla army to join us there! He said that submarines do come to the island, but infrequently.

When we left Amparo after a month to go back to Gomoco, Mercedes was squatting by the river, still looking for her boat, her eyes squinting against the powerful smoke of her native cigar. She stood up to wave good-bye, but I saw her turn to scan the river again for her boat before we were out of sight.

⟾◆⟽

Khalil Khodr offered us a ride on his launch, the *Calape*, when it was time for us to go upstream to Gomoco. On his way to Bunawan, he would drop us off at the Land of The Floating Houses where the Gibong flows into the Agusan.

My father decided to take the offer—even though a motor launch would be more visible to the Japanese than three native *barotos*—because the trip would take only three days instead of ten. We tied our rented *barotos* to the *Calape* and joined the crowd on the decks. Other people were hitching rides, too.

Our trip downriver had been languid and restful, but now *Calape* struggled against the current; her engine spluttering with indigestion because it was trying to run on alcohol distilled from palm juice. The crowd on deck was the usual wartime mix of hungry pigs and crying babies. Chickens tied to poles were gasping with thirst. The noise and the smell of the engine forced me into my mother's lap, where I breathed through a towel and hid from the confusion.

Over the noise of his engine, Khalil told us of his adventures and narrow escapes on missions against the Japanese.

"One night we were coming back from Negros. We were bringing guns back from a sub landing. We hit heavy seas and were about to run out of fuel. It looked like we'd be out there for the Japs to find in the morning, and then we bumped something in the dark and it turned out to be a barrel of diesel fuel! Our subs sink a lot of Jap ships around here, and it must have floated off the deck as the *maru* went down!"

He told us that the guerrillas had learned to disarm mines that floated loose in the sea and to use the explosive to make cartridges. Bright-yellow picric acid (phenol) explosive worked wonders when rubbed into tropical ulcers.

"It's better to have a guerrilla who can think than one with only a big education," he said.

A long, noisy day on board *Calape* brought us to Esperanza on the Agusan, where the Wawa River flows in from the east. We hung up our mosquito nets and ate cold rice and avocados for dinner.

The second day was even harder for *Calape;* the river was swifter and sometimes the motor gave up and the boat sagged against the bank, panting and wheezing. Many times that day Khalil sweet-talked his engine back to life, and the men pushed us away from the bank. The boat wore a ragged cover of palm fronds as camouflage in the hope that we would look like floating brush. We prayed that a plane overhead would not notice that the floating brush on the river towed three *barotos.* Our engine was so noisy we couldn't hear the planes coming—we could only see them when they were nearly overhead, and that gave us only a short time to take cover. Twice, during that long, noise-filled day, we pulled under protecting trees along the bank to hide from Japanese planes that passed overhead.

The moon lit the dock at Talacogon. Too tired to start a fire so that we could cook our rice, we walked the grass-grown streets looking for a place to sleep.

All twenty-five of us found the same place: a large room above a Chinese general store. Because we were American, all courtesies were shown to my mother and me. The Chinese owner escorted us, before anyone else, up narrow stairs, past blond bundles of hemp in the storeroom, and into a dusty, cavernous room. He lit a smoky lamp and stayed with us. He had only one good eye, which was in shadow. The sunken lid of his blind eye caught light from the little lamp. My mother grew more and more uneasy as she looked at the closed door and thought of the narrow stairway that separated us from the moonlit street.

Suddenly she stood, grabbed my hand, and said to our Chinese host, "I go now. Thank you very much."

My father was at the bottom of the stairs, bringing in the bedrolls.

"I'm done in," he said, still not quite well. "All we have to do is get the nets up, and I'm calling it a day."

"We're not going back in there. Let's go to the padres in the convent."

"But I've made all the arrangements and paid the Chinaman."

"No, please, let's go to the padre. I can't climb those stairs again."

My father was too exhausted to argue. "You and your notions!" was all he could say.

We crossed the moonlit square to the convent. Father Alphonse's long Dutch face, glowing behind an auburn beard, came straight from a Rembrandt. There were buttons from his chin to his shoes on his worn black cassock. I wanted to count "Rich man, Poor man . . ." down those shiny buttons. I had never seen so many to count in all my life.

Priests traveled the rivers and jungle trails all during the war, running their missions and tending to the faithful. Their arrival in the towns and barrios of Mindanao always caused a fiesta. Many priests quietly worked with the guerrillas, carrying messages as they went from barrio to barrio. Others remained neutral, but they all kept their flocks together.

We felt safe with the priests in the mission, and in the morning, they opened their diminishing supplies and shared a large breakfast with us. Before he went next door to celebrate Mass, the other priest, Father José, gave us a blessing in Latin, his hands extended toward us and his head bowed. He had buttons, too.

Noon of the third day found us at the Land of the Floating Houses, where the Gibong flows into the Agusan. *Calape* chuffed up to the largest of the floating houses, tied up, and silence returned.

Diosdado Cajada's hospitality was joyful. It was his house that my father had saved during the terrible typhoon.

"Sir, I learn from you great knowledge to save my family. Many times I could sell rope, but I never sell. There could be more typhoon. Thank you, sir."

His house sat in the center of a large raft made of hardwood logs; it floated on the river and was tied by a strong jungle vine to a tree on the shore. Mr. Cajada said that the tree was as important a part of his family as the house was because it had stood through many floods.

Inside the house, there was a small shrine to the Virgin on the Singer treadle sewing machine. I wondered at the candle burning; we were so careful of our candles. I thought Mr. Cajada must be very rich to be able to burn a candle in the daytime.

We shared the family's stove, which was a box of sand with three "burners," each one three rocks surrounding hot coals, to cook our meal.

Madre Cajada's dining room table was a thick slab cut from a giant tree. She washed it by tying it with a long vine and tossing it into the river to swing in the current. When our meal was cooked, she pulled our table in, clean and dripping, and served us. We ate our rice and slipped our avocado skins directly into the river through the bamboo floor.

Mrs. Cajada asked for our avocado seeds. The typhoon had destroyed all the avocado trees at her *kaingin*. "This avocado is very good kind," she said.

There is much to be said for this mode of living. In rainy season when the river rises, you live high among the branches of ancient trees. In dry season when the water recedes, you float close to the rooty shore in a different dooryard every year. The flowing water carries troubles away, and peace and contentment say, "Why hasten on? All good will shall come to you if you turn not away from it."

Calape went noisily up the Agusan toward Bunawan, and we loaded our things into the *barotos* to go on toward home.

⇒•◆•⇐

July 27, 1943. I never thought I would be glad to return to Gomoco once I left it, but the cannas and balsams in Mary's flower garden were a cheerful sight when we broke into the clearing from the trail. The palm-thatched house, tucked deep in the jungle, looked so wonderfully safe after our time so close to the Japs in Butuan. The change was good for us, though; it taught us to appreciate the good water that does not need boiling, our mattresses, and the swimming pool in the mill tank. Food is much more plentiful here than it was when we left a month ago. The natives in the nearby valleys have been planting, and often we have five different kinds of vegetable at dinner.

A letter to Fred Feigel from my father:

July 25, 1943. News from down river: First, the Japs are getting very much stronger in Mindanao. Childress (a Major in the guerrilla army) says they are about to make a strong effort to break up the insurgent organization. Second, the Japs have been building fast launches and the coasts are not expected to be as safe as they have been for the last few months. I think that right where we are now is the best possible place to be for the rest of the year. If your house is too bad for the rainy season, consider coming back to Last Resort.

You asked me for some cigarettes and a pair of shoes. All the cigarettes that have ever come in were a few that the crew members of the subs handed out. And there is as much chance of getting a pair of shoes as of getting a slice off the moon. Amparo hasn't a thing. I never saw such poverty-ridden places as those I was in on my trip.

In the five weeks we were away, Charlie had begun raising chickens with the energy and enthusiasm that marked all his ventures. Chickens roosted everywhere, on beds in empty rooms, in empty cupboards, and even on the rafters over the dining table. Mother took to calling the mess house the Inn of the Floating Feather.

Charlie was still in the *bolo*-making business, making blades in the blacksmith shop from drill steel he found in the mill building. He was in partnership with some Filipinos now, and the camp rang with hammers beating steel against the anvil.

He had cleared about an acre of ground near Philomena's house where *camote* vines made a dark green carpet. He hoed furiously there in the early morning, then he fed the pig he was fattening for a special event—the Liberation, he told me. He tended his setting hens and made sure his *bolo* makers were at work.

Charlie rolled his own cigars from tobacco that came tamped into bamboo tubes. He treated the rough leaves with sugar and wrapped them tight, sealing them with rice paste. Sometimes he tied the cigars with a cord that he slid inward as he smoked.

The *cargadores* brought his *tuba* to Gomoco in long bamboo poles. All but the bottom segments were removed, and the *tuba* traveled safely over the trail. The poles were tied together in varying lengths and reminded me of the organ at the convent in Talacogon. Amiable bargaining began, half in English and half in Manobo, and finally the men would pour the cloudy amber fermented palm juice into Charlie's *frascos*.

"Drink it," he would say to my parents. "Drink lots of it. It's good for you, lots of vitamins!"

But my mother made her share into vinegar for our salads.

August 8, 1943. Twenty months of war in the Pacific. For several weeks now, we have been relying on messages of world news from Nelson Kellogg. Our diesel oil is too precious now to use except for bargaining. He has an optimistic way of writing down the broadcasts, and they always cheer us. Munda, in the Solomons, fell to the Americans yesterday, and the Allies invaded Sicily last month. Maybe, maybe, maybe, MacArthur will come to the Islands in time to play Santa for Christmas. It is so hard to keep tamping down hope in the attempt to be sensible.

Mustard-colored parrots, hard to see in the sunlit leaves, are screeching from across the stream. Later, monkey families will come just before sundown and chatter among themselves. In the brief dusk of evening, lemurs often sail like huge kites. Startling

in their swift appearance, nearly lost in perfect camouflage
among the shadowed trees, they glide with webbed limbs out-
spread to land on tree branches. Folding their furry sails around
them, they climb higher up the tree to glide through the jungle in
arching swoops.

A python came to the chicken coop one night. We awakened to alarms from the hens. My father killed the snake with his *bolo*. In the morning, my mother coiled it up and cooked it in a pot. We thought the cats would like a change from their rice diet, but they would not touch it. We offered the snake, all tenderized now and still coiled like a spring, to the chickens. They pecked it to the bones in revenge.

Charlie said, "What did you give it to the chickens for? We should have eaten it. It's good, tastes like chicken!"

My mother said she hoped she never got to where she had to eat a snake.

The same week, the last two pigs left Gomoco. They had put on a little weight since the starving days of the rainy season, but they needed a better home. Charlie traded them for three bags of rice. They went off to a *kaingin* by the river bound to poles and muzzled so they couldn't squeal on their way. My mother and I watched them go and hoped they would eat coconut meat and ripe corn for the rest of their lives. The biggest pig, Duchess, had always been mean and dangerous; I remembered her chasing me during the hungry months of rain, and I wasn't sorry to see her leave.

August 20, 1943. So it's come to this: a broody hen chooses a
place behind my books for a nest, and I do not shoo her away. I
watch her busily arranging things to suit her fancy, that secret,

expectant look on her face. I'll just quietly leave the room to her and see what happens.

Jaime had provided us with only a quarter of a wild pig for all the shotgun shells my father had given him, so my father went out one day to hunt for himself. He sat motionless all day, trying to catch the elusive pigs eating nuts from a certain tree in the jungle. He came home, stiff and grumpy and without a pig, having learned that the Filipinos were right in saying that "shooting the wild pig is never-never, sir."

Instead, he brought home the most wonderful insect I have ever seen. Five inches long, it had three wings on each side that were perfect copies of green leaves; each leg joint protected by a tiny "leaf." Its eyelids looked like tiny bits of bark protecting a bright bead. When it moved, all its parts fluttered and shambled as if it couldn't hold together.

To be so hungry for meat and then only to bag a creature that was a link between the animal and vegetable kingdoms! We stared at it and knew that God was truly playing tricks.

We couldn't keep anything so delicate, so I waded across the river, carrying the treasure carefully to the edge of the jungle. When I let him go, he sat where I put him on the trunk of a tree for a while and then shuffled to the other side. He matched his world so well that I couldn't find him again.

August 29, 1943. Maximino paid us a visit, after avoiding us for many months. He gave me two lipsticks, a square of white outing flannel, some sugar-cake and five pesos on account. The five pesos was prewar money. It would not be honorable, he said, to give me emergency money when I had given him hard currency.

*He still owes me ten pesos that he says he will give me after the fi-
esta in Novele, when he hopes to win at the cockfights. I am glad I
didn't give up on him last Christmas when everyone was teasing
me about being taken. Life is difficult for everyone in this war.*

My mother made a shirt for Opren. For one little shirt for her
child, Philomena made six large *cambos* to store our supplies in.
She cut armloads of bayonet palms in the jungle, slit the sharp
edges away with her *bolo,* and dried them in the sun. When the
fronds were pliable, she wove sweet-smelling baskets that were
big enough for me to play in.

Philomena was raising three children in her small hut by the
river. Opron, who had learned English quickly, was liaison officer between Philomena and my mother. He could charm quinine pills from my mother like no one else.

"My sister, Ameliana, do like this," he would say, teeth chat-
tering and muscles jerking in perfect imitation of a malaria attack.

"She is very sick. Please, ma'am, keeneena."

My mother was able to resist anyone else who asked for our
precious quinine because she was sure it was traded and not
used for healing. She had never seen Ameliana have the chills
and then the fever, but Opron got his "keeneena," anyway.

Another day, he spent one whole afternoon leaning in our
window while my mother was at the treadle machine. She ig-
nored him, knowing he wanted her to sew for his family again.
She had only one sewing machine needle left and did not want
to sew anything more for Philomena's family.

Finally, since there was no break in her reserve, he said,
"What of the pants of Opren? He has *camisa,* but now no pants. I
will give you chickens." He smiled his dimpled smile.

Wearily, she made a pair of shorts from a pillow tick.

I asked Opron where his father was; no one had ever seen him. Opron looked at the sky and said, "He is like chicken, but like boy."

My mother looked at me. She didn't understand.

"He's an angel now," I said.

Gossip tells me that Pedro Balthazar was fatally boloed in a fight during a fiesta, in Rosario. Philomena is alone now, and is raising her children as best she can by pounding our clothes on the rocks of Kagomay Creek. I find it hard to believe that her husband now is an angel.

Months before, we had scraped the last of the prewar flour from the barrels in the *bodega*. Now that the weather was as hot and as dry as it can get in the tropics, we started a new industry—flour making. The vendors brought loads of cassava, and we washed the knobby roots in the river with coconut-fiber brushes, peeled them, and sliced them into thin wafers. We dried the cassava wafers in the sun on galvanized iron sheets borrowed from the mill roof until they were crisp as potato chips.

Julio and Opron pounded the cassava chips in the rice mortar. Pounding in a mortar is a skill; the heavy pole must hit the very bottom of the mortar during the pounding or the contents splash over the edges of the mortar and are wasted.

Sometimes little Ameliana would step in to the rhythm of the pounding and three poles pounded the cassava in a triple beat set by their chanting. After the pounding, we sifted the powder through green net curtains that someone had abandoned. At the end of the day, we ran for the river to wash away the dust from our white eyebrows and dusty arms.

Bending in the blasting sun to sift the flour over and over again to get all the flour we could from the cassava roots was miserable, dusty work, but pancakes made from our cassava flour and Lieutenant Mester's baking powder, dripping with coconut-and-sugar syrup, were my reward. We hoped to have enough cassava flour to last the rainy season.

PART
3

HOPING AND ESCAPING

September 19, 1943. It's true! The Japs have left Butuan! That means that we are no longer trapped at the head of these four rivers. Perhaps they will leave Surigao as well, and we can go back to our ruined mine. It would be great to find some of the things that were looted from our house. I have heard who has my Chinese rugs. Other news is good, too. Italy has surrendered only a few weeks after we invaded them. The Russians are chasing the Germans out of their country and will soon retake Smolensk. Oh, how can I say the news is good when it means so many young men are dying? Bob could be one of them fighting in a far land. Perhaps, wherever he is, he is safer in the Philippines than he would be in the Army. I never stop worrying about him.

It was a bountiful time for us at Gomoco. Vegetables and fruit came up the trail in the vendors' *bonkils*. We had plenty of rice and cassava flour. (Our own vegetable garden, however, was a disappointment. The only crop that the jungle soil could grow well was okra, and only Charlie could eat it.) We needed the vendors to bring us vegetables; they came because they needed our goods. For five chickens my mother traded a gray-

and-white print linen dress she had bought in Manila. She promised a bright print blouse to a man who would bring fresh fish.

The traders also wanted our diesel oil, but they were having a harder and harder time wheedling it from us. The war seemed endless, and we were afraid to let our supplies get too low. We were not likely to find a barrel floating down our river like Captain Khodr!

"Only pity me. Buy for even what," the vendors would say hopelessly after their long and fruitless walk. My mother would relent and buy whatever she could.

September 20, 1943. We have over 180 eggs and nearly fifty coconuts. I have learned to cook rice with coconut milk. We find it delicious. Coconut honey is time-consuming to make, but it brightens our meals. I grate coconut meat, mix it with coarse brown sugar and a little water. Then I squeeze the mass with my hands to extract a creamy sweet milk. What a treat it is to have something sweet and nourishing. It's called malado. *We haven't needed to use any of Douglass' "iron rations." The scale in the bodega says that Douglass weighs 143 pounds. He's still thin from the dysentery. I weigh 128, which is heavier than normal! Mary weighs 65 pounds. I think that must be about right for a nine-year-old. I guess this tedious food is getting us by.*

Life at Gomoco was easier now. Fear of a surprise visit by Japanese soldiers abated; the guerrillas seemed to be keeping them busy. My parents were happier than I had seen them in a long time. Perhaps they were reliving the days during the Depression when they had lived isolated in the Sierra Nevada in

California. They were free now of the dissension that had haunted all the days at Gomoco.

One lovely afternoon I remember: After siesta, I led my parents out of the camp and up the creek farther than they had had time to go before. I showed them shallows where Opren and Opron had taught me how to catch river shrimp, and we sank up to our necks in the deeps. The green of the jungle was pierced by long shafts of light. Mother had brought her jar of melted soap shampoo and we stopped to wash our hair. We floated, our long hair floating around us, and then brushed it dry on a sunny rock.

We waded home through the clear waters, the jungle all around us.

Small things filled my days; I tended my little flower bed, checked for eggs under our hens' warm feathers, and played with Opren and Opron.

"Callao, callao!" The hornbill high in the trees called. I imitated the bird, "Callao, callao," my voice a perfect nasal sound.

"Never do like callao!" Opren said. He crossed himself because he knew two religions. "They watchmen for *anitos*. They no like to make laugh to them. They come look you with bad eyes, hurt you with sharp nose!"

We passed a *balete*, a parasitic vine that surrounds and smothers a jungle tree and then stands alone in the tree's place. The boys bowed to the *diwatas* who lived in the *balete*.

"When moon bright, you listen with ears. You hear *kituyapi* [nose flutes] come from *anitos*. They teach you music if you not talk for two days."

I knew about *anitos*. They were also jungle spirits, but not so powerful as the *diwatas*. They did good deeds, but they also were watchful and could punish minor infractions.

September 22, 1943. This morning I broke the last lamp chimney. It shattered into a thousand pieces when I flipped the mosquito net out of the way as I made the bed. We had patched a hole with paper months ago and patched and patched again as the flame charred the paper. Now the chimney is gone, and our little red lamp will be smoky and fitful as it lights our room at night. Bedtime will be even earlier now. Mary is making a wind chime to hang in our window by gluing a little bit of my raveled-sock thread to the bits of glass. She's learned so well the lesson that we cannot waste a thing.

Juanito, who had cooked for us before the days of Ah Hing, brought us chickens from his *kaingin* by the Sulibau. He was the one who had taken my mother and me to Rosario so many months before. He told us that Ramon, a houseboy who had been at Gomoco when the number of refugees was large, was dead.

"But why?" my mother asked. "He was so young!"

"He was murdered, ma'am," said Juanito.

"How can that be? I am so sorry. He was such a happy boy."

"He repented his marriage, ma'am, because his wife all the time want money, all the time he no have. His wife go home with baby. Then Ramon alone again. Happy. Bye and bye, he see *parientes* of wife. He forget they angry, take cool drink, get fever, then die."

"But that's terrible! He was so bright and funny. He can't be dead!"

"Is Manobo way, ma'am. The drink is sweet, but you drink, you never talk again. Just make noise with fat tongue, get fever, and die. The *parientes* of the wife of Ramon wait a long time to get chance to kill. Not good to give back wife."

September 23, 1943. Today planes went by five different times. Charlie saw them and said they were very fast with red wings and silver bodies. The piece of sky above our green well in the jungle is small, and I was not at the right angle to see them, but the sound of the motors was very loud. How wonderful it would be if they were ours and the attack we have been waiting for is about to come.

The planes went by so fast, and there were so many of them, that we couldn't hear their motors clearly. We all believed that the Japanese couldn't build a proper engine, and that their engines had an unsteady sound, as if someone pumped the accelerator. We believed that an American plane had a strong, steady sound.

Maximino came in toward the end of September and said that he had once had my mother's money and was on his way to bring it to her. Then he was elected vice mayor of Novele and he had spent her money "to have a blowout."

"Do not worry, ma'am, your money is safe with Maximino!"

September 30, 1943. We must be getting hopeful about leaving here, for we have made a contract for two barotos to take us down the long rivers when we can go forth from this lost land and find the world again. Domingo Orlandez, the baroto maker, says the wood of lanigpa *or* colantas *is best. He selects the trees where they grow, fells them and hollows them out where they fall. The craft are sturdy, no seams, no caulking—just a tree hewn into a boat. Long and narrow with outriggers attached, they are almost unsinkable.*

Two of Charlie's baby chicks disappeared from a new brood, and Charlie accused our cat, Miss Puss. I had carried her home from Rosario when we were first at Gomoco. He said that he had pardoned her once because she had rid the camp of rats, even though he had seen the last of a chick's yellow feet disappearing down her throat.

"I let her off once, but no more. She's eating my chicks, and that's it. Chickens are food, and we can't afford to have a cat that's a thief."

"But she has two kittens," I argued. "They'll die without her! Please. Please."

"They're old enough to look after themselves now. They don't need her. But I tell you I'm going to keep an eye on 'em, because she could have already taught 'em to eat my chicks!"

So Plug Tail (Filipino cats have a gene that deforms their tails; Plug Tail's tail was doubled over and over and was very short) and Smiley Face would be orphans.

My mother offered two of our pullets—even the one we had trained to eat cockroaches!—to make up for his loss.

"Nope. Soon as I finish my dinner, I'm gonna drown that cat!"

I accused Charlie's cat, Big Tom. No response.

I left the table in tears and ran home to my cat. I carried her to the assay office, hoping to lock her in, but my father saw me and made me bring her back. He said that I couldn't go against Mr. Martin, that Miss Puss was only a cat and that we had to live with Charlie. It was more important to have a happy group to live with than to have a cat. We had other cats, he said. He didn't understand my desperation. Miss Puss was one of the few beings to have been with us almost all the time, and she was my friend. My own friend, I had brought her home from Rosario.

I sat with her on my lap in our room and waited for Charlie to come with his sack. Her kittens curled up on my pillow, and I had never been so sad.

Then I heard shouting up by the mess hall, and my mother ran to tell me that Julio had found a python asleep above the door where the hen nested. Julio had killed the snake and found two undigested chicks inside.

Charlie came to apologize and told me he now knew my cat was innocent. I accepted his apology, hugging my hot and squirmy cat.

October 3, 1943. A letter came from Lt. Mester down at Amparo. He says that three of the escaped prisoners left for Australia on the submarine that came in last month. I am sure that by now our letters must be home. It gives me comfort to think they know we are all right.

I wonder what the next news that comes up the green trail will be. It may throw us into a fever of packing. I should sew for Mary while I have a machine. Mine at Mother Lode is stolen, and anyway there will be no electricity where we used to live, if we go there. If Fertig's army really routs the Japs, then maybe we can go back to our homes, now emptied by looters.

The demand for cloth was so great and our supply so small that my mother ripped the ticking off a mattress left in the empty rooms. She put the kapok stuffing in a *cambo* and washed the ticking in the river.

The ticking was drying in the sun when a group of vendors came up the trail. They came from Bunawan, farther into the interior than the barrios where most of our traders came from. They had not seen such bounty in months, and they fell on it— two or more pulling on an end. *"Que mucho, que mucho?"* Eager brown faces surrounded my mother; hands grabbed at her to get her attention. Five "real" pesos, not "emergency money" or

Japanese "Mickey Mouse" money, but five prewar pesos took the cloth. She sold the kapok, too.

She felt like a thief until she found that she, having no idea of the rate of inflation on Mindanao after nearly two years of war, had given the cloth away. A pair of men's pants was worth a horse in some parts of the island.

———◆———

I was playing with Ameliana on the hard-packed dirt under Philomena's house when I heard a freight train coming through the jungle. The noise moved toward us, and the trees began to shake. Philomena and Carmelina, Ameliana's oldest sister, tumbled out of the *nipa* house and fell to their knees. "Santos, Santos, Santos," they cried, and crossed themselves.

By this time the jungle was dancing, and the ground shivered like a great animal shaking off irritations. The trees swayed and shook, and then the freight train rumbled off in the other direction, leaving us stupefied.

We looked at one another for a while, and then Philomena ran back up the ladder to make sure that her charcoal iron had not tipped over.

After the earthquake, my father and I went on an expedition to look for damage and found only that water in the mill tank we used for swimming had splashed out and that some of the bamboo troughs that brought water down the hill from the spring had jumped apart.

As we retied them, I said, "Daddy, Philomena told me that an earthquake like that means that there will be many changes soon."

"She may be right, you know. We'll have to watch and see, won't we?"

In the night, Plumy Tail, my gorgeous, vain rooster—who spent his nights on the windowsill in the room the Welbons had used at the other end of our little building because he was too elegant to sleep where ordinary chickens slept—set up a fearful racket. We all arrived at the door of our room at the same time, wanting to save him from whatever was attacking him. There was silence and I knew my pet was dead, but then my father yelled, "The chicken's all right, but we have to get the wildcat!"

We had heard of *musangs* who came to eat chickens in the night, but had never seen one. The dictionary calls them palm civet cats. Sometimes, when chickens were missing in the morning, Julio would say, "*Musang* take chickens." Other days, he would say, "Python." We never knew how he knew the difference.

"Bring a lamp and a gun!" my father called.

Plumy Tail, bleeding from the head and minus most of his magnificent tail feathers, was hiding behind the rice barrel. Mother grabbed him and handed him to me and then ran for my father's Enfield rifle and our fading flashlight.

"You do go in for guns! I only meant the pistol under my pillow!"

My mother came back with the pistol and found my father taking aim with the rifle. She shone the flashlight at the rice barrel where the *musang* had run in panic.

Just then Charlie's *bolo* makers, roused by all the yelling, came into the line of fire. My mother got them to safety on our porch and then held the light again as my father shot and missed. The terrified *musang* ran around the edges of the room as my father emptied the pistol.

The civet cat was dead, shot once in the head, by the time Charlie Martin arrived, his huge pajamas wrapped around his waist like a *dhoti*. His bent and iridescent bifocals glinted from under his hat.

"What's going on here? I thought it was the Invasion!"

Then we all looked at my father. In the light of Charlie's kerosene lamp, he stood on the porch holding his pistol and the *musang*.

He was triumphant and completely naked.

———⟫⟨———

October 13, 1943. Bob Crump came back to camp to get tools and supplies for the guerrillas. He brought letters from friends on the coast where he has been since he joined the United States Armed Forces in the Philippines (USAFP). Hearing what our friends are doing to help the resistance unsettled us, and Douglass decided to go down river to Army Headquarters. He hopes to find a way to look after Mary and me and still help the cause.

All those twenty-two months, we had only been guests at Gomoco Goldfields Mining Properties, the tiny mine in the jungle that sheltered us. We had been there so long, and the needs of the guerrillas were so great, however, that my father packed up a great many things that belonged to Gomoco to take to the Army. My father opened the *bodega* and took food that the U.S. Army had sent to us at the surrender to the ad hoc Army now fighting the Japanese. Now the *bodega* shelves were almost bare.

He took all the one-inch pipe he could scavenge for the guerrillas to make homemade guns. A meter of pipe could be fashioned into a *paliuntod* that shot nails (also requested from the stores at Gomoco). There would never be enough guns, even though the submarines were coming more often.

My mother and I were to wait at Gomoco with Charlie until my father came back with news and a new plan. He expected to be gone about two weeks.

The *cargadores* settled their loads on their backs and filed across the river. My father waved good-bye and disappeared into the green. We waved bravely, my mother and I, having seen it happen so many times before.

This time it was different. My mother and I were alone with only Charlie in the camp; my father was going close to the Japanese without us, and we might never see him again. My mother panicked almost immediately, and after a few minutes spent trying to quell her fear, she said, "Go play with Ameliana. I'm going to try to stop him."

She was swallowed up by the jungle, too. For a little while, I could hear her calling, but only the wind in the jungle answered. Then she remembered me and turned to run toward the camp. No, she thought, I must catch him, and she turned again toward the Sulibau River landing where the party had planned to spend the night.

I couldn't possibly play docilely with Ameliana. I was truly alone now, with one parent alone in the jungle chasing the other down the trail. As night fell, Ameliana and I splashed across the river and ran down the trail, too.

"Mommy, Mommy!" My voice was small in the green vastness. Not too far from home, we found my exhausted mother sitting on a log, trying to get her mind together.

We cried and clung together on the path, Ameliana watching, and all three of us went back to Gomoco in the brief tropic twilight.

"If we get up really early, Mommy, can't we catch them at Kelloggs' before they load the *barotos*?"

"That's what we'll do," she said.

By morning, however, she had given up the idea of catching him. She would take me, as planned, to Kelloggs' for a visit of a few days. We would go at leisure and not in panic.

Julio carried our bedrolls and our rice pot on our trip to Kelloggs' *kaingin* on the Sulibau. I was delighted to be going off for a few days, and Julio looked forward to dancing in the barrio nearby and courting Maria.

Two years before, he had not had a word of English, but just a few days before, he had said to my mother, "Ma'am, I am to marry. I dance for Maria at the fiesta."

The Kelloggs set places at their table for us on their wide veranda. I was happy to be with so many people and to hear family chatter. The young girls were looking forward to the dancing later, and there was a feeling of anticipation in the air that was new to me. Gomoco had too few people now, and they lived in suspension in a waiting jungle.

At dusk, Alma Oliva, Mr. Kellogg's wife, led us to the little house she had built at the edge of the clearing as a hostel for travelers on the river. The fiddles and drums began to play at a neighbor's house, and then the dancing began on the hard-packed earth beside it. I could hear bare feet slap the ground, and I knew that Julio was happily dancing for his Maria.

We lay under the mosquito net and talked about Daddy's trip on the river. If he was really lucky, we decided, and caught *Calape* each way on the river, then the shortest wait we would have was fourteen days. If he missed the launch and had to go by *baroto*, then we would wait much longer. Perhaps even a month would go by without him. We could rely on the bamboo telegraph for bad news, but it was likely that the first we would know about his trip would be from him.

I fell asleep, and in the morning found my mother lying wide awake beside my sleeping father.

"Mary! You can't tell a soul. Daddy met Captain Ball and Major Childress in Talacogon. They were on the way to Gomoco to tell us that a message came from Australia. Daddy's going to stay here to help the guerrillas, but you and I can ride on a submarine! And after that, maybe we can go home!"

Home! I could barely remember it. There were cars there and telephones and schools and children my own age. It must be a magical place, home. Everyone seemed to long for it and to talk about it, but I wasn't sure what it was. I knew there were aunts and cousins to know, but they were scattered. Where would we live? Near some of them? In Reno again? I longed for a "normal" life and knew that living in a jungle mining camp surrounded by an enemy was not "normal." I wanted real friends, not imaginary ones or native ones whom I was taught to patronize.

A trip on a submarine sounded wonderful. I had always loved the steamer trips to Manila and back. Leaning over a ship's rail to watch the bow chew the blue water to white foam was endlessly entertaining. I would like an ocean voyage again.

While we were at Kelloggs', my father made all the arrangements he could for our trip down the Agusan. Only one of the *barotos* he had contracted for was ready. He canceled the second one and rented another, and then we walked back to Gomoco for the last time.

We could tell no one why we were so suddenly leaving the quiet place in the jungle that had kept us safe. We just were leaving; that's all. Opron questioned me all the time; he knew there was more to our story than we were telling. Ameliana stood near my dolls, hoping that we would give her one.

My mother made me pajamas from her last piece of cloth and a woolen coat from a tweed cape that somehow had followed us from Nevada in our six years of wandering in the Philippines.

October 20, 1943. I can't go. I can't go. We have escaped capture this long. It's crazy to risk everything on a perilous escape by submarine. I can't leave Douglass. I know he's not really well. His teeth trouble him. He will not leave these islands. He says he must help get rid of the Japs and be here to protect Mother Lode when he can get there. I can't leave Bob, wherever he is. I can't risk Mary. I can't go. I go through the day doing what I should be doing, but at night I can't sleep. I can't go. I don't have the courage.

When she told my father that she wasn't going, he was stunned.

"Are you jungle jolly? How can you even think of passing up this chance?"

"I just can't go. I'm safe here. I can't leave you here when the war is just about to heat up. Even if we make it safely to Australia, how could I live and not know about you?"

"I can't believe you. I had just about decided that you weren't going to fall apart on me, and now you pull this! At least think about getting Mary out healthy."

"I am thinking about Bob. I can't leave the Islands if I don't know what's happened to him!"

"But you can't do anything about Bob! He's as good as on another planet. Don't you see? You have to go."

"Why do I have to go? We're doing fine here. We're comfortable here. How can I manage alone in Australia with a nine-year-old child? I'll have no money. I can't even remember how to drive!"

"All I have thought about for two years is getting you and Mary out of this. I sent a letter to MacArthur about the American civilians on Mindanao on the last bomber that went to Australia. I never told you, but I wrote him again when I heard about the subs coming in. I begged him to get you out. I pulled out all the stops, reminded him of the dinner parties in Manila before the war, about how Mary used to play with his son at the Manila Hotel. I've talked to Fertig, asked him to talk to Parsons, who's coming in and out with the subs all the time. If you don't go, you'll defeat all I've worked for. Do it for Mary. She can't be here much longer without being permanently damaged. At least get her out."

She gave up and packed our few belongings for the *cargadores* to carry down the trail. Rice for the trip, *camotes* and vegetables, a few quarts of diesel oil to use for trading, a few toys for me. She took the *musang* skin from the wall of the *bodega* where it was drying and tucked it into her bag as a souvenir.

The muslin curtains that Mother made after our trip to Rosario came down—bamboo curtain rods and all—to pay our way down the river.

"Ameliana, you may have one of Mary's dolls."

Ameliana wanted them both—how could she choose? First she held Sally, the cuddly doll with the soft body, but then she saw Virginia, the Scarlett O'Hara doll with the marvelous dresses. In the end she chose Sally, and Virginia went to one of the Kellogg daughters.

It seemed wrong to me to leave the hen sitting on her box and not to see her chicks hatch. What would happen to the goats and the kid I had seen being born? Charlie was staying at Go-moco, carrying on as caretaker as he had been when the war began. He promised he would take care of all my friends, even Miss Puss.

We ate a last breakfast with Charlie on the veranda of the mess house, and then as we left the table, the cats rose and rubbed around our ankles as we went down the steps of our lit-tle house to wade across the river.

The *cargadores* settled the loads on their backs, fell into line, and began the hike to Kelloggs'. We fell in behind them, and Go-moco was gone.

October 25, 1943. The dappled shade of the forest played on an-other safari as we passed along the overgrown trail leading through the jungle to the lowlands by the river. Leaves and vines formed tunnels for us to bow beneath as we picked our way along the trail. Sunlight spattered through the leafy archways and shone on cargadores bent under suitcases and boxes, rice cambos, five-gallon gasoline tins used for kettles. Philomena and her chil-dren left Gomoco with us to find a new way of living, and Opren and Opron scampered ahead of us on the trail through sunlight and shadow like two small elves.

Ameliana carried her doll.

⊰•◆•⊱

October 26, 1943. Our departure from Kelloggs' landing resem-bled a Saint's Day fiesta. The schoolteachers from Rosario and Cabantao, the faithful vegetable vendors and their families all gathered on the shore to wave good-bye. We have been a source of income for them, and I'm sure they are sorry to see us go. Old

Pedro came down river from Rosario to catch me before I got away because the sewing-machine needle he had begged from me in trade did not fit his machine. I had tried to tell him so at the time, but since he thought I was trying to keep him from getting it, I gave it to him for thirty eggs. Today he wanted reparation for a bad bargain. I gave him a pair of Mary's socks to unravel and let him keep the needle. He was delighted even though the eye is in the wrong end. It will sew better than no needle at all.

Ah Hing emptied a sack of *camotes* into the *baroto* for a *despedida* gift. He couldn't spare the sack; there were so few. He told my mother that another baby was on the way, and she gave him the little bit of white flannel that Maximino had given her as part of his debt. She hoped Loling could use it for a diaper for the new baby.

The Kelloggs gave us twelve chickens. Everyone tried to persuade us to stay inland. The Agusan valley was dangerous, they said; the Japs were up and down the river all the time. What could we be thinking of to leave our safe place in the mountains?

We couldn't say.

Our instructions from the guerrillas were to be at Esperanza at the confluence of the Agusan and Wawa Rivers by the first of November.

We settled into the *baroto* for the trip, and I heard my mother say—mostly to herself, but a little to me, "We are heading for Esperanza—that means 'hope' in Spanish. I hope that's a good omen."

We made good time down the rivers. By now, they were familiar paths, and we waved greetings to barrio people who gathered on the shore to watch us float by. There hadn't been time to build a thatched roof over the boat this time; we were cold and wet the day it rained and burned by the sun the next.

At Talacogon, we paid a last visit to the priests and their long buttoned soutanes and returned a pile of dog-eared prewar magazines to them. *Calape* happened to be tied up at the bamboo dock, and we paid Captain Khalil handsomely for a ride downriver with him. My father worried all the way that rumors of increasing Japanese presence on the river were true, and he was relieved to get to Esperanza on October 29. We saw only the Japanese mail plane that flew up the river in the morning and back in the afternoon.

At Esperanza, we rented a *nipa* house.

"I am honored to give you my house, sir, but I am sorry for the roof. You will be wet in the rain," said our landlord. "Before the Hapons come, sir, I never have hole in *nipa* roof! Never! Now I run from Hapons, I have no money, I have no time. I am sorry for my poor house."

The floors were resilient as we walked through the rooms, and my father said they reminded him of "rubber ice."

"When I was a little boy in North Dakota, when the ponds were first freezing, we used to skate as fast as we could across the thin ice in the middle of the pond. If you got going really fast on the thick ice, you could make it across the thin ice to the other side. It sagged under you like these floors. What stupid little boys we were!"

I couldn't imagine my sober father, who worried about our safety so much, could possibly have been a boy who took such chances.

I leaned on the windowsill of José Pebillo's house in Esperanza, looking out on a palm-lined street and the grassy shore of the Wawa River, trying to imagine ice and cold water and bare trees against gray skies. Someday soon, I thought, I might be cold. I might even wear a scarf and mittens to build a snowman.

Our kitchen had a sandbox big enough for three groups of three stones to set our pots on. Such a large stove was a luxury. It meant that Julio could cook more than one dish at a time.

Maria has rejected Julio's proposal of marriage, and he has come with us to Esperanza to forget his troubles. The last time he went dancing, she ran from him to hide in the cornfield. Maria's mother is the one who really wants the match because she thinks that Julio would be a source of cloth. We have often paid him with filter cloth from the mill instead of money.

I was happy to have Julio with us. He was a good friend. In two years we had taught each other little bits of our languages. I loved to listen to the endless native songs he sang as he squatted to tend our smoke-blackened pots. He carried water from the Wawa River in long bamboo poles that leaned against the woven walls of the house. He was strong and could pour a thin stream of water from the hollow pole into a small rice pot without wasting one drop.

In the slow hours we spent in the kitchen, he told me the tale of the golden god. Far up the Wawa River there was once a tribe who possessed a golden image of a foreign god. The god protected the tribe from disaster for many generations. In return, the *datu* of the tribe cared for it in a special house. Legend said that the tribe would die if they lost the statue, and so they were careful with it and told no one why they had such good fortune and so many healthy children. Then, one day, there was a terrible typhoon, much worse than the one we had seen at Gomoco.

The river rose far higher than memory could recall and swept away the barrio and the villagers. Only the *datu* survived. He spent the rest of his life searching the riverbanks for the golden god.

And then Julio said to me, "When my father young man like me, he live in Cabantao near Gomoco. People say that golden *kwan* found near river here in Esperanza. Maybe they find it. I don't know, I think true. Old men say it now in America."

November 1, 1943. How quiet everything is. The large rivers flow together quietly here. They slip by, the water shining like wide mirrors. I was used to our noisy little Kagomay Creek at Gomoco. This is a day of anxious waiting. We keep listening for the river launch, thinking that it may bring news from Head-quarters. Occasionally an airplane goes by to the West of us to remind us that the world is at war. The engine's uneven sound tells us that it's Japanese.

Runners sent out by Colonel Fertig were finding other Americans who, like us, had been hiding in remote parts of Mindanao. In small groups they came; a few arrived at Esper-anza each day.

Calape chugged into town one afternoon with the Mearses aboard. No word of them had ever come to Gomoco over the bamboo telegraph, and I think my parents had counted them as dead. We had visited their logging camp just before the war began, and I could remember their large house that perched over a blue bay. Now they were sick and exhausted after two years alone. I watched a tearful reunion on the shore.

Thin, pale Thelma Briggs came to Esperanza by herself. Moros murdered her husband early in the war during a robbery, and she had found her way to a haven in a convent. It was hard to find a place for her to sleep because she had to have her head pointing a certain direction as she slept and the bamboo flooring ran the wrong direction for her to lie comfortably. I found her quirk strange because my mother said it was a Mohammedan custom to face Mecca. Why, I wondered, would a woman follow the customs of the people who had killed her husband while she watched?

Then the party from Prosperidad arrived. We hadn't seen the Welbons and Glenda and Stevie Crytser for eight months. They had a difficult time after they left Gomoco. The *cargadores* they hired when they left Gomoco had turned on them and taken the lengths of fabric they had counted on for trading. Helen lost that pink ring again (I was glad!), and seven hundred pesos in cash. The recent months had been a little easier because Colonel Fertig had made emergency money available to American civilians who needed it.

Stevie was now two and had learned to walk and to talk since we had seen him. He was the mascot of the Americans gathered on the shore waiting for a submarine that might or might not come, and he delighted us all.

The Martins came from Leyte to wait at Esperanza. Charlotte Martin had come to the Philippines as a tiny child and could speak pidgin, too. In the evenings on the veranda of the house, she and I entertained the waiting refugees with long conversations in pidgin.

"Aaaah, my podder is bery seeck, and my wipe is fregnant. We hab no rice, we hab no feesh. Only pity me, sir, you hab flenty money, bery reech, and we hab notting!" We would finish the dialog with a long, high-pitched wail of anguish amid gales

of laughter from our audience. After two years of surviving because of the kindness and generosity of the Filipinos, we could
still ridicule them. It isn't comfortable to think about.

*November 3, 1943. It is wonderful to see all these people after
having been alone for nearly six months. I had secretly thought
that no one else would attempt this escape. I am relieved that
there will be other civilians with Mary and me on the voyage
through enemy-infested waters.*

I listened to the grown-ups catch up on news and marvel at
the miracle of the submarine that might come to spirit us away.

"Fertig's done an amazing job getting all these renegades to
work together as well as he has. You know he just went down to
Oriental Misamis and declared himself commanding general!
And then he rigged up a radio and finally got Australia to believe he wasn't a Jap with the old codes. It took Charlie Smith—
remember him?—and Hedges to sail to Australia with a secret
code to convince Australia there really were Americans out here
in the woods!"

Somebody else said, "The first submarine came to Mindanao from Australia last March and Chick Parsons was on it!"

I remembered Chick Parsons—he was a businessman in
Manila whom my father used to deal with. I remembered his
white smile in his tan face.

"Chick Parsons really knows these Islands! I heard he came
in here on that first sub with guns and medicine, and that he
also brought communion wafers to the priests! Imagine knowing how much that would mean to the natives! What a guy!"

*November 8, 1943. The Mearses, who arrived here the other day
from Anaken, talked to Chick Parsons when he came ashore last*

March. They say that his agents on Luzon report that most of the Americans there have been interned in Manila. Some Brent School students are with them, so Bob must be there. I don't know why Waldo didn't find him. Perhaps it's better than being out in the hills; they say the Japanese have combed the island, looking for Americans. This is the first, even indirect, word we have had of him in over two years. It comforts me. I think we would know any terrible news of him.

One evening after most of the refugees had come to the waiting place, the Filipino deputy governor of Agusan Province invited all of us for dinner. Together, we walked up the grassy trail along the Wawa River to his house, which stood back from the river in a peaceful stand of palm trees.

I sat with the adults at a long, shiny wooden table and ached for the formal speeches to end because smells of delicious food were coming from the kitchen. When the plates of food began to arrive, I realized that poor Ah Hing had never been a cook.

The meal began with *lumpia,* a Filipino spring roll of river shrimp, hearts of palm, and garlic. There was a sweet-and-sour sauce to dip them into. Chicken roasted in banana-leaf wrappings and lemongrass arrived with steaming rice. Then, when it seemed I had eaten more at this one meal than I had in two years, the servant brought us pork *adobo.* Marinated in vinegar, soy sauce, and peppercorns, the *adobo* hit my tongue like an electric shock. There were vegetables, of course, and fruits and sweet rice cakes to end the meal.

Because we had had a special meal, a toothpick tree was passed from person to person. The soft green part of the palm leaf was removed, and only the dry spines remained. Each person broke a piece off and passed the frond along. We cleaned our teeth and burped noisily to show how much we appreciated a fine meal.

As the sun went down, we sat on the veranda of Mr. Villareal's house, and, while the grown-ups talked, I watched the *tuba* gatherer collect palm sap. He ran up each tree on notches cut on the inside curve and disappeared into the fronds to pour the day's accumulation of juice into a bamboo tube tied to his belt. The palms rustled as he worked. Soon his palm juice would be *tuba*, and I hoped some would find its way to Charlie far away at Gomoco.

Mr. Villareal gave us a meal to remember in a country filled with hardship. I hope we understood that. Later in the war, after living through a savage Japanese attack that leveled Esperanza, he died of hunger in the jungle.

———◆———

Esperanza, on the two slow rivers, made me uneasy. I was used to the protection of the green jungle and the noise of our small river. There was too much space around me in Esperanza, and the Japanese were always in the back of my mind, even as I played with Filipino children or listened to the adults reminisce about days "before the war." I watched the mail plane fly just to the west of us on its daily route between Davao and Surigao and hoped they weren't looking our way.

One day, I overheard my father tell Bill Mears that he hoped the sub would come soon.

"I don't like having so many of us all in one spot. One quick Jap party could follow a rumor and wipe us out, easy," he said.

Mr. Mears, who was British, puffed on his pipe filled with rank wartime tobacco and said, "Umm."

I felt a chill, remembering my father's unease on the trip downriver to Esperanza.

I heard the Martins tell the story of a mining engineer on Panay who, with his family, had eluded the Japanese for many months. When a Japanese search party found their hideout, the man shot his wife and daughter and then killed three soldiers before he was killed as well. It was better to be dead when the Japanese soldiers found you. I remembered the day that Swede Swanson had told my father he would have to kill us if the Japs came, and I knew that the Martins' story was true.

The month before, the Japanese had given independence to a puppet government that offered ten thousand pesos to anyone who captured a guerrilla. I knew that the Japanese considered us guerrillas because we had not volunteered to become prisoners, and I couldn't imagine why ten thousand pesos—even if it was "Mickey Mouse" money—would allow us to go free any longer.

We waited for Wendell Fertig, Commander of USFIP, to come up the river from his headquarters in Amparo. Our fates were in his hands. He would know if there really was a sub on the way to take us out, and when. He would get us out of the Islands before the bounty hunters came. He might possibly have some answers to questions about our lives after an escape.

I seemed to worry alone while the grown-ups waited and gossiped.

My parents' plan for my father to stay with the guerrilla army was subject to Fertig's desires. When my father returned civilian registration forms to Fertig's headquarters in Amparo on November 3 he said in a note: ". . . my departure will be contingent upon your advice . . ."

Fertig replied, "Will see you within the next few days. We have need for men who know the country. Will discuss it when I see you."

Late one afternoon, we heard the sound of a boat coming upriver. The motor sounded faintly, then louder, then fainter again, then loud.

"Mommy, do you hear that engine?"

"Yes, dear."

"Mommy, I think it's the Japs coming for us. Daddy, where can we hide?"

"Be still, Mary. It's all right. Really."

"But I *know* it's the Japs coming! Can't you hear the motor? It's not steady, like an American! It comes and goes like a Japanese one. Please, we have to run!"

The terror was overwhelming. No one listened to my cries, my warnings, my certain knowledge that terrible events were coming closer every minute. I remembered the story of the engineer and his family on Panay, but the adults chatted on the veranda and allowed the boat to come closer.

I didn't know which was worse, my fear or my inability to make anyone take action. I knew in my soul that the approaching launch was Japanese, but I was powerless to save us. I stood apart from the careless grown-ups, unable to leave them, unable to stay close to the riverbank. Panic filled my whole being. I couldn't die alone; I had to die with my parents, the way I had always lived.

Suddenly, I knew that I couldn't die at all, and that the most important thing to do was save myself. I bolted across the town to the house farthest from the boat landing. I stopped to vomit as I climbed a bamboo ladder, and then folded myself as small as I could behind a rice-filled *cambo*.

There I waited for the worst I could imagine. I had heard many stories from the vendors about the Japanese and the way they buried people up to their necks and left them in the sun, about the way they cut people apart with their bayonets before they died. They beat people who forgot to bow deeply to them; they burned towns. "Hapons very bad mans. Very bad," was the way each story ended.

I waited a long time, and then, exhausted, I curled up and fell asleep behind the *cambo*.

It was a long time before they found me. Colonel Fertig had arrived by guerrilla launch with news that a submarine would be here in a few days. He had a camera, and all of us who were going to be on it were gathering for picture taking.

The photograph shows me sulking, nestled against my mother, my head averted from the camera. I was happy that the Japanese had not come, but I was also angry that the adults had been so complacent.

November 11, 1943. A dog burst through the bamboo wall of the kitchen last night and ran off with the leg of pork Julio had so carefully cooked for Colonel Fertig's arrival at Esperanza. We served the last two chickens from Charlie's despedida gift instead. The Colonel had much to tell of former friends. He said we could try to send money and a message to Bob with Doctor Montalvan, the doctor who helped Douglass at Amparo. He goes frequently to Luzon as a guerrilla spy.

We tried to simulate a happy gathering, but there was a weight in each person's heart. Slanting shadows from a waning moon lay across the porch; the palms lisped and clicked in the river wind, and the wide band of the Wawa lay like a silver sash

upon the dark lands. Over all hung the shadow of war, of danger,
apprehension and uncertainty.

I know that the two of us were thinking, with a dull ache in
the breast, of Douglass staying here in the guerrilla, of our son
wherever he may be, and of Mary and me slipping away to sea in
a submarine in the wild hope of reaching Australia.

At dinner, Colonel Fertig spoke to the group,

"I wish I could stay longer with you all—it's really been wonderful to be with such a large group of friends of former days, but
I have a lot to get done before I can get you out of here. If your
means of escape really does rendezvous with us, I have to get a
crew organized that can move what comes in to places where it's
needed. I hope you'll interpret what I am saying, as I don't want
to speak directly. I'm sure you'll understand that. It's been a privilege to be with you, and good luck until we meet again."

Fertig left a letter with us that answered many of our questions:

November 9, 1943

To All Civilian Repatriates:

You are being repatriated as a result of some very
hard work on the part of the personnel of the armed
forces of the United States. It is requested that you show
your appreciation for these efforts by refraining from
discussing any military or guerrilla activities in the
Philippine Islands, especially those which have taken
place since the surrender of our forces on May 10, 1942.

The safety of our troops in the Tenth Military District may depend upon our ability to keep our activities out of the newspapers and off the radio until such

time as the War Department desires to release this information.

You will find that every effort has been made to make you as comfortable as possible under the circumstances, and that General MacArthur, who is responsible for the repatriation of civilians, has completed the necessary arrangements for your trip to your final destination.

With the kindest good wishes, and the hope that your stay in the Tenth District has left at least a few good memories, I am,

Sincerely yours,

Wendell Fertig

Colonel, AUS, Commanding

That night, there was another powerful earthquake. Our bamboo house swayed like a hammock. Outside, Filipinos tumbled from their houses and formed a human chain to keep anyone from falling into opening fissures.

It took a long time to get back to sleep after the disorienting shock of the earth being seized by such power. Just as I drifted off to sleep, I heard my father say to my mother, "Did you ever hear rapids here before? I hear the rivers."

In the morning, we found that the Wawa now joined the Agusan over a ripple of rapids. The two rivers no longer slipped together noiselessly as they had before.

<hr />

Once again, an earthquake meant change and movement as much for us as it did the land.

Lieutenant (bamboo rank) Frank Duff brought Colonel Fertig's message from Headquarters at Amparo the next evening to tell us to be ready to go to the rendezvous point early the next morning.

There was a separate note for my father, which made the escape much easier for my mother and me:

November 14, 1943

Dear McKay:

SWP [Southwest Pacific] advises that all husbands who are out of concentration should accompany wives at least to Australia. They are interested in getting some civilians down there who know the Philippines. In view of these instructions I believe it advisable that you plan on going out. You can undoubtedly report there and come back with the first wave.

Fertig

Julio leaned against the wall of José Pebillo's house when he heard we were going where he could not follow us. Tears slipped from his tightly shut eyes and slid down his cheeks. My mother gave him the *carahay* that he had used to cook our rice for so many months and the last bit of filter cloth from the mill at Gomoco, but still he wept. I hugged him, hoping to stop the tears, but he was inconsolable until my father gave him our brand-new *baroto*.

The tears stopped. Perhaps now Maria would change her mind when he came home in his own *baroto*, worldly, traveled, and rich.

The whole barrio of Esperanza knew we were leaving Japanese-occupied Mindanao long before the launch arrived at the rickety bamboo landing, which looked more like a fish trap than a pier. Everyone had seen American cigarettes and magazines that were coming in from Australia. There were pictures of MacArthur with "I Shall Return!" slogans almost everywhere by November of 1943.

"Good-byes" were likely to be forever.

Though they were sad to say good-bye that morning, the women begged us to give them anything we could spare. My mother opened her straw *tampipi* and gave away almost everything in it. She saved one dress and a pair of slacks to wear in Australia and gave away the rest. Her last two needles and a pair of sewing scissors went to our landlady, Mrs. Pebillo. I saw the *musang* skin and the letter opener Bob Crump had carved for her birthday in the pack as she tied it for the last time.

We traveled half a day down the river toward Butuan, stopping at Amparo, the Military headquarters. There, waiting for us, was a group of military men who will join us on our escape. Some of them are escapees from the Penal Colony. It's good they are young, because their faces show marks of great hardship. They will report to Australia, be retrained and, to a man, they say they want to come back to finish this war.

Our little launch became part hospital as men helped Jim Burchfield—he's fifteen now—carry Evelyn aboard and lay her on a rattan cot. Helpless from a long illness of typhoid fever, her emaciated body has no strength to support her undernourished frame. Jim is tired and serious beyond his years; he has looked after his mother all alone for too long.

The launch, with its new passengers, headed toward the sea. The river was wider now and brown. We hugged the curving riverbank with its protective overgrowth, turning often in the river delta. I realized that the launch that had frightened me a few days before had followed these same curves and that was why the engine's sound had not been steady.

We passed Butuan, now battered and burned after many battles between the guerrillas and the Japanese. The once-tidy town was not as I remembered it. Helen Welbon gasped when she saw the skeleton of her prewar house. She had lived near the river and the sawmill where her husband made lumber out of logs that his partner, Nelson Kellogg, had sent down the Agusan in the days before the Japanese had stopped the old life in the tropics. Helen was leaving for Australia without Roy, who was going to work as a radio operator for the guerrillas. She knew her life would never be the same again.

Soon after passing Butuan, we came onto the open sea and turned west toward the barrio of Nasipit on Butuan Bay. I stood on the tiny deck of the launch and felt an unfamiliar sea breeze on my face. The glare off the open sea was dazzling, but I scanned the waters, both hands curved over my eyebrows, looking for the periscope of the American submarine I was sure was nearby.

Others were scanning the sea, too, but they were looking out for a Japanese patrol boat. The Japanese were regular in their habits, and the crew of our boat was reasonably sure that we were crossing the sea at a safe time of day. I didn't think of being afraid; all this was too exciting, but the adults knew more than I did and were uneasy and very quiet.

The sun dried the salt on my lips and I licked them often, partly to moisten them and partly to taste the salt. Captain Martin stood beside me as we chugged toward Nasipit.

"You shouldn't lick your lips out here, Mary. They'll get chapped and maybe bleed," he said.

I had never heard of chapped lips. It was another new phrase.

Late in the afternoon, sharp-prowed outriggers met our little boat and took us through the breakers to the beach at Nasipit. The fishermen held their *bancas* steady in the sea as we climbed from the launch to the smaller boats. They paddled hard until we beached on dry land. These coastal boatmen had different skills from the men who boated on the inland rivers; they knew about tides and surf, and our *grumetes* knew shoals and currents. I don't know how Mrs. Burchfield got ashore. Perhaps Jim carried her again.

Lieutenant Duff led us through the desolated village of Nasipit. Tall *tigbao* grass grew in the streets after two years of war. Long feathery plumes waved over our heads as we followed our leader to a house on a bluff above the bay. The ground floor of the house had been a Japanese *sari sari* store. The bare room and glassless cases were not as pleasant as the walled patio behind it, and we drifted outside.

Soon three rocks over a fire were supporting a boiling coffeepot, and the patio filled with all of us who waited to escape.

There was still no word from Wendell Fertig. We waited, not knowing how we would meet a submarine, or when, or even if we would meet one.

There was rice cooking over the fire when the sound of a powerful engine—a very powerful engine—set up a roar through the quiet town. The sound simply began. It hadn't come from a distance.

Someone yelled, "It's the sub!"

We ran through the *tigbao* grass to the end of the bluff, and there, in the sea hammered golden by the sunset, was the ship we waited for. Water still drained from her decks as she made her way carefully to the concrete pier on the deep-water side of the point. She was black and menacing, alert sailors on deck manning her guns.

"Isn't she beautiful," someone whispered.

"Oh, yes . . . ," came the answer.

She wasn't beautiful. She was low in the water, her conning tower abruptly breaking the line of her deck. She was built for war and for stealth, but this day she was a miracle—our dream of escape from violent death by bayonet, or a slow death by disease—come to life.

The submarine disappeared from sight as she rounded the point and drew up to the pier just below us.

My impulse was to follow and never lose sight of the ship again, but we had to stay at the sari-sari *store until the ship was unloaded and we could embark. We straggled back to rekindle the fire, make more coffee and curb our impatience as best we could. Night had come; the firelight shone on the faces around the fire and lit the faces of curious natives gathered in an outer ring.*

The people around that fire had many stories to tell. Three of the men were Marines who had survived the Bataan Death March, then had escaped from a labor camp on Mindanao. They joined the guerrillas and were now going home to be the first to tell the story of the brutal days after the fall of Bataan where young men, who were marched in the heat from Bataan to a brutal prison camp, collapsed from thirst and hunger and were beaten to death by their captors.

There were two sailors from a PT boat—one still wore his white sailor hat, now dingy, at a rakish angle. They claimed their PT boat sank two Japanese cruisers before they lost it in battle and they began a two-year-long trek from Cebu to Nasipit. Two of the Norwegian sailors from the *Ravenaas* were there. Now, two years after their ship sank on December 8, 1941, they spoke a little English; but they still held aloof in the background like Indians. Later, I learned that some of the military men were unstable and were being repatriated by Fertig to get them out of his way, but that others were being sent home because they were too weakened by two years in the jungle to be of service to the guerrilla army.

There were eight of us who had started out at Gomoco: the Burchfields, Glenda and Stevie, Helen Welbon and the three of us, and eight others who had come to wait at Esperanza.

There would be thirty-two extra people aboard a submarine built lean for war.

"She must be a big ship if she can take all of us aboard," someone said.

"I heard she's one of two extralarge subs built for carrying cargo. She's got close to a hundred tons aboard. We'll be here a couple of days, I bet, waiting till they get it all on the trails out of here."

Then a man in the whitest shirt I had seen in two years came into the circle around the fire. He was Chick Parsons, a friend from prewar days in Manila—the first person from the outside world I had seen since the war began.

Tired and weary grown-ups had been my companions for two years. They wore handmade shoes and faded, patched clothes. Here was a man who buzzed with good health. His smile shone white in a tanned face. He wore shiny leather shoes. He was confident and strong, not cautious like those of us who had survived two years of defeat.

My parents stood stock-still. I pulled on my mother's skirt. "Mommy, it's the man who taught me to swim!"

"Chick!" My mother spoke first. "I can't believe this. Are you really here?"

He gave her a quick hug and then shook hands with my father, who was unable to speak. His mouth opened to speak and then tears rolled down his cheeks. I learned then that tears can show the deepest emotions a man can feel.

Commander Charles Parsons of the U.S. Navy joined us at our campfire and shared a cup of our ersatz coffee without a grimace. He told us that the Red Cross would meet us in Australia, and that we would be there until we were all strong and healthy. Then perhaps we would get home to the States. He had worked on organizing our escape since his return to Australia after his first trip into Mindanao the previous April. He would be staying this time again, and would see us in Australia on his next time there.

I looked around the gathering and saw that no one could believe that the wait was almost over. Even when we heard and saw the submarine, the moment seemed unreal. Now that a man many of us had known before the Japanese had changed our lives was really with us, we could begin to believe that we might soon be safe. My father's tears still made his blue eyes bright, but now he seemed a little giddy. My sober, serious father was animated and happy!

"Now," the good friend said, "you can go down to the pier any time you're ready."

I was wild to see the submarine up close, to be near it and to hear it, but my parents felt a sudden need to write another message to my brother. Chick Parsons had a network that reached Manila, and perhaps a farewell message would reach him.

By the flickering light of a stubby candle, Douglass and I tried to fit words together in a letter to be given Bob if we never reach Australia. We tried to tell him about insurance policies, and bank accounts. It was difficult to be coherent, but we closed the letter with a flourish of brave words and I felt better about leaving.

⟹•◆•⟸

We gathered our things and walked down the white coral road, which was shining in the moonlight. The night rippled with excitement. I skipped beside my parents, ran ahead, then came back to them. The road to the submarine seemed longer than the rivers we had traveled.

We heard the activity on the pier before we saw it. Bright lights run by the sub's generators cast wavering shadows of palm trees on the road and flickered behind the tree trunks. I heard men grunt as they caught the weight of their loads. Officers called directions to men, who ran with their loads up the hill past us. Other men ran down the hill to claim another load.

The brightest lights I could remember lit the pier.

Yellow lamplight and soft candlelight had been my companions; tonight I was seeing blue-white light that made me squint. The night outside the light was blacker than ever, though a lopsided moon hung in the sky.

An endless line of American sailors in blue denim carried off the ship cases of sending and receiving sets for the coast watchers. There were replacement parts for radios, too, because the submarines were supplying, mainly, the coast-watching efforts of the guerrillas. Cameras and film from Australia, along with orders to take pictures of the beaches and terrain of Mindanao, landed in the hands of guerrilla officers. Then came crates of guns and ammunition. My mother hated the guns, even though they might win the war; they were meant for killing, she said. Medicines (among them antimalarial atabrine, which would soon turn the guerrillas yellow), bandages, cases of cigarettes, flashlight batteries, and mantles for Coleman lamps landed on the dock. Typewriters, typewriter ribbons, and carbon paper appeared, for even an ad hoc Army has paperwork. Magazines and books and pictures of General MacArthur came up the ladder of the conning tower for propaganda.

Millions of pesos in counterfeit Japanese occupation money came to undermine the wartime economy. Printing plates and paper arrived, too, so that the guerrillas could print legal currency of their own.

Shoes and clothing, so scarce now in the Islands after two years of war, served as dunnage to keep the angular boxes from shifting in the submarine's curved interior. Bags of denims and blue Navy shirts and lengths of cotton came off the ship and replaced the tattered clothes of the guerrillas. I saw a sailor give a man his shirt.

It seemed like chaos, but there was a plan. Colonel Fertig of Mindanao, Colonel Kangleon, the guerrilla leader from Leyte, and Major Ingeniero, from Bohol, oversaw hundreds of men who loaded their shares into *bancas* and *lorchas* for trips across the Visayan Sea. *Cargadores* carried it out on the trails to the interior of Mindanao.

A fifteen-piece band in white uniforms was a classic example of Filipino flair. The arrival of a submarine carrying precious supplies was an Occasion. Occasions must be celebrated properly and formally. Therefore a band wearing clean, starched, and pressed uniforms must play American songs and marches to make the Americans know that the Filipinos appreciate the moment.

"Anchors Aweigh" blasted cheerily as we came onto the pier, followed by "The Stars and Stripes Forever." I overheard two officers:

"Where the hell are we? Hollywood? Jesus, the Japs could be anywhere and they strike up a band! I'll be glad to get out of here; that's for sure. This place gives me the creeps."

"Me, too, we're only six air miles from the closest Japs," said his friend.

Then a sailor said to me, "Are you coming with us? It's going to be an amazing trip with kids on board!"

He gave me a Hershey Bar. Melty and sweet, it coated the roof of my mouth and slid down my throat slowly. Sweet as sugarcane juice, but smooth and thick, it made my cheeks ache as the saliva responded to a long-forgotten taste.

Sweating sailors took a moment from the unloading to buy souvenirs from the Filipinos. They bought *bolos* and baskets, and the Filipinos were delighted to get American money. My mother caught the fever; she bought a pair of carved and brightly painted wooden clogs that she would never need.

I bought a pair of fancy bakya with hand-woven abaca bands to hold them to the feet. It would be I—who had been the one to buy goldfish, parrots, cats and cockatoos—to buy something frivolous!

We refugees sat on our straw suitcases, clutching our bundles and watching the scene. A box went by labeled "Sulfaguanadine."

"What's Sulfaguanadine, Mommy?" I asked.

"I don't know, dear. Maybe it's a new medicine. Before the war, there was a new drug called Sulfanilimide, but I never heard of this one. There are probably lots of things at home we've never heard about."

Colonel Fertig came over to say good-bye.

"Well, Mac, have a good trip," he said to my father. "We'll see you back here in a few months, I guess. Give the boys Down Under all the news, and come back to finish the job."

"Quite a scene here, Colonel," my father said.

"Well, it turned out all right, but I'll tell you I lost some sleep after that earthquake. I didn't know what had happened to this dock, and the sub was too close to turn away. There should be some sandwiches along in a minute."

He was right. One of the galley crew arrived with a huge platter of ham sandwiches. Right behind him, a sailor carried Cokes. At first we couldn't touch the food. It was hard to realize that we were looking at bread made with yeast, at fresh green lettuce, at mayonnaise and mustard, at wasp-waisted bottles of Coke.

Then we reached out, chose, and bit. Rich, tangy, familiar, the sandwich was too rich. I couldn't eat more than three bites. I couldn't swallow the Coke, either. It stung my mouth, and the bubbles hurt my nose. It was too sweet.

"Mommy, what should I do with this? I can't eat it. Rice is better."

"Just put it down. It's all right."

The fatty ham sandwich and the Coke lay heavily on the Hershey Bar. I sat miserably by my parents waiting for the last boxes to come off the ship. It was close to midnight, and the day had begun a long time ago.

"I'm going to be sick!"

Afterward I felt better and wondered how I was going to do without rice and *camotes*.

"Okay, let's go!" The order came at midnight, on schedule. We picked up our bundles to walk toward the ship. The scene was lit by smoky palm-leaf torches and flickering flashlights now that the ship's lights were back on board.

Commander Latta was at the gangplank to welcome us to his ship, *Narwhal*.

"Are you Mary?" asked the captain. "We're going to have a good trip with you aboard! We'll do our best to make you like your ride with us."

We turned right and walked along the ribbed deck to the ladder of the conning tower.

The band played "God Bless America" as we boarded the submarine. "Philippines, My Philippines" rang out as I climbed the gray-painted steel ladder. Then, with a last look at the dark land, I descended into a white-painted metal world.

———⊳◦⊲———

We dropped down the ladder into the control room, which contained a mass of dials too confusing to focus on. The civilians walked to the forward torpedo room. The military men and the two Norwegian sailors turned in the other direction and went aft.

We went along the companionway, passing the wardroom, the galley on the right, the officers' rooms on the left, then through a thick bulkhead, down a couple of steps, and into the torpedo room.

Our new home.

The first things I saw were four shining copper hatches at the far end of the room, two on each side of the hull. One above the other, they covered the tubes where the torpedoes lay waiting for enemy ships. There were only two torpedoes to replace the ones in the tubes. The sub was stripped to carry supplies into the Islands and was traveling lightly armed.

The space that had recently held boxes of ammunition was filled now with cots made up for us. Evelyn Burchfield, too sick to stand, had been strapped to a chair and let down through the fore escape and intake hatch. As we came into the room, I saw her in her chair, being surrounded by our bundles as the sailors brought them on board.

My bunk nestled in the ribs of the curving hull and above the torpedo on the rails leading to the torpedo hatch. My father's was wedged under an elbow pipe, and my mother slept in a row of three cots, head-to-foot, that lined the passageway between the torpedoes and the rest of the ship.

Trolleys and pulleys ran along the edge of the room and were used to move torpedoes into place. I was taking in the steel ribs of the hull curving over me when the engines came to life. There was no way to tell that we were moving, but I knew we were leaving Mindanao. Maybe forever.

November 15, 1943. Mary and Douglass are completely at ease. I wonder why I do not feel afraid. The frantic urge for exit that I had feared hasn't seized me. I am holding Mary's anting-anting. Native women in Esperanza gave her the charm, a spent bullet on a fine chain necklace made of wild boar's hairs, and said, "This is for you, Mary. It will keep you safe." Perhaps it is well I am leaving this land of spirits and superstition, of belief in diwatas and wak-waks.

There was no time to settle into bed. I went with the others to the wardroom for a briefing on how to travel by submarine.

Captain Latta told us that he and his crew were happy to be on the unusual mission of bringing civilians out of occupied Philippines.

"You are the first group of women to be taken out of the Islands. We have taken civilian men but never women and children. If you can take the heat and hardship of this voyage, then we'll know we can rescue other families, too. I think you can take it. Look what you've been through already!

"I hope you clearly understand that you are on a warship whose mission is to attack and sink enemy ships. We will go after any targets we find, regardless of your presence. I ask you now, in case of enemy contact, to be quiet, calm, and to stay out of the crew's way.

"I am sorry that the decks are off-limits to the passengers; we need to be ready for battle at any moment. We spend most of our time, I assure you, cruising peacefully on the surface. Please read our magazines and books, use our games. I hope you have a pleasant voyage. If you find the torpedo room hot, please feel free to use an officer's cabin if there's one empty. They are cooler. Now, I am sure you are tired. We always have a trim dive at five A.M. You'll be wakened by two blasts on the horn. The trim-dive hour is not far off. Good night."

Captain Latta gives me courage. He is so calm and so much in command of his ship. The crew respects him and now I know we'll be safe. After he said good night, a young blushing officer explained to the women that only the thinnest of paper could go into the head. His fellow officers leaned in the door, delighted by his embarrassment. Then he showed us how to flush the head. There was a chart with complicated directions, and I had the feeling that I could bring the whole Pacific Ocean aboard and sink the ship if I made a mistake.

There is no water for bathing, except "condensate." The women can use the officers' cabins for dressing, and are invited to eat their meals at the officers' mess.

After the trim dive, any other dive during the day means that we are either hiding or attacking.

Mary went to sleep in her bunk high on the ribs of the hull. She was disappointed that there were no portholes. She had so counted on watching the fish.

"BLEEEAGH! BLEEEAGH!" At five A.M., the ship tilted and settled into its morning dive. Our ears felt the pressure, and we sat up in our bunks waggling wide-open jaws. It was a funny sight, seeing so many people wrapped in sheets and sitting up in bed singing a soundless song.

In about twenty minutes, the siren sounded again, the ship tipped upward toward the surface, and we took our turns in the wardroom for breakfast. Hot oatmeal with butter and sugar! I had forgotten. Corn Flakes. Bacon. Strawberry jam.

Then we all took our turns visiting the pharmacist's mate. He had thought he would find a group of weak and sickly people to take care of and was amazed to find us so well after our two years in the jungle. I did have a tiny tropical ulcer on one leg, though. Ulcers were hard to get rid of where I had come from; they usually just got bigger and deeper, and they indicated that a person's resistance to infection was low. When the pharmacist treated my sore, it was the first time I had seen Band-Aids with a little red string to tear the wrapper. His magic salve and the good food we ate cured the ulcer in a few days.

The wardroom became our hangout. Off-duty officers slid onto banquettes behind the green-baize tables and drank coffee that waited, always hot, on an electric plate. (An electric plate!) When the men were going back to the bridge at night, they wore red goggles to keep their eyes used to seeing in the dark.

One night, when the men knew us a little, they told us how they almost didn't get to Nasipit to get us. A Japanese cruiser spotted them in the Mindanao Sea the day before they were to be at the rendezvous. Narwhal *endured several hours of depth-charging, and then nearly was lost when she came in to shore. She ran aground in the uncharted inlet and only a high tide and some expert blowing of the forward tanks got her free. They said they were about to scuttle her and join us in the jungles!*

I played Cribbage and Hearts with the men in the wardroom. Our cards at Gomoco had been limp and worn; the submarine's cards were crisp, and I could shuffle them like a Reno gambler. I stunned the officers when I shot the moon in a game of Hearts, and they played more warily after that. "That's some nine-year-old," one young officer muttered, but he didn't know how many hours I had spent playing cards under a mosquito net at Gomoco.

November 16, 1943. Major Dobervich, a Marine, happened into the wardroom in the afternoon. He is one of the ten men who escaped from the Davao Penal Colony after being taken prisoner when Bataan fell. He told us more about the brutality of the Japs toward our soldiers. They used our boys as slave labor, they beat

them, gave them no medicines, fed them vermin for food. Here
below the waterline of an unknown sea I heard, firsthand, details
of cruelty and torture on the Bataan Death March that the world
knows nothing about.

I got better about eating rich foods. Grilled-cheese sandwiches, lettuce, ham, fresh bread, and cherry pie made in the
galley all made me feel like a princess in a fairy tale where every
wish comes true.

In just a few days, *camotes* and greens faded from my mind.

The women took turns washing dishes in the galley to make
up for the extra work we caused. My mother and I filled the sink
with hot running water (hot running water!) from a faucet (a
faucet!) and filled the sink with soapsuds. We plunged our arms
up to the elbows in the bubbles and washed the plates over and
over again just for the fun of it.

The second day at sea we had a tour of the ship. We saw the
four noisy engines—named Matthew, Mark, Luke, and John by
the crew—that drove the ship on the surface of the sea. There
were huge, silent batteries that powered the submarine when it
was submerged. I looked through the periscope, turning it full
circle, and looked for a ship. All I saw was a gray sea, its surface
gathered into little rippling waves.

The periscope was in the center of the control room rimmed
by panels of red and green lights and dials that the men called
the Christmas tree. All the lights on the Christmas tree had to be
green before the command "Take 'er down!" could be obeyed.

We saw crates of supplies in the cold rooms and fresh
pineapples and bananas that had come from Mindanao. The
sailors were happy to have fresh fruit, but they never knew
what a sacrifice it had been for the Filipinos to give it.

November 17, 1943. I asked Charlie Eckart, who had duty in the forward torpedo room, if he had thought he would have to put up with a bunch of hysterical women when he learned that his ship was going in for rescue work.

"Yes, I did at first, but now I think all of you could take it with the rest of us, and even if you knew we were lost, you wouldn't turn a hair."

Charlie's alternate was George Zelina, who sat with his back to us all day reading adventure stories. He didn't like us, said that he had joined the submarine fleet to get away from women, and here he was on a submarine full of them.

My mother, who had lived with my quiet father and knew how to coax a silent man to talk, finally got George to tell us that he thought we had been stupid to stay in the Philippines when a war with Japan had been so obviously on the horizon.

"You should have left when you could," George said. "You got yourselves in a jam that the U.S. Navy has to risk a ship and crew to get you out of."

Charlotte Martin and my mother told him that MacArthur himself had told them there was no reason to leave the Islands because any war the Japanese might dare to start would be a short one and over in less than a month. George softened a little then, and turned his chair to face his motley crewmates who hung feminine laundry in his torpedo room.

Before I left the ship, he gave me his submarine pin. I suppose he didn't think it was my fault that I had been caught in a war.

The third day out, in the Molucca Sea, we felt the pressure of submarine warfare. We neared a Japanese convoy and, spotted by the enemy, suddenly dived. We stayed underwater for a long time.

November 18, 1943. Tension in the air, following us down companionways, sitting with us at meals and staring back from the eyes of fellow passengers. The crewmen are busy and have no time for us. We are off Halmahera and are chasing a convoy. Books, bridge, nothing holds the attention.

Helen Welbon went to her bunk and turned toward the wall, curled into a large ball. I thought she was a terrible coward.

The Japanese planes made a dolphin of *Narwhal*. The double horn "Submerge!" sounded many times that afternoon. When a single sound of the horn, "All Clear," sounded, relief spread among us as we reached the surface of the sea. The waters, though, were filled with enemy ships and aircraft, and soon the double sound of the horn would send us down again.

I watched the sailors, usually so cheerful and happy to spend time with me, become professional and serious as they ran to their battle stations. I could see them relax when an All Clear sounded. The grown-ups I had known so long were quiet, too. Cards were dealt in a Bridge game, but they lay unsorted as the players waited for an "All Clear" or heard another "Take 'er down!"

I am in the Ward Room, riffling the pages of a magazine, not having any luck at reading it. I was invited to play Bridge, but I cannot concentrate. Neither can the players, I notice, though they are trying. Captain Latta appeared in the doorway just now. He stood there a while, playing with a yellow pencil, and finally said, "You are on borrowed time, and it's not over yet. You signed on to this trip with us and you should know the situation." As he turned to go back to the command of his ship, I thought of Lorca's poem about the bullfighter: "At five in the afternoon. It was ex-

actly at five in the afternoon. The rest was death, and death alone at five in the afternoon." How will it come, by depth charges? By bombs? Long, slow suffocation? I must be numb, for I don't feel very different. I just reach for my lipstick. Courage is of the heart and soul, but a dash of red on pallid lips can keep courage alive.

Later, after it was all over, Captain Latta told us what he meant by "borrowed time." We had surfaced once in a rain-squall and could no longer see the Japanese ships. Captain Latta continued his hunt anyway; he was commander of an attack ship in wartime, and hunting the enemy was his duty. Planes pursued us, and, as we neared the convoy again, we were attacked. Four men came through the hatch in five seconds before one of the dives and saw Japanese torpedoes coming at us as they ran for the ladder. Two "tin fish" missed our stern, one by twenty feet and the other only by a little more.

We borrowed time twice that Thursday—once when the torpedoes just missed us and again when the ship went out of control and plunged to more than three hundred and fifty feet during a dive. The pressure made the ship creak, the captain told my father; and a column in the middle of the ship, bigger than I could put my arms around, bent visibly, paint chipping, before the ship stopped plunging toward the bottom.

After I heard the story from my father, I looked at the column and saw the chipping paint.

Captain Latta and I shared the disappointment of losing a chance to sink a Japanese ship: he because sinking ships was his mission, and I because I thought I should be witness to more than just a ride on a submarine! I had been two years in a war and had seen only three bombs fall silently in the distance. I wanted my submarine to sink a Japanese ship on my voyage.

After that day, the voyage was never again as dangerous. We were nearing friendly waters.

I discovered a phonograph in one of the crewmen's cabins. I played "You Are My Sunshine" over and over and over. It was a new song for me, and I couldn't stop hearing it just one more time. The men gave me the run of most of the ship and rummaged in their duffel bags to give me presents. I still have a silk hat ribbon that says *"S. S. Narwhal"* and George's submariner pin.

Stevie Crytser was two and a half and was missing a lot of the time. Several times a day, he rode back to his mother on a strong sailor's back. "I'm bringing this kid back to you, ma'am! I think he was AWOL!"

Friday, November 19. "Clear Sailing" was the report from the bridge and we had only the routine morning trim dive. It was a surprise, then, to hear the siren again in the late afternoon. Then a voice came over the loudspeaker: "This is Father Neptune welcoming you to the Southern Hemisphere. I now proclaim you Trusty Shellbacks!" In a way, we ducked the Equator and did not cross it at all, for we had dived under it!

Saturday: Navy beans for breakfast, an old Navy tradition. Reports from the watch say they took pictures of small outrigger fishing boats manned by natives with black curly hair. Land was visible in the Banda Sea, perhaps Amboina. A huge three-tiered white birthday cake came from the Galley to Lieutenant Jonathan Hine, who said he would have to eat double for his twin who was flying over New Guinea.

On Sunday, my mother went up onto the bridge to see the sunrise.

The other women had been invited to go up on deck, but not me. I thought I had been forgotten by the commander; but finally the call came and I could go up the conning tower again. I had been below water level for nearly a week and now I was out in the wind and sun again. How glorious to feel the wind in my face! The Arafura Sea was an opalescent pearl, rimmed with clouds piled on the horizon. The sun split the mists with daggers of light that struck the sea. I looked down the long black hull of the ship, her guns menacing and powerful, and saw the wake churning behind us. Then a danger signal shortened my stay, and I ran for the hatch. We submerged that time for 35 minutes.

I didn't think it was fair for the grown women to be allowed on deck when I could run and climb faster and better than they could. No one invited me to go on deck, though I waited for a special favor.

On Monday night, November 22, 1943, we came in to Port Darwin, Australia.

———⊰•◆•⊱———

Exactly a week after *Narwhal* had come into sight at Nasipit, at six in the evening of November 22, 1943, we were on deck amidships, our bundles at our feet, watching the red hills of Australia and the broken, bombed buildings of Darwin grow blurry in the dimming light. When an Australian special-purpose vessel, the *Chinampa*, drew alongside, *Narwhal*'s men were at their deck guns.

We had spent two years hiding from the Japanese, but now that we were in Australia where we felt safe, we found we were top secret. Instead of sailing directly into Darwin Harbor, we went farther west. The captain watched for a single light in the darkness; one minute later, another light blinked, and a small cabin cruiser approached us.

When the Australians gave the correct codes, lines tied the two vessels together, and we crossed over to the Australians.

"Good-bye, don't forget me!" called a sailor.

"Stevie, gimme a smile!"

We didn't want to leave that miracle ship, and there were tears from many of us as we herded onto the deck of the smaller one, but there was no time for sentiment.

Captain Latta saluted us all, and *Narwhal* slid quickly out of sight in the black sea. Within three days, she began her eighth war patrol and was on her way back to Mindanao.

A doctor and two nurses met us on board the Chinampa as we left the Narwhal. We surprised them, too, with our relatively good health. They were ready for stretcher cases. Even our sick lady, Evelyn Burchfield, could walk off the Narwhal after seven days of Navy food!

The smaller boat brought us to shallow water, and we moved to boats that could land us on a beach. Javanese, whose heads were wrapped in batik turbans, rowed the dinghies onto the pebbly shore. Nothing surprised me anymore, but the memory of those dark men with high cheekbones in the flickering night is sharp.

The lanterns moving on the shore threw wild shadows from the mangrove trees. I walked up a path in the steaming hot night holding my mother's hand and met a cloud of buzzing gnats that tried to climb into my eyes.

A light shining in the dark led us to the Officers' Club of the "Lugger Maintenance Station" outside of Darwin, where the Allied Intelligence Bureau (AIB) organized and equipped the secret submarine trips to occupied Pacific Islands.

On the screened veranda, gnats danced around electric lights and made cotton-candy halos around them. We tried to push the gnats away from our faces with a quick wave of a hand. British officers welcomed us, delighted to see, at last, the people they had worked so many weeks to bring out of Japanese territory.

Cold drinks came on trays, followed by mutton sandwiches and pickles. The night was oppressively hot; there was no escaping the torment of the gnats, though we swatted at them constantly. One of the officers congratulated us on learning the "Darwin salute" without any instruction at all.

Then we met Colonel Allison Ind, who was in charge of *Narwhal*'s mission. He was a member of the Allied Intelligence Bureau, the organization coordinating clandestine operations in the Pacific.

For the first time, we heard the other side of our story: how plans for the rescue were made in Australia, and how complex those plans were. Our arrival at Darwin was completely secret. Secrecy required us to get out of Darwin before dawn the next morning and before anyone saw us anywhere near the secret "Lugger Maintenance Station."

"We'll be taking you by air to Brisbane, and then to a Red Cross hostel north of there, where we'll feed you up and get you ready to go home on a troopship! Any word of where you came from, or how you got to Australia, will jeopardize the people left in the Islands—both guerrillas and civilians. The Japanese have promised to kill three prisoners for every one person who escapes."

A terrible cry escaped my mother.

"Why didn't you tell us this before we left? My son is still there! I would never have put him in danger like this if I'd known. Oh my God, I didn't know!"

In all the war, this was the only time I saw her near hysteria. She had left her son in the Islands, only to be told that the Japanese would take reprisal for our eluding them. My father must have known this, but he made no move to comfort her. The crease between his eyebrows deepened, and he put his finger to his lips.

I knew I would never tell who we were, or how we got to Australia—no matter who asked me. I could protect my big brother from the Japanese by my silence. It was important.

A U.S. Army doctor and nurse had flown from Brisbane to care for us, though only Mrs. Burchfield needed immediate attention. Lieutenant Willa Hook, who had herself escaped from Corregidor by submarine in 1942, led the women to a back veranda where nine cots, sheets tightly pulled over them and mosquito nets waiting to enfold us, were lined up in the half light.

A Red Cross kit sat precisely in the middle of each cot. A folded scratchy gray blanket was folded around a gray woolen bathrobe, lipsticks, and toothbrushes. My kit had a strange little suit made of cotton flannelette that wouldn't have fit a monkey.

I loved, however, the brand-new toothbrush wrapped in cellophane. My last one, from the Chinese store in Rosario, had worn out long before we left Mindanao. For a long time I had been rubbing my teeth with a finger dipped in salt. The new brush was strong and made my teeth feel clean. The sweet taste of mint lasted in my mouth a long time. I decided that I liked toothpaste much better than salt.

We lined up for roll call before the sun came up and climbed into military ambulances to go to the airstrip. We ate cold sandwiches as we bounced along a broken road. There were strange-looking trees in the graying light, and broken buildings of the airport destroyed by Japanese bombs in 1942 were black silhouettes as the sky lightened.

There was no building at the airport; we waited at the edge of a field that stretched off in every direction. A plane sitting under a chicken-wire net covered with a few branches was a Liberator named "Old Hickory." The soldiers who had spent two years as guerrillas ran to touch her.

We waited, numbly patient and exhausted. The sun came up; the heat got worse. We waited. Finally two dots in the sky became two C-47s that landed near us. The pilots got out, stretched, and yawned while the crew carried our bags aboard and laid mattresses on the steel deck.

The soldiers went aboard "Cold Turkey," and the civilians climbed into "Hairless Joe." The mattresses were the only amenity aboard that cargo plane, aside from a steel bench along the plane's right side.

"Have your blankets ready!" called Nurse Hook. "You'll need them."

The heat was pounding on the metal skin of the plane, and I didn't even want to touch my blanket. I sat on the hard bench next to my father and watched our ascent over the red land. Always the geologist, he showed me mineral deposits far below.

"That rosy color," he said, "might be cinnabar—that's mercury ore."

I remembered the tragic day at Gomoco when the last thermometer broke. I had played with the mercury, an impossibly heavy drop that tickled as it rolled around in the hollow of my palm. I broke the drop into tiny droplets and gathered them again into one big ball like globules of fat on the surface of soup.

Later he pointed out an orange color on the land below. "Iron deposits," he said, but by now I was too cold and sleepy to stay with him, and I curled up on a mattress at his feet and slept.

November 23, 1943. Dark trees lining dry riverbeds wind their aimless courses across the withered plains. It seems uninhabited and uninhabitable, changeless and unchangeable. Below us a great stillness prevails, broken only by a spiraling whirlwind and our own flying shadow.

The plane landed and rumbled over a rough field. We were at Cloncurry in the middle of the Australian continent. The heat blasted us and the glare blinded us as we walked to the airport mess hall. Australian desert heat is different from tropical heat; this heat made me cringe and want to cry.

It was hard to eat mutton and potatoes and canned beans in the hot metal hut; but the IXL brand of gooseberry jam was familiar from before the war, and I filled up on bread and jam.

On the second half of our two-thousand-mile trip across Northern Australia, we knew to be near as many blankets as possible when the cold attacked as we rose into the sky.

I watched idly, as if from windows of another world, as Nurse Hook's firm fingers braided Mary's long, fair hair in tight French braids that pulled her eyes up at the corners. Mary was so sleepy that her nodding head jerked against the strands of hair in Willa's hands, each bob of her head waked her a little less until I covered her with a Red Cross blanket and she joined the other blanket-wrapped cocoons on the mattresses.

The pilot left the cockpit to check on us and said, "This is absolute zero for being without oxygen masks!" I was cold to the core of my being. Now I, too, joined the sleepers.

———◆———

There is a river laced with bridges in Brisbane. There are houses with red-tiled roofs. As our olive-drab bus moved through the city on our way north, I saw cars honking in traffic, people wearing shoes walking on sidewalks. They had no idea how extraordinary they were.

Colonel Courtney Whitney, an old friend from Manila days, now Chief of Guerrilla Operations for the Philippines; Colonel Pete Grimm, also from Manila; and Alex Taylor of Ilo Ilo were foremost in the delegation to meet us at Brisbane. There was an ambulance from the 42nd General Hospital ready to take over immediate care of the sick. They had all anxiously awaited our arrival, for we were the first group of Americans from the surrendered Philippines.

Tears were in our eyes, but we would not break to weeping. There were tears, too, in the eyes of Army officers who met us and who had known by coded messages of our perilous voyage. To reach out and touch the hands and hear the voices of friends whom we had known on the other side of war's chasm was indeed moving.

Our first thought was to find Bob through the Red Cross. The latest bamboo telegraph had told us he was in Santo Tomás, but his name was not on that list—or any list of prisoners. Courtney Whitney could not find him on any military lists, either. The Chief of the Red Cross offered to start a search in the

Berne office in Switzerland, but he said that the search could take eight or nine months. I said sadly, "Never mind. A search might be dangerous for him. We can't dare bring his name to the Japs' attention now, can we, Douglass?"

Our second thought was to send a cable home announcing our safety. "No," Courtney Whitney said, "I'm sorry, but you forget you are a military secret. No one must know where you came from or how you got here." Orders—and honor—keep us silent. We are orphans again, this time in custody of the Red Cross.

Everything in Australia was different from the Philippines. The trees had pale trunks that shed their bark in long strips. Some trees had a smoky haze of leaves. The spicy smell of eucalyptus filled my nose. The road led us north along the coast past the Glass House Mountains, cores of ancient volcanoes carved to strange shapes by time. It was amazing to me to be able to see long distances; the jungle had enclosed me for so long.

As we came closer to the beach town where we would stay, the edges of the road were sandy white with red-stemmed plants that I had never seen before.

It was the Red Cross's mission to bring us back to the world, and they picked a perfect place. They rented two boarding-houses in Caloundra, seventy miles north of Brisbane, from two enormously fat Irish spinsters who were monumentally genteel. The sisters invited us to tea now and then while we lived there, confiding once to my mother that they "tended to run to fat."

The sisters had solved the Australian gnat problem by crocheting doilies weighted with tiny seashells along the edges. The sisters Corcoran covered every glass and teacup with a dainty doily made by their pudgy fingers.

I wondered, as I drank sweet tea and listened to their idle talk, how they had bent over on the beach to collect the shells for their doilies.

My father didn't respond to the good food and easy life the way the rest of us did and soon went to Brisbane for more medical attention and to be "debriefed" by the Army there. One day he came back to see us, but I ran away in tears and couldn't talk to him. The Army dentists had pulled out all his aching teeth, and he was waiting for the new ones. He wasn't my father; his attempts to keep his face from collapsing reminded me of the ancient toothless women of Mindanao who had squatted beneath their houses and smoked their small cigars with the lighted ends burning inside their mouths. They had been beyond my comprehension; and now, it seemed, so was he.

December 10, 1943. Douglass is optimistic about his health, and once the infection from his teeth is gone and he has told the authorities all they want to know about the Islands, he will go back. I don't think I can bear it when I have to say good-bye. If only he could be here with us enjoying this lovely place. I know he won't relax until he has the mine running and producing gold the way it was in '41.

The beach, where long even combers rolled, was only a run over a white dune. I learned to catch the waves and ride them onto the sand. In that long Australian summer, we swam at night under the stars, phosphorescence glowing around our bodies.

My mother pointed out the Southern Cross and other constellations we had never seen before. We watched the water go down the bathroom drain the opposite way from the Northern

Hemisphere. We thought that we remembered water going down the drain clockwise in the Northern Hemisphere, but now that we were in the Southern Hemisphere, we couldn't be sure what we remembered.

"You know why we can't remember, Mary?" my mother said. "It's because we haven't really watched water going down a drain for a long time! We've been tossing pans of water out of a window!"

We were safe now. We couldn't get back to the States, and there was nothing to do but be taken care of. The rooms were comfortable, there was all the rich food we had ever dreamed of: Australian lamb and beef, fruit and vegetables. Desserts came with pitchers of cream. I learned to eat oatmeal by burying a large lump of butter in its center and covering it all with white sugar. White sugar was better than the half-refined brown sugar at Gomoco.

Mrs. MacArthur came out from Brisbane to welcome us to freedom, and I presented her with an enormous bouquet of flowers. She offered Stevie Crytser a piece of fruit, but he hung back and pouted.

"I only like bananas," he said.

I started school. My new friends and I walked barefoot up the path lined with blue gum trees and marched into class to "Me and My Gal" played on a tinny piano. There were large maps on the wall with the British Empire all in pink. There was plenty of paper and pencils. I learned to spend "thrippences" and crack my knuckles. (My new school friend, Margaret, told me that I would have as many boyfriends as cracks of the knuckles, and I soon was eligible to have at least ten.) There were eucalyptus leaves with rubbery outer coating that I learned to blow into little balloons.

While we were at Caloundra, another submarine brought Americans from the Philippines. They looked tired and ragged even to me.

Some of the group came from Panay, an island just to the north of Mindanao. I heard them tell a terrible tale. Perhaps twenty Americans lived for quite a long time in safety in the hills, as we had at Gomoco. One day the Japanese came after them. In the group were missionaries who had spent time in Japan and could speak Japanese fluently. They did not run, but thought that Japanese words spoken softly could save them.

From their hiding places farther up the mountain, the ones who had run told of the awful silence in the camp below. There were no shots, only a black plume of smoke as the camp burned. Days later, a Filipino scout dared to take the path down to their old camp.

The Japanese had slaughtered all the missionaries with bayonets, even the children and old people.

The rest of the group, which included a mother and her newborn baby and a pregnant woman, walked barefoot over mountain trails to a rendezvous with the *Narwhal*.

Among the sixteen new arrivals was Jean Feigel. She reported that, in a furious attempt to stop the guerrilla activity, the Japanese had assaulted the Agusan valley, burning barrios and villages that we knew well. They burned Esperanza to the ground. The Japanese finally got to Gomoco Goldfields. They arrived from three directions and spent three weeks looking for us. In their thoroughness, they would have found La Casita— and us. They would not have taken us prisoner.

Alberta Stumbaugh and Helen Louise, who had left Gomoco to live more cheaply on the east coast of Mindanao, were
on the submarine with Jean. Helen Louise was still quiet and
shy. I envied her trip on the submarine because *Narwhal* attacked and sank the *Omi Maru*. Captain Latta got his quarry that
time, but I wasn't there when he did it.

In the second group of refugees there was a man whose
name I have forgotten. I remember very well that he betrayed us
all by telling the townspeople of Caloundra where we had come
from and how we had escaped. It had been hard for me to explain my American presence in the little country school, but I
kept my vow of silence. I despised that man for his stupid
weakness, but I had no power to punish him. He endangered all
the prisoners left in the Philippines and the ones who worked to
save us. The only way I could punish him was to remember
every facet of his face and to forget his name.

I had a tenth birthday at Caloundra. My school friends came
to the party, and there was no shortage of candles in Australia!

———◈———

Early in February, my father came from Brisbane. He was as
grim and miserable as I had ever seen him. Because the Army
would not send a civilian back to the Islands by submarine, he
had volunteered to serve in the armed forces. An X ray given
during the physical showed serious silicosis, and he was rejected for active service. All his plans for being in the Philippines for the Liberation were crushed.

"Scuttlebutt tells me that a big troopship is on its way from
the States. MacArthur assures me that he'll get the refugees out
as soon as he can, so it sounds as though you might get ready to
go home. I still have more work to do here, but I imagine they'll

send me home, too, now. Maybe I can do some work for Mother Lode in San Francisco while the war winds down."

He went back to Brisbane to the Army headquarters as a civilian and continued to tell them all he knew about the Islands, the beaches, and the terrain of Mindanao. He didn't stay long with us at Caloundra, and my mother and I went on with our new life without him.

One Saturday afternoon, after my half day at school, my mother and I were bobbing in the green sea waiting for a perfect wave when we saw a large ship out at sea sail past us on its way to Brisbane. Its lines, and the way it moved in the water, reminded us of the *President Coolidge*, which had taken us from San Francisco to Manila nearly seven years before.

On Tuesday morning, February 15, 1944—three months to the day after we left Mindanao—my mother and I were aboard that ship and ready to go home. Once again, there wasn't time to say good-bye to friends. We left late at night, spirited out of Caloundra the way we had come.

All the dignitaries who had welcomed us in November came to say farewell. Mrs. MacArthur, too.

We stood on the deck, waving and waving, and I saw my father turn toward his work with the Army as the slice of water between the ship and the dock widened and we headed for home. He promised the Army would send him home when his work was completed.

In peacetime, the big troopship had been the *Matsonia*, so the towels in our first-class cabin said. She had carried passengers in luxury back and forth across the Pacific before the war, but now she was carrying fifteen hundred troops, and unnumbered Red Cross women, Army nurses, and Australian war brides.

This was the ship voyage I had been looking for when we boarded *Narwhal*. The ship was large, and she cut through the seas leaving a white wake. I loved the sound of the engines and the slight roll of the ship. Our cabin was large and fitted with a wall of drawers for putting our few things in. Mrs. Burchfield had known General MacArthur many years before when he was a young officer in Mindanao. We were traveling in first-class cabins as his personal guests!

Civilian passengers could not be on deck at night, but I remember wakening to see my mother dressing in an officer's uniform. She was tucking her long hair into a cap so she could sneak up to the moonlit deck. It was an escapade she enjoyed and talked about for the rest of her life.

One night in the lounge, I yelled, "Bingo!" and made my way through the crowd to the stage and collected ten dollars and fifty cents. When the money was in my hand, I announced that I was going to bed. The whole room burst into laughter. Later I learned that most people stay until they lose their money again. Not me. I needed money for my new life in California.

After four days, we docked at Auckland, New Zealand, for twenty-four hours. Then we made our lone, zigzag way across the Pacific. Not even a lighted cigarette could be on deck at night, and we kept our life jackets with us all the time. A shell-shocked soldier escaped the psychiatric ward and ran naked to leap into the sea. We circled for an hour to look for him, even though we should never have slowed in such hostile waters. Finally we sailed on across the cold ocean. I watched the wake for a long time that day, wondering how the world could be such a cruel place.

It was an early morning in March 1944 when I saw the low, green hills of California. We ran parallel to the hills for what seemed like a long time, and the wake grew straight in friendly waters. Then the engines of the ship slowed as we approached the Golden Gate.

As we went under the Golden Gate Bridge ("Why is the Golden Gate Bridge red, Mommy? I thought it was golden."), a roar of cheers came from the soldiers on the decks below. Their voices swirled around the ship with the gulls. The sound made my chest want to burst.

I looked up and learned that, from underneath, the great bridge looks unfinished.

—————

My father's brother, Cam, met us in San Francisco on March 2, 1944. He carried a copy of a letter Bob had written the previous August to my mother's Canadian sister. Bob had said he was doing well and there was lots of time for reading! That news was what my mother had been longing to hear, and I know it filled her heart. The news was more than six months old, but it was news—and he had sounded well. It made being home sweeter than she had hoped it would be.

As my uncle drove us to his house in Berkeley, I marveled at the bridges and the bay and the green hills spread before me. My uncle even remembered to show me the custom—now forgotten—of blowing the car horn as we passed through the tunnel between the two bridges!

No one knew quite what to do with us. How could we get ration books? Clothes were hard to find, and housing even more impossible. My parents' insurance policies and assets were frozen in Reno because we had been missing, and my mother had no money. My mother's family came one after the other to make sure we were alive, and the house in Berkeley bulged.

My mother had a seriously infected finger resulting from a needle prick she got in Australia, and she soon went into Alta Bates Hospital. My aunt marched me to the nearest grammar school, and I started school in the United States for the first time in my life. They gambled and put me into the fourth grade. I could read better than anyone in the class, and I knew more arithmetic than they did, but I couldn't jump rope or throw Jacks or play kickball.

When a flaxen-haired little girl named Jane invited me home to play, I had my first friend. I know her still.

In a few months, my father came home, and enough money was found to buy a house in the Berkeley hills. He found a desk in the offices of Mother Lode Mines' American legal firm and became a commuter to San Francisco. He was planning as best he could the reopening of the mine. Soon, however, his "shipyard worker's cough" was rediagnosed as tuberculosis, and he went to a sanatorium where bed rest and rich foods were the cure.

I think 1944 was harder for my mother than the war had been. We had no car, and I can remember her toiling up the hill from the streetcar, carrying groceries. She spent whole days getting the fifty miles and back to see my father, who was desperate at his inactivity. Often she took a train to San Francisco, stopped at the law firm for papers for him, and then continued to the peninsula by another train.

The war wore on, and there was no new news from Bob. The war in the Pacific looked to be endless because the war in Europe was to be won before the United States turned to liberating the Philippines.

My mother left no diary of those days, but I know she spent sleepless nights alone.

PART

4

THE AFTERMATH

On Monday, December 8, 1941, while people were trying to accept the news of the attack on Pearl Harbor, great silver bombers flew over Baguio, the summer capital of the Philippines, where my brother went to boarding school. My brother watched them proudly, thinking that the U.S. Air Force didn't waste any time getting after an attacker.

The bombers flew over the mountain city, but dropped their bombs on Camp John Hay, U. S. Military Headquarters in Baguio. The Japanese bombed the city for a few days because Baguio was an important commercial and mining center. The largest concentration of Americans outside of Manila lived amid pine trees in the cool, mile-high town. Americans and British operated rich gold mines in the mountains near Baguio. Many of the Japanese who lived there soon became important officials in the occupation—an indication that the attack had long been planned.

People from outlying areas began to congregate at Brent School after it stopped teaching classes on December 12. News of Japanese activity, and awareness of The Rape of Nanking, all over the Far East made them wish for safety in numbers.

Baguio is in a canyon, which made the approach of enemy planes impossible to see until they were directly overhead. Bob and a friend, Bud Oss, whose parents also lived on an outlying island, volunteered to climb Mount Santo Tomás to be lookouts. The mountain was shrouded in clouds as they took up their watch. A north wind parted the clouds, and through their binoculars, the boys saw an armada of Japanese ships discharging small boats full of troops. The clouds cleared during the day, and they had a panoramic view of the invasion of the Philippines. They could not see any opposition to the landing. They telephoned the information to Baguio, and soon the terrible news, "One hundred and ten ships in Lingayen Gulf!," came to us in Mindanao. We, of course, didn't know who had flashed the news. Bob was soon ordered to come back to safety and away from the invading troops.

Japanese troops arrived in Baguio on December 27 and began rounding up Americans and seizing their property. They dumped them and their possessions at the school.

Each family was searched thoroughly for weapons—even scissors were confiscated—and valuables, then pushed into the gym. Machine guns were aimed into the room. If there was no room for more people, a soldier with a bayonet easily created more. The crowding was so tight that my 180-pound brother was lifted off his feet. There were no beds or mattresses provided, nor any room to spread the ones that people brought with them. Most people spent the night sitting with their knees pulled up; Bob actually got some sleep on the eight-inch-wide mantelpiece. The Japanese "forgot" to provide food. Diarrhea soon appeared, and sick people spent all their time standing in line, using the scanty facilities, and then joining the line again.

Each person was given a four-inch square of newspaper to use. The septic tanks overflowed, and misery stalked everyone.

In time, amid the confusion, a few people began to take charge and to try to create some order. Bob, strong and free to move without encumbrances, joined a group who had permission to walk to the market. They found stale bread and several industrial-size tins of Spam. Those sandwiches were the first food the prisoners had had in several days.

The Japanese demanded every automobile to be surrendered, but they needed volunteers to drive them to their precinct. To escape the awful conditions in the barracks, Bob—loving cars, anyway—volunteered to drive them for the Japanese. When he went to collect the cars, the servants of the owners slipped him food and water. When he was finished with the job, he carefully threw all the sets of keys, unlabeled, into a box, bowed, and presented them to the soldiers.

On December 29, the Japanese ordered a march from the school to the military camp that they had bombed a few days before. They could have moved their prisoners in cars and trucks, but they wanted to shame the Americans and cause them to lose face as they straggled across the town carrying their few belongings.

Bob and his friend, Chuck Lerberg, filled their duffle bags with clothing and anything of value they could find, hung the bags on a strong pole, and carried them swinging from their shoulders on the five-mile walk across town. Two mattresses slipped and shifted on top of the pole as they walked to Camp John Hay, so recently bombed by the Japanese.

There were several empty barracks there, but the Japanese put all 500 internees into one building designed to hold 180 soldiers. It did no good to be angry or to make demands; the Japanese were in no mood to be generous. They were retaliating for the treatment they themselves had suffered in internment in the few short days between December 8 and the time they took control.

Order slowly began to be made; an ad hoc committee formed to deal with the Japanese. Among the missionaries was a woman who spoke an extremely elegant form of Japanese. At first she hid her skills from the troops and reported their intentions, but she soon became interpreter for the camp. The beauty of her language awed the rough soldiers, and she was able to get concessions from them that another interpreter might not have done. People learned to live in such crowded conditions that a person was happy to have a "home" as large as a mattress.

Committees were formed to collect garbage, work in the chow line, and deal with the needs of a community. Bob, because he was young and strong, was put on the wood crew, which left the camp every day to log the surrounding hillsides and to bring firewood back to camp. The job gave him a change in scenery that other internees never got, and also made it easier for Filipinos to slip him extra food and necessities. The work was hard, but it was exercise for his young body; as the years passed, though, the job became difficult because available trees were farther and farther from the camp while, at the same time, food rations diminished and his energy decreased.

A few months later, the camp moved to Camp Holmes, just outside the city, where the prisoners remained for two and a half years. This camp was larger, perched on a hillside. Conditions eased in the new camp, and the internees learned to deal with the Japanese. One Japanese commandant was benign and did what he could to make conditions better. So benign, in fact, that during his trial in Japan after the war, internees pleaded for him and—unlike other prison-camp commandants—he was acquitted of atrocity by the Army Tribunal.

During the middle part of the war, food was plentiful enough. Most people in the camp had outside resources, and it was possible to buy food privately to augment the paltry thirty-centavo daily allowance the Japanese Intelligence Office provided. Bob soon ran out of money and borrowed from Chinese businessmen, promising to pay the debt after the war. After the war, my father paid the debts gratefully—postwar peso for inflated Japanese peso.

A mining family that we had known from prewar days took Bob in, and he shared their family events. The school set up classes again, and Bob finished high school about on time, in the middle of 1942. He had been accepted at Duke University, but the war made that an impossibility. He did get in, however, at the University of California when they agreed to accept his pencil-written high school diploma dated September 1942.

My brother will tell only a few stories about his years as a prisoner, and he resists dwelling on the worst memories. Once the guards caught him hiding notes in his shoes as he left the camp. They beat him and broke his glasses, but he doesn't say much more than that about the experience.

Usually, he tells funny stories like the one about the wood crew trying to fell a tree on a guard sleeping on a sunny hillside. They succeeded only in frightening the guard, though, because the tree wasn't quite tall enough.

Bob learned to steal chickens by saving whole corn kernels and tying a thread through a hole drilled in one kernel, then scattering the corn. A chicken with a thread down its throat cannot squawk and can be reeled in and quietly dispatched. He says the hope and suspense of waiting for a chicken to swallow the kernel with the thread is heart-stopping, but that the joy is great when you can tuck it into your shirt for the walk back to camp.

Mostly, Bob spent his time waiting for the war to be over the same way we did. There were poker games, and Bridge games, and classes to go to. Classes met; there were concerts and lectures and plays, all devised to make the time pass.

An exchange of prisoners took place in September 1943. Bob sent a letter through the Red Cross to my mother's sister in Canada, giving as much news as he could. The typewritten letter, dated August 20, 1943, in which he tells his family not to worry about my parents and me—he had had no direct word of us.

> However, I know definitely that they are well. I have had indirect word from Manila through a friend of the family that they are well, so don't worry about them. As for me, I'm getting along very well. The weather is swell and I get plenty of exercise and sunshine, and I have had plenty of time to read some good books.

The only letter he ever received came from the same aunt in 1944. She, too, could say little, but she told him that I was doing well in the fourth grade. From that he could deduce that somehow we were "home."

As the war went badly for the Japanese, life in the camp deteriorated. After two young men escaped to the guerrillas, the camp commandant was replaced by a repressive, cruel man whose brutality and unfairness made life nearly unbearable. He reduced food rations, and the internees grew thinner and weaker.

In December 1944, just after Christmas, and after the American invasion of the Philippines had begun, the Japanese abruptly moved their prisoners to Manila. They said it was because Manila was an Open City. There were far too few trucks for the five hundred men, women, and children; and though I have read about it in diaries and history books, I have heard Bob talk about that trip only once. It was hot as they reached the lowlands from their cool, misty mountains. They sat on their dwindled belongings in the burning sun in misery without food or water. Dysentery and other sicknesses attacked the youngest and the weakest. He tells of holding a woman by the hands so she could lean out over the end of the truck to defecate.

He says that they survived the trip from Baguio to Manila because a storm in the China Sea prevented American planes from getting enough fuel to harass the Japanese that week. American planes, if they had been flying, would have strafed the unmarked trucks.

Bilibid Prison in Manila was the destination of those weak and hungry civilians. In Spanish fashion, the ancient prison buildings were built in spokes around a central guardhouse. Bilibid had been scheduled for demolition in 1941, but the Japanese kept military prisoners there in unspeakable conditions all during the war. Now the Baguio civilians joined them. There were rats and lice and bedbugs to contend with. Food rations—only cracked corn already visited by weevils that ate the nourishing germ of the grain—dropped from three hundred grams a day to two hundred grams. Finally, people began to die. The climate in Baguio had saved them, but now in Manila's lowland climate, it was too hard for many to go on.

Manila had been an Open City in 1941, but it was not an Open City in 1945. The shelling grew more intense as the American Army drew closer. Army Intelligence didn't know that civilians had come to Bilibid so late in the war, and that meant that Bilibid remained on the front lines for several days. During the shelling of Manila, in early February 1945, Bilibid's thick Spanish walls were more protecting than confining.

The way Bob laughs when he tells stories of the battle for Manila makes me realize how surreal those days were. He giggles when he talks about washing his last pair of shorts and hanging them on the clothesline in the courtyard. As he walked back to his building, a mortar shell landed in the yard. He turned to see only smoking shreds of his shorts, leaving him to wear what he was using for underwear—a Japanese loincloth called a *fundoshi*.

Here are my brother's words, written just after he came home:

> One evening about sundown, there was a steadily growing rumble in the north. It grew louder and louder and just at dusk the point of the advancing army came roaring up Quezon Boulevard. They had every gun going full blast. They swept past the walls of our prison. Eight tanks and about six truckloads of men chased 20,000 Japs across the Pasig River. The air was full of flying shells. There was so much noise that we in the prison could hardly think. I was thankful that the Japs had put us behind the twenty-foot-thick

walls of Bilibid Prison. The walls kept most of the hot stuff over our heads.

Outside a couple of tired and dirty GIs were taking shelter next to the wall. They figured that it would be a lot safer inside that wall than outside. We didn't know they were there, nor did they know we were inside. When they heard us talking, they thought we were some of their buddies. One of them called out, "How did you get in there?" The guy next to me called back, "What we want to know is, how do we get out? We have been in here for thirty-seven months!"

Those two GIs were the liberators of our camp as far as I am concerned.

In a few days, Bob and his old friend, Chuck Lerberg, found a tank crew lost in the city. They gave directions, and the soldiers—all about their same age—asked them to join them for a tour of the city. He tried, when one of the soldiers gave him a weapon, to shoot a Japanese soldier. His glasses were long gone, and the boy who learned to shoot in California missed this quarry. Courtney Whitney, adjutant to General MacArthur and a friend of our family's, sent a search party out looking for Bob and chewed him out for being so stupid as to risk his life in a battle.

Mother and Daddy and I were next to the radio all during the Battle of Manila, learning every day of the destruction but never hearing a word of him. We scanned the lists in the *San Francisco Chronicle,* and at last a telegram from Washington reported him safe in Manila and in fair condition.

My father wrote Bob through the Red Cross on February 17, 1945:

A picture published a few days ago showed two fellows pushing a cart carrying two men to a hospital. One of the fellows pushing the cart was about your age and build and resembled you. I wonder if you were the one.

Bob's name came up on the lottery to take the first repatriating troopship home; and on March 30, 1945, my mother, my aunt and uncle, and I stood on a pier on the Embarcadero in San Francisco and finally spotted him—high above us as the ship eased up to the pier—leaning on the rail of the *Jean Lafitte,* smiling calmly—coming home as if he'd been on a pleasure trip.

Hours later, it seemed, he joined us onshore and we drove through the streets of San Francisco to a skyscraper on Post Street where the Red Cross, or the Army perhaps, did more processing.

It's odd to remember the numbness we all felt. There was too much to tell; there were too many changes in all of us to know where to begin again. We had to tell him that his father was lying in a tuberculosis sanatorium south of San Francisco.

We five squeezed into my uncle's 1940 Mercury Coupe to drive to the hospital, and there we had our reunion. My father wrote my mother the next day:

> Our son has returned to us free and sound in body and spirit. You, of course, in your calm faith, knew he would. I hoped he would. We saw him last a boy; he's back a man! He's made of Damascus steel, but you were the smith. I most humbly give you full credit.

At the University of California Bob became a student again. He was drafted, of course, but during the medical examination, one doctor noticed his prison-camp history and asked him to take the eye examination again. The second examination qualified him to carry a white cane if he wanted one, and he went back to classes.

And then, briefly, our family was reunited under one roof. After eighteen months in the sanatorium, my father's tuberculosis seemed contained, and he came home to build his strength. By that time I was an adolescent, and it embarrassed me to have him walk slowly up and down our block in his maroon bathrobe. He went back to work again in San Francisco to make plans to go back to his ruined mine.

The Philippines was our home, the center of my father's life. We three left Bob at the University in Berkeley in 1947 to go back to the mine on Mindanao.

We found near disaster all over the Islands. Manila was second only to Warsaw in destruction; one hundred thousand civilians died when the departing Japanese set fire to the Pearl of the Orient. At Mindanao Mother Lode, an American Air Force firestorm destroyed the mine buildings. Even our house, across the canyon from the mill, took a firebomb. The porcelain toilet lay, melted, in the ruins of our house, but the gardenia tree still bloomed bravely under a smothering vine that grew in from the jungle. Nearly everything we owned was gone, though my father paced off his coordinates and dug up the Leica he had buried in the backyard in 1941.

In shattered Manila, my mother and I lived near the American School in a Quonset hut built on the foundations of a house destroyed in the bombing. My father shuttled between Manila and Mindanao. He was distracted and moody and difficult to live with. He didn't want my mother and me to be in the Islands. He said it was too difficult for white women to live in with the hardships of a city struggling to rebuild. My mother would not leave; she said her place was with her husband. I lived with tension and muffled arguments between my parents—I often heard my mother's voice rising toward hysteria and my father's voice grow silent. They drifted apart—he preoccupied by his work and she aching to take part in the social life of postwar Manila. I tried to mediate, to bring them together, but I was not old enough to understand their relationship. I began to spend all the time I could at the American School.

The second year we were in Manila, my mother had serious surgery. No one, of course, told me that the cancer had been discovered too late. Their respective illnesses then became each one's private battle, and they had no energy to put toward mending their marriage.

Reflecting on their lives, I see that the war years were perhaps their happiest years. In hiding from an implacable enemy, they had faced uncertainty and fear together. They worried about their son together. They built La Casita together. They had a young child to teach and to protect. An intimacy developed in those two years they could never recapture in peacetime.

My father strained his precarious health by working too hard at putting the mine back into operation. Long negotiations with the War Damage Commission, restaffing and rebuilding the devastated buildings, used up his strength. His lungs failed again, and in the same month both my parents flew home to California to enter hospitals. I stayed with friends until school finished and flew home alone in April 1949 at the end of ninth grade.

My father died in May, and my mother died in August. They had survived the war, playing cards of good luck and intelligence dealt to them by Fate, and escaped death at the hands of Japanese soldiers. Five years later they died of diseases they could not control.

My aunt came from Vancouver the last few days of my mother's life. Even though she clung to me one morning in our kitchen in Berkeley crying, "Why can't it be me? I can't bear to lose her," I still could not imagine my mother dying, not even when we saw her in terrible pain in the hospital in San Francisco. Numbly, I heard my mother's last words to Bob and me: "Be honest and have good lives," and we left her for the last time.

My practical aunt, soon after my mother died, hid her grief and invited women in to pick through my mother's closet. I felt like a picture on the wall watching them try on her shoes and take away her clothes. This can't be happening, I thought. It just can't be, but it is.

My aunt took me to I. Magnin's in San Francisco and bought me more elegant clothing than I had ever had and took me home with her to Vancouver.

Bob stayed in the house in Berkeley to finish school, and I joined a boisterous and busy family.

I felt suspended and spinning alone without my parents, but the Canadian family was too interesting and too much fun for me to stay apart for long. To be honest, a part of me felt a great relief to be free of my troubled parents; I could never have helped them to be happy, though I had tried. Fifteen-year-olds are selfish and want freedom. It was only many years later, when I learned more about them from my aunt, who had loved them both, that I could fully grieve.

I was at last living a normal life in a place where ordinary lives were led. There were no shattered buildings, no hidden tensions. My uncle taught at the University of British Columbia, and there was a stability in my new life I had hungered for. I finished high school in Vancouver and a year of university, then completed my degree at the University of California in Berkeley.

Bob and I each married happily and have four children and seven grandchildren between us. We have led our lives since the war in a normal, uneventful fashion, except that Bob soars in gliders high above the Sierra Nevada, and I travel the world whenever possible. In our differing ways, we both choose freedom and motion, perhaps responding to the war years that held us tightly in small places.

THE AFTERMATH

The war scattered everything and everyone in our lives. Possessions, friends, business associates all disappeared or changed so much that they were unrecognizable.

Nearly all the people with us before and during the war survived. Some we never saw again.

Dionisio, our houseboy, returned shortly after we did—the bamboo telegraph works in peacetime, too! He had guarded my mother's carved Chinese chest with infinite care and gravely returned it to us. Twice a year he washed and aired the Chinese linens my mother bought from the peddler, and his wife, Consuelo, ironed them and repacked the chest. I use them still on holidays.

After Jean left for Australia, a Japanese sniper killed Fred Feigel in July of 1944 on the Bunawan River not far from Gomoco. Jean joined the Red Cross in Australia and was in France at the end of the war, then went to work in occupied Japan. I have talked to some of Fred Feigel's family, but none of them knows what happened to Jean.

Helen Welbon went to Australia with us on *Narwhal* in November 1943, and Roy, who stayed on to fight with the guerrillas, was cut down in an ambush the following January. He was buried in front of the little church in the barrio of Baroy on Mindanao.

The Smith family reunited in Santo Tomás Interment Camp in Manila and returned to Mindanao Mother Lode after the war to begin operation of the gold mine. Together, Larry Smith and my father had flooded the tunnels at the beginning of the war. In 1941, the mine produced a million pesos' worth of gold concentrate each month; in 1947, the miners could never find ore in the concentration they had had before. After my father died, Larry stayed on to mine copper instead of gold.

He lived in the Philippines for nearly sixty years. He wrote me:

> Whitey Crenshaw and I flipped a coin in 1949 after the war to see who would go to Gomoco to get the 5850 pesos we buried, and he won. He took two employees with him and brought the fire extinguisher back with every peso right inside the glass jar containers. We had taken this with us when we left the mine in 1941—all that was in the safe. We returned it 7½ years later to the same safe at Mindanao Mother Lode.

Charlie Martin stayed free on Mindanao all during the war and was there to meet the Americans when they arrived. I heard that as an old man in his native Texas, he became deaf, and was killed while crossing a street by a pickup truck that he couldn't hear.

Bob Crump joined the U.S. Army as the war began; as a captain in the guerrilla army, he was in charge of storing and allocating supplies the submarines brought to Mindanao. He had a camera and during the war took a few rolls of film that he sealed in glass jars. Evelyn Burchfield had the green and moldy rolls developed in San Francisco, and Bob has given me photographs that exactly match my memories. He did pan enough gold for a wedding ring. When I asked him over the phone—the first time I talked to him—if my father was a son of a bitch, Bob was surprised and said, "Yes." Then he remembered who I was and tried to retract.

I met Glenda Crytser before she died, and she refused to tell me anything about those days with my father. She was lovely and gracious, just as I remembered her, and she told me they had had a wonderful life after she and Stevie were reunited with her husband. They lived lightly and happily in the Virgin Islands for several years. I have met Steven at reunions. He is rueful that he remembers nothing of his adventures in jungles and on submarines.

Life was never again as much fun for Waldo Neveling as it was on Mindanao. Glenda wrote me once to tell me she remembered Waldo saying to her during the war: "Don't you worry about me! I'm having the time of my life!" For a time after the war, he worked again at Mindanao Mother Lode. A lifetime of smoking harsh Filipino tobacco left him with emphysema. One day, in Arizona, where he lived after the United States gave him honorary citizenship for his contribution to the guerrillas, he could stand no more of old age and illness and he went for a walk without his oxygen and died.

I found Jim Burchfield, too, splitting his time between Ohio and Florida. His father, David, was in Santo Tomás after being held in Davao. His family never went back to the Philippines— his father knew seven Filipino dialects, but he never needed them to sell real estate in Kentucky. Mrs. Burchfield recovered from the typhoid that nearly killed her and lived until 1991!

We never heard from the Jarvises again, though I believe that they ended up in Santo Tomás with the others.

Commander Latta of *Narwhal* took command of another submarine, *Lugarto,* toward the end of the war and was lost in the China Sea. *Lugarto* was one of the last submarines the Navy lost in World War II. At reunions, I have been able to thank the very crewmen and officers who took us out of Mindanao. They all remember the brass band.

As I grew up, I was never sure that there really was a gold statue that Julio told me about in Esperanza, though I believed him when I was nine. As there is always a grain of truth in the bamboo telegraph, so Julio's story was true as well. The Golden Image of the Agusan is in the Chicago Museum of Natural History. Javanese miners lived in the Agusan valley in the thirteenth and fourteenth centuries, and their statue was found at the edge of the Wawa River in 1917. It is twenty-one-karat gold and weighs four pounds. It was made in the fourteenth century.

In the two years we spent in the Philippines after the war, there was never time to go back to Gomoco. A highway now leads from Surigao to Davao, slicing through the jungle near where we were. Perhaps the jungle has been clear-cut and is no longer dreaming in the moonlight. Mindanao is troubled now, and Americans who go there now do so accompanied by armed guards. Lives are often short in the third world, and I would probably never find Opren or Opron or Ameliana or any of the Filipinos who were gentle and kind in the vortex of a war.

Utang na lo-ob is central to the Philippine way of life. Each Filipino feels a sense of debt and obligation to everyone who helps him, and he honors those obligations. It is *walang hiya* (shameless) not to repay kindness.

The Filipinos protected and supported Americans in countless heroic ways during World War II. There is no way to thank them for keeping thousands of us alive and safe.

I remain *walang hiya*. I cannot repay my debt of obligation.

GLOSSARY

abaca hemp, a banana-like plant, from which rope is made

amah a woman, usually Chinese, who cares for children

bakya a wooden clog, often carved and brightly painted

banca a seagoing canoe, usually with a sail and outriggers

baroto a dugout canoe, with outriggers, usually propelled with poles; an inland vessel

barrio from the Spanish, it usually means a village

bodega a warehouse

bolo a machete

bonkil woven backpack, usually with a headband

calape, kalape a tasty fish that lived in the Agusan River

cambo a woven storage basket

camote a potato-like tuber, but stringy, like a yam (ca-mo-tee)

carabao a water buffalo

carahay a clay cooking pot

cargador from the Spanish, a man who carries cargo

carretela a light, brightly painted, horse-drawn cart

cogon grass a tall grass with razor-sharp leaves

colintasin a Mindanao measurement of weight

crudo crude oil or diesel oil

271

despedida   a Spanish word used to describe a good-bye party

frasco   a hand-blown glass bottle

ganta   a dry measure equal to twelve cups (eight chupas equal
     a ganta)

grumete   a boatman

kaingin   a temporary farming plot in the jungle

kwan   a thingamajig

lavandera   from Spanish, a washerwoman

lorcha   a sailboat meant for the open seas

mestizo, mestiza   a person of mixed blood

Moros, Moras   southern Mindanao was converted to Islam—
     the Spanish for Moor

nipa   a fan-shaped palm used to make roofs and walls

palay   unhulled rice

parientes   from Spanish, parents, and also the extended family

peso   Philippine currency; before the war a dollar equaled two
     pesos

pidgin   a Chinese corruption of the word "business." By
     extension, a *lingua franca* between foreigners and natives

piña camisa   a man's dress shirt made from pineapple fiber

sala   a Spanish word—we used it to mean living room

sari sari   a general store, often run by Chinese

tampipi   a woven suitcase

tao   a Filipino peasant

tienda   a small shop

tigbao grass   a tall, gracefully waving plumed grass

tuba   fermented palm-tree sap

wak-waks   evil spirits that can assume animal form; they steal
     children and eat their livers

BIBLIOGRAPHY

Crouter, Natalie, *Forbidden Diary*. New York: Burt Franklin & Co., 1980.

Demetrio, Francisco R., SJ, *Dictionary of Folk Belief and Customs No. 2*. Cagayan de Oro, Philippines: Xavier University, 1970.

Dissette, Edward and Adamson, H. C., *Guerrilla Submarines*. New York: Ballantine Books, 1972.

Francisco, Juan R., *Essays in Ancient Cultural Relations*. Manila: National Bookstore, 1971.

Haggerty, Edward, *Guerrilla Padre in Mindanao*. New York: Longmans, Green and Co., 1946.

Hartendorp, A. V. H., *The Japanese Occupation of the Philippines*. Manila: Bookmark, 1967.

———, *The Santo Tomás Story*. New York: McGraw-Hill, 1964.

Heib, Harley F., *Heart of Iron*. Lodi, California: Pacifica Publications, 1987.

Ingham, Travis, *Rendezvous by Submarine*. Garden City, N.Y.: Doubleday Doran and Co., 1945.

Ind, Allison, *Allied Information Bureau: Our Secret Weapon in the War Against Japan*. New York: McKay Co., 1958.

Jamboy, Evelyn Mallillin, *The Resistance Movement in Lanao, 1942–45*. Iligan City, Philippines: Coordination Center of Research and Development, Mindanao State University-Iligan Institute of Technology, 1985.

Keats, John, *They Fought Alone*. New York: J. B. Lippincott Co., 1963.

Lesse, William Armand, *Drake's Island of Thieves: Ethnological Sleuthing*. Honolulu: University Press of Hawaii, 1975.

MacArthur, Douglas, *Reminiscences*. New York: McGraw-Hill, 1964.

Manchester, William, *American Caesar*. New York: Dell Publishing, 1983.

Manikan, Gamaliel L., *Guerrilla Warfare on Panay Island*. Manila: Sixth Army Military District Veterans' Foundation, 1977.

McKay, Harriet Mills, unpublished manuscript, *No Conqueror Comes*.

Miles, Fern Harrington, *Captive Community, Life in a Japanese Internment Camp, 1941–45*. San Angelo, Texas: Mossy Creek Press, 1987.

Nid, Anima, *The Head-hunting Tribes of the Philippines*. Novaliches, Philippines: Cultural Foundation of Asia, c. 1985.

"Papers in Mindanao Ethnology, No. 2–3." Marawi City, Philippines: University Research Center, Mindanao State University, 1979.

Pomeroy, William J., *The Philippines: Colonialism, Collaboration and Resistance!* New York: International Publishers, 1992.

Romulo, Carlos P., *Filipino Heroes of World War II*. Makati, Philippines: Agro Printing and Publishing House, c. 1980.

Sams, Margaret, *Forbidden Family: A Wartime Memoir of the Philippines, 1941–45*. Madison, Wisconsin: University of Wisconsin Press, 1989.

Spencer, Louise Reid, *Guerrilla Wife*. New York: Thomas Y. Crowell Co., 1945.

Schreuers, Peter, *Caraga Antigua 1521–1910: The Hispanization and Christianization of Agusan, Surigao and East Davao*. Cebu City: University of San Carlos, 1981.

Stahl, Bob, *You're No Good to Me Dead*. Annapolis, Maryland: Naval Institute Press, 1995.

Stevens, Frederic H., *Santo Tomás Internment Camp, 1942–45*. New York: Stratford House, 1946.

Wise, William, *Secret Mission to the Philippines: The Story of the "Spyron" and the American-Filipino Guerrillas of World War II*. New York: E. P. Dutton Co., 1968.

Whitney, Courtney, *MacArthur, His Rendezvous with History*. New York: Alfred A. Knopf, 1956.

Willoughby, Charles A. and Chamberlain, John, *MacArthur, 1941–51*. New York: McGraw-Hill, 1954.

DATE			